280
SELECTED MODERN
ENGLISH ESSAYS

Oxford University Press, Amen House, London E.C.4

GLASGOW   NEW YORK   TORONTO   MELBOURNE   WELLINGTON
BOMBAY   CALCUTTA   MADRAS   KARACHI   LAHORE   DACCA
CAPE TOWN   SALISBURY   NAIROBI   IBADAN   ACCRA
KUALA LUMPUR   HONG KONG

SELECTED
MODERN
ENGLISH
ESSAYS

LONDON
OXFORD UNIVERSITY PRESS
NEW YORK TORONTO

This selection of Modern English Essays *was
first published in* The World's Classics *in 1925,
and reprinted in 1925, 1927, 1930, 1931, 1933,
1937. Reset in 1940, and reprinted in 1945, 1949,
1956, and 1962.*

PRINTED IN GREAT BRITAIN

LIST OF ACKNOWLEDGMENTS

(1925)

THIS is the third anthology of Essays in *The World's Classics;* of these the first, selected by Mr. William Peacock, covers the three centuries from Bacon to R. L. Stevenson; the second, selected by S. V. Makower and Mr. Basil Blackwell, gleans over the same field but adds a few later writers to the end of the nineteenth century; the present selection is from writers working in the twentieth century, and most of them happily still alive.

Acknowledgment is hereby made to the following authors for kind permission to include essays, and to the publishers whose names follow theirs in brackets for confirming those permissions: Mr. Max Beerbohm (and to Messrs. William Heinemann); to Mr. Hilaire Belloc (and to Messrs. Methuen); to Mr. R. W. Chapman (and to the Delegates of the Clarendon Press); to Mr. G. K. Chesterton (and to Messrs. Methuen); to the late Mr. Joseph Conrad; to Mr. Basil de Selincourt (and to the Delegates of the Clarendon Press); to Mr. E. M. Forster (and to the Hogarth Press); to Mr. John Galsworthy, to Sir Edmund Gosse (and to Messrs. W. Heinemann in respect of both); to Mr. E. V. Lucas (and to Messrs. Methuen); to Mr. Robert Lynd (and to Messrs. Mills and Boon in respect of 'The Humour of Hoaxes'); to Mr. W. S.

Maugham (and to Messrs. W. Heinemann);
to Mr. J. M. Murry (Messrs. William Collins);
to Mr. H. W. Nevinson (and to Messrs. James
Nisbet); to Mr. Gilbert Norwood; to Lord
Rosebery (and to Messrs. Hodder and Stough-
ton); to Mr. George Saintsbury; to Mr. J. C.
Squire (and to Messrs. Hodder and Stoughton);
to Mr. L. Pearsall Smith (and to Messrs.
Constable); to Mr. G. S. Street (and to Messrs.
Constable for one essay, and to Messrs. Martin
Secker for two others); to Mr. H. M. Tomlinson
(and to Messrs. Cassell).

For the essays by Austin Dobson, Maurice
Hewlett, Alice Meynell, and William Hale
White, thanks are due to their personal repre-
sentatives.

The following publishers have kindly per-
mitted the use of essays by the authors whose
names follow theirs in brackets: Messrs. Edward
Arnold (A. Clutton-Brock in *Modern Essays from
'The Times'*: I am indebted to the editor of *The
Times Literary Supplement* for identifying the
author); Messrs. Jonathan Cape (Samuel
Butler); the Delegates of the Clarendon Press
(W. P. Ker, Sir Walter Raleigh); Messrs. J. M.
Dent (W. H. Hudson); Messrs. Duckworth
(Mr. R. B. Cunninghame Graham, Edward
Thomas); Messrs. Methuen (A. Clutton-Brock);
and Mr. Elliot Stock (Mr. Augustine Birrell).

H. S. M.

CONTENTS

A*

William Hale White
('Mark Rutherford')
1831–1913

THE BREAK-UP OF A GREAT DROUGHT

FOR three months there had been hardly a drop of rain. The wind had been almost continuously north-west, and from that to east. Occasionally there were light airs from the south-west, and vapour rose, but there was nothing in it; there was no true south-westerly breeze, and in a few hours the weather-cock returned to the old quarter. Not infrequently the clouds began to gather, and there was every sign that a change was at hand. The barometer at these times fell gradually day after day until at last it reached a point which generally brought drenching storms, but none appeared, and then it began slowly to rise again and we knew that our hopes were vain, and that a week at least must elapse before it would regain its usual height and there might be a chance of declining. At last the disappointment was so keen that the instrument was removed. It was better not to watch it, but to hope for a surprise. The grass became brown, and in many places was killed down to the roots; there was no hay; myriads of swarming caterpillars devoured the fruit trees; the brooks were all dry; water for cattle had to be fetched from ponds and springs miles away; the roads were broken up; the air was loaded with grit; and the beautiful green of the hedges was choked with dust. Birds like the rook, which fed upon worms, were nearly starved, and were driven far and wide for strange food. It was pitiable to see them trying to pick the soil of the meadow as hard as a rock. The everlasting glare was worse than the gloom of winter, and the sense of universal parching thirst became so distressing that the house was preferred to the fields. We were close to a water famine! The Atlantic, the source of all life, was asleep, and what if it should never wake! We know not its ways, it mocks all our science. Close to us lies this great mystery, incomprehensible, and yet our very breath depends upon it. Why should not the sweet tides of soft moist air cease to stream in upon us? No reason could be given why every green herb and living thing should not perish; no reason, save a faith which was blind. For aught we *knew*, the ocean-begotten aërial current might forsake the land and it might become a desert.

One night grey bars appeared in the western sky, but they had too often deluded us, and we did not believe in them. On this particular evening they were a little heavier, and the window-cords were damp. The air which came across the cliff was cool, and if we had dared to hope we should have said it had a scent of the sea in it. At four o'clock in the morning there was a noise of something beating against the panes—they were streaming! It was impossible to lie still, and I rose and went out of doors. No creature was stirring, there was no sound save that of the rain, but a busier time there had not been for many a long month. Thousands of millions of blades of grass and corn were eagerly drinking. For sixteen hours the downpour continued, and when it was dusk I again went out. The water-courses by the side of the roads had a little water in them, but not a drop had reached those at the edge of the fields, so thirsty was the earth. The drought, thank God, was at an end!

JUDAS ISCARIOT—WHAT CAN BE SAID FOR HIM?

Judas Iscariot has become to Christian people an object of horror more loathsome than even the devil himself. The devil rebelled because he could not brook subjection to the Son of God, a failing which was noble compared with treachery to the Son of man. The hatred of Judas is not altogether virtuous. We compound thereby for our neglect of Jesus and His precepts: it is easier to establish our Christianity by cursing the wretched servant than by following his Master. The heinousness also of the crime in Gethsemane has been aggravated by the exaltation of Jesus to the Redeemership of the world. All that can be known of Judas is soon collected. He was chosen one of the twelve apostles, and received their high commission to preach the kingdom of heaven, to heal the sick, raise the dead, cleanse the lepers, and cast out devils. He was appointed treasurer to the community. John in telling the story of the anointing at Bethany says that he was a thief, but John also makes him the sole objector to the waste of the ointment. According to the other evangelists all the disciples objected. Since he remained in office it could hardly have been known at the time of the visit to Bethany that he was dishonest, nor could it have been known at any time to Matthew and Mark, for they would not have lost the opportunity of adding such a touch to the portrait. The probability, therefore, is that the robbery of the bag is unhistorical. When the chief priests and scribes sought how they might apprehend Jesus they made a bargain with Judas to deliver Him to them for thirty pieces of silver. He was present at the Last Supper but went and betrayed his Lord. A few hours afterwards, when he found out that condemnation to death followed, he repented himself and brought again the thirty pieces of silver to his employers, declared that he had sinned in betraying innocent blood, cast down the money at their feet, and went and hanged himself.

This is all that is discoverable about Judas, and it has been considered sufficient for a damnation deeper than any allotted to the worst of the sons of Adam. Dante places him in the lowest round of the ninth or last of the hellish circles, where he is eternally 'champed' by Satan, 'bruised as with ponderous engine,' his head within the diabolic jaws and 'plying the feet without.' In the absence of a biography with details, it is impossible to make out with accuracy what the real Judas was. We can, however, by dispassionate examination of the facts determine their sole import, and if we indulge in inferences we can deduce those which are fairly probable. As Judas was treasurer, he must have been trusted. He could hardly have been naturally covetous, for he had given up in common with the other disciples much, if not all, to follow Jesus. The thirty pieces of silver—some four or five pounds of our money—could not have been considered by him as a sufficient bribe for the ignominy of a treason which was to end in legal murder. He ought perhaps to have been able to measure the ferocity of an established ecclesiastical order and to have known what would have been the consequence of handing over to it perfect, and therefore heretical, sincerity and purity, but there is no evidence that he did know: nay, we are distinctly informed, as we have just seen, that when he became aware what was going to happen his sorrow for his wicked deed took a very practical shape.

We cannot allege with confidence that it was any permanent loss of personal attachment to Jesus which brought about his defection. It came when the belief in a theocracy near at hand filled the minds of the disciples. These ignorant Galilean fishermen expected that in a very short time they would sit on twelve thrones judging the twelve tribes of Israel. The custodian of the bag, gifted with more common sense than his colleagues, probably foresaw the danger of a collision with Rome, and may have desired by a timely arrest to prevent an open revolt, which would have meant immediate destruction of the whole band with women and children. Can any position be imagined more irritating than that of a careful man of business who is keeper of the purse for a company of heedless enthusiasts professing complete indifference to the value of money, misunderstanding the genius of their chief, and looking out every morning for some sign in the clouds, a prophecy of their immediate appointment as vicegerents of a power that would supersede the awful majesty of the Imperial city? He may have been heated by a long series of petty annoyances to such a degree that at last they may have ended in rage and a sudden flinging loose of himself from the society. At any rate, Judas was not guilty of cool, mercenary treason, for he was impulsive exceedingly. Matthew, and Matthew only, says that Judas asked for money from the chief priests. 'What will ye give me, and I will deliver Him unto you?' According to Mark, whose account of the transaction is the same as Luke's, 'Judas . . . went unto the chief priests to betray Him unto them. And when they heard it, they were glad, and promised to give him money.' If the priests were the tempters, a slight difference is established in favour of Judas, but this we will neglect. The sin of taking money and joining in that last meal in any case is black enough, although, as we have before pointed out, Judas did not at the time know what the other side of the bargain was. Admitting, however, everything that can fairly be urged against him, all that can be affirmed with certainty is that we are in the presence of strange and unaccountable inconsistency, and that an apostle who had abandoned his home, who had followed Jesus for three years amidst contempt and persecution, and who at last slew himself in self-reproach, could be capable of committing the meanest of sins. Is the co-existence of irreconcilable opposites in human nature anything new? The story of Judas may be of some value if it reminds us that man is incalculable, and that, although in theory, and no doubt in reality, he is a unity, the point from which the divergent forces in him rise is often infinitely beyond our exploration; a lesson not merely in psychology but for our own guidance, a warning that side by side with heroic virtues there may sleep in us not only detestable vices, but vices by which those virtues are contradicted and even for the time annihilated. The mode of betrayal, with a kiss, has justly excited loathing, but it is totally unintelligible. Why should he have taken the trouble to be so base when the movement of a finger would have sufficed? Why was any sign necessary to indicate one who was so well known? The supposition that the devil compelled him to superfluous villainy in order that he might be secured with greater certainty and tortured with greater subtlety is one that can hardly be entertained except by theologians. It is equally difficult to understand why Jesus submitted to such an insult, and why Peter should not have smitten down its perpetrator. Peter was able to draw his sword, and it would have been safer and more natural to kill Judas than to cut off the ear of the high priest's servant. John, who shows a special dislike to Judas, knows nothing of the kiss.

According to John, Jesus asked the soldiers whom they sought, and then stepped boldly forward and declared Himself. 'Judas,' adds John, 'was standing with them.' As John took such particular notice of what happened, the absence of the kiss in his account can hardly have been accidental. It is a sound maxim in criticism that what is simply difficult of explanation is likely to be authentic. An awkward reading in a manuscript is to be preferred to one which is easier. But an historical improbability, especially if no corroboration of it is to be found in a better authority, may be set aside, and in this case we are justified in neglecting the kiss. Whatever may have been the exact shade of darkness in the crime of Judas, it was avenged with singular swiftness, and he himself was the avenger. He did not slink away quietly and poison himself in a ditch. He boldly encountered the sacred college, confessed his sin and the innocence of the man they were about to crucify. Compared with these pious miscreants who had no scruples about corrupting one of the disciples, but shuddered at the thought of putting back into the treasury the money they had taken from it, Judas becomes noble. His remorse is so unendurable that it drives him to suicide.

If a record could be kept of those who have abjured Jesus through love of gold, through fear of the world or of the scribes and Pharisees, we should find many who are considered quite respectable, or have even been canonised, and who, nevertheless, much more worthily than Iscariot, are entitled to 'champing' by the jaws of Sathanas. Not a single scrap from Judas himself has reached us. He underwent no trial, and is condemned without plea or excuse on his own behalf, and with no cross-examination of the evidence. No witnesses have been called to his character. What would his friends at Kerioth have said for him? What would Jesus have said? If He had met Judas with the halter in his hand would He not have stopped him? Ah! I can see the Divine touch on the shoulder, the passionate prostration of the repentant in the dust, the hands gently lifting him, the forgiveness because he knew not what he did, and the seal of a kiss indeed from the sacred lips.

Samuel Butler

1835-1902

RAMBLINGS IN CHEAPSIDE

WALKING the other day in Cheapside I saw some turtles in Mr. Sweeting's window, and was tempted to stay and look at them. As I did so I was struck not more by the defences with which they were hedged about, than by the fatuousness of trying to hedge that in at all which, if hedged thoroughly, must die of its own defencefulness. The holes for the head and feet through which the turtle leaks out, as it were, on to the exterior world, and through which it again absorbs the exterior world into itself—'catching on' through them to things that are thus both turtle and not turtle at one and the same time—these holes stultify the armour, and show it to have been designed by a creature with more of faithfulness to a fixed idea, and hence onesidedness, than of that quick sense of relative importances and their changes, which is the main factor of good living.

The turtle obviously had no sense of proportion; it differed so widely from myself that I could not comprehend it; and as this word occurred to me, it occurred also that until my body comprehended its body in a physical material sense, neither would my mind be able to comprehend its mind with any thoroughness. For unity of mind can only be consummated by unity of body; everything, therefore, must be in some respects both knave and fool to all that which has not eaten it, or by which it has not been eaten. As long as the turtle was in the window and I in the street outside, there was no chance of our comprehending one another.

Nevertheless, I knew that I could get it to agree with me if I could so effectually button-hole and fasten on to it as to eat it. Most men have an easy method with turtle soup, and I had no misgiving but that if I could bring my first premise to bear I should prove the better reasoner. My difficulty lay in this initial process, for I had not with me the argument that would alone compel Mr. Sweeting to think that I ought to be allowed to convert the turtles—I mean I had no money in my pocket. No missionary enterprise can be carried on without any money at all, but even so small a sum as half a crown would, I suppose, have enabled me to bring the turtle partly round, and with many half-crowns I could in time no doubt convert the lot, for the turtle needs must go where the money drives. If, as is alleged, the world stands on a turtle, the turtle stands on money. No money no turtle. As for money, that stands on opinion, credit, trust, faith—things that, though highly material in connection with money, are still of immaterial essence.

The steps are perfectly plain. The men who caught the turtles brought a fairly strong and definite opinion to bear upon them, that passed into action, and later on into money. They thought the turtles would come that way, and verified their opinion; on this, will and action were generated, with the result that the men turned the turtles on their backs and carried them off. Mr. Sweeting touched these men with money, which is the outward and visible sign of verified opinion. The customer touches Mr. Sweeting with money, Mr. Sweeting touches the waiter and the cook with money. They touch the turtle with skill and verified opinion. Finally, the customer applies the clinching argument that brushes all sophisms aside, and bids the turtle stand protoplasm to protoplasm with himself, to know even as it is known.

But it must be all touch, touch, touch; skill, opinion, power, and money, passing in and out with one another in any order we like, but still link to link and touch to touch. If there is failure anywhere in respect of opinion, skill, power, or money, either as regards quantity or quality, the chain can be no stronger than its weakest link, and the turtle and the clinching argument will fly asunder. Of course, if there is an initial failure in connection, through defect in any member of the chain, or of connection between the links, it will no more be attempted to bring the turtle and the clinching argument together, than it will to chain up a dog with two pieces of broken chain that are disconnected. The contact throughout must be conceived as absolute; and yet perfect contact is inconceivable by us, for on becoming perfect it ceases to be contact, and becomes essential, once for all inseverable, identity. The most absolute contact short of this is still contact by courtesy only. So here, as everywhere else,

Eurydice glides off as we are about to grasp her. We can see nothing face to face; our utmost seeing is but a fumbling of blind finger-ends in an overcrowded pocket.

Presently my own blind finger-ends fished up the conclusion, that as I had neither time nor money to spend on perfecting the chain that would put me in full spiritual contact with Mr. Sweeting's turtles, I had better leave them to complete their education at someone else's expense rather than mine, so I walked on towards the Bank. As I did so it struck me how continually we are met by this melting of one existence into another. The limits of the body seem well defined enough as definitions go, but definitions seldom go far. What, for example, can seem more distinct from a man than his banker or his solicitor? Yet these are commonly so much parts of him that he can no more cut them off and grow new ones, than he can grow new legs or arms; neither must he wound his solicitor; a wound in the solicitor is a very serious thing. As for his bank—failure of his bank's action may be as fatal to a man as failure of his heart. I have said nothing about the medical or spiritual adviser, but most men grow into the society that surrounds them by the help of these four main tap-roots, and not only into the world of humanity, but into the universe at large. We can, indeed, grow butchers, bakers, and greengrocers, almost *ad libitum*, but these are low developments, and correspond to skin, hair, or finger-nails. Those of us again who are not highly enough organised to have grown a solicitor or banker can generally repair the loss of whatever social organisation they may possess as freely as lizards are said to grow new tails; but this with the higher social, as well as organic, developments is only possible to a very limited extent.

The doctrine of metempsychosis, or transmigration of souls—a doctrine to which the foregoing considerations are for the most part easy corollaries—crops up no matter in what direction we allow our thoughts to wander. And we meet instances of transmigration of body as well as of soul. I do not mean that both body and soul have transmigrated together, far from it; but that, as we can often recognise a transmigrated mind in an alien body, so we not less often see a body that is clearly only a transmigration, linked on to someone else's new and alien soul. We meet people every day whose bodies are evidently those of men and women long dead, but whose appearance we know through their portraits. We see them going about in omnibuses, railway carriages, and in all public places. The cards have been shuffled, and they have drawn fresh lots in life and nationalities, but anyone fairly well up in medieval and last-century portraiture knows them at a glance.

Going down once towards Italy I saw a young man in the train whom I recognised, only he seemed to have got younger. He was with a friend, and his face was in continual play, but for some little time I puzzled in vain to recollect where it was that I had seen him before. All of a sudden I remembered he was King Francis I of France. I had hitherto thought the face of this king impossible, but when I saw it in play I understood it. His great contemporary Henry VIII keeps a restaurant in Oxford Street. Falstaff drove one of the St. Gothard diligences for many years, and only retired when the railway was opened. Titian once made me a pair of boots at Vicenza, and not very good ones. At Modena I had my hair cut by a young man whom I perceived to be Raffaelle. The model who sat to him for his celebrated Madonnas is first lady in a confectionery establishment at Montreal. She has a little motherly pimple on the left side of her nose that is misleading at first, but on examination she is readily recognised; probably Raffaelle's model had the pimple too, but Raffaelle left it out—as he would.

Handel, of course, is Madame Patey. Give Madame Patey Handel's wig and clothes, and there would be no telling her from Handel. It is not only that the features and the shape of the head are the same, but there is a certain imperiousness of expression and attitude about Handel which he hardly attempts to conceal in Madame Patey. It is a curious coincidence that he should continue to be such an incomparable renderer of his own music. Pope Julius II was the late Mr. Darwin. Rameses II is a blind woman now, and stands in Holborn, holding a tin mug. I never could understand why I always found myself humming 'They oppressed them with burthens' when I passed her, till one day I was looking in Mr. Spooner's window in the Strand, and saw a photograph of Rameses II. Mary Queen of Scots wears surgical boots and is subject to fits, near the Horse Shoe in Tottenham Court Road.

Michael Angelo is a commissionaire; I saw him on board the *Glen Rosa*, which used to run every day from London to Clacton-on-Sea and back. It gave me quite a turn when I saw him coming down the stairs from the upper deck, with his bronzed face, flattened nose, and with the familiar bar upon his forehead. I never liked Michael Angelo, and never shall, but I am afraid of him, and was near trying to hide when I saw him coming towards me. He had not got his commissionaire's uniform on, and I did not know he was one till I met him a month or so later in the Strand. When we got to Blackwall the music struck up and people began to dance. I never saw a man dance so much in my life. He did not miss a dance all the way to Clacton, nor all the way back again, and when not dancing he was flirting and cracking jokes. I could hardly believe my eyes when I reflected that this man had painted the famous 'Last Judgment,' and had made all those statues.

Dante is, or was a year or two ago, a waiter at Brissago on the Lago Maggiore, only he is better-tempered-looking, and has a more intellectual expression. He gave me his ideas upon beauty: 'Tutto ch' è vero è bello,' he exclaimed, with all his old self-confidence. I am not afraid of Dante. I know people by their friends, and he went about with Virgil, so I said with some severity, 'No, Dante, il naso della Signora Robinson è vero, ma non è bello'; and he admitted I was right. Beatrice's name is Towler; she is waitress at a small inn in German Switzerland. I used to sit at my window and hear people call 'Towler, Towler, Towler,' fifty times in a forenoon. She was the exact antithesis to Abra; Abra, if I remember, used to come before they called her name, but no matter how often they called Towler, everyone came before she did. I suppose they spelt her name Taula, but to me it sounded Towler; I never, however, met anyone else with this name. She was a sweet, artless little hussy, who made me play the piano to her, and she said it was lovely. Of course I only played my own compositions; so I believed her, and it all went off very nicely. I thought it might save trouble if I did not tell her who she really was, so I said nothing about it.

I met Socrates once. He was my muleteer on an excursion which I will not name, for fear it should identify the man. The moment I saw my guide I knew he was somebody, but for the life of me I could not remember who. All of a sudden it flashed across me that he was Socrates. He talked enough for six, but it was all in *dialetto*, so I could not understand him, nor, when I had discovered who he was, did I much try to do so. He was a good creature, a trifle given to stealing fruit and vegetables, but an amiable man enough. He had had a long day with his mule and me, and he only asked me five francs. I gave him ten, for I pitied his poor old patched boots, and there was a meekness about him that touched me. 'And now, Socrates,' said I at parting, 'we go on our several ways, you to steal tomatoes, I to filch ideas from other people; for the rest—

which of these two roads will be the better going, our father which is in heaven knows, but we know not.'

I have never seen Mendelssohn, but there is a fresco of him on the terrace, or open-air dining-room, of an inn at Chiavenna. He is not called Mendelssohn, but I knew him by his legs. He is in the costume of a dandy of some five-and-forty years ago, is smoking a cigar, and appears to be making an offer of marriage to his cook. Beethoven both my friend Mr. H. Festing Jones and I have had the good fortune to meet; he is an engineer now, and does not know one note from another; he has quite lost his deafness, is married, and is, of course, a little squat man with the same refractory hair that he always had. It was very interesting to watch him, and Jones remarked that before the end of dinner he had become positively posthumous. One morning I was told the Beethovens were going away, and before long I met their two heavy boxes being carried down the stairs. The boxes were so squab and like their owners, that I half thought for a moment that they were inside, and should hardly have been surprised to see them spring up like a couple of Jacks-in-the-box. 'Sono indentro?' said I, with a frown of wonder, pointing to the boxes. The porters knew what I meant, and laughed. But there is no end to the list of people whom I have been able to recognise, and before I had got through it myself, I found I had walked some distance, and had involuntarily paused in front of a second-hand bookstall.

I do not like books. I believe I have the

smallest library of any literary man in London, and I have no wish to increase it. I keep my books at the British Museum and at Mudie's, and it makes me very angry if anyone gives me one for my private library. I once heard two ladies disputing in a railway carriage as to whether one of them had or had not been wasting money. 'I spent it in books,' said the accused, 'and it's not wasting money to buy books.' 'Indeed, my dear, I think it is,' was the rejoinder, and in practice I agree with it. Webster's Dictionary, Whitaker's Almanack, and Bradshaw's Railway Guide should be sufficient for any ordinary library; it will be time enough to go beyond these when the mass of useful and entertaining matter which they provide has been mastered. Nevertheless, I admit that sometimes, if not particularly busy, I stop at a second-hand bookstall and turn over a book or two from mere force of habit.

I know not what made me pick up a copy of Æschylus—of course in an English version—or rather I know not what made Æschylus take up with me, for he took me rather than I him; but no sooner had he got me than he began puzzling me, as he has done any time this forty years, to know wherein his transcendent merit can be supposed to lie. To me he is, like the greater number of classics in all ages and countries, a literary Struldbrug, rather than a true ambrosia-fed immortal. There are true immortals, but they are few and far between; most classics are as great impostors dead as they were when living, and while posing as gods are, five-sevenths of them, only Struldbrugs. It comforts me to remember that Aristophanes liked Æschylus no better than I do. True, he praises him by comparison with Sophocles and Euripides, but he only does so that he may run down these last more effectively. Aristophanes is a safe man to follow, nor do I see why it should not be as correct to laugh with him as to pull a long face with the Greek Professors; but this is neither here nor there, for no one really cares about Æschylus; the more interesting question is how he contrived to make so many people for so many years pretend to care about him.

Perhaps he married somebody's daughter. If a man would get hold of the public ear, he must pay, marry, or fight. I have never understood that Æschylus was a man of means, and the fighters do not write poetry, so I suppose he must have married a theatrical manager's daughter, and got his plays brought out that way. The ear of any age or country is like its land, air, and water; it seems limitless but is really limited, and is already in the keeping of those who naturally enough will have no squatting on such valuable property. It is written and talked up to as closely as the means of subsistence are bred up to by a teeming population. There is not a square inch of it but is in private hands, and he who would freehold any part of it must do so by purchase, marriage, or fighting, in the usual way —and fighting gives the longest, safest tenure. The public itself has hardly more voice in the question who shall have its ear, than the land has in choosing its owners. It is farmed as those who own it think most profitable to themselves, and small blame to them; nevertheless, it has a residuum of mulishness which the land has not, and does sometimes dispossess its tenants. It is in this residuum that those who fight place their hope and trust.

Or perhaps Æschylus squared the leading critics of his time. When one comes to think of it, he must have done so, for how is it conceivable that such plays should have had such runs if he had not? I met a lady one year in Switzerland who had some parrots that always travelled with her and were the idols of her life. These parrots would not let anyone read aloud in their presence, unless they heard their own names introduced from time to time. If these were freely interpolated into the text they would remain as still as stones, for they thought the reading was about themselves. If it was not about them it could not be allowed. The leaders of literature are like these parrots; they do not look at what a man writes, nor if they did would they understand it much better than the parrots do; but they like the sound of their own names, and if these are freely interpolated in a tone they take as friendly, they may even give ear to an outsider. Otherwise they will scream him off if they can.

I should not advise anyone with ordinary independence of mind to attempt the public ear unless he is confident that he can out-lung and out-last his own generation; for if he has any force, people will and ought to be on their guard against him, inasmuch as there is no knowing where he may not take them. Besides, they have staked their money on the wrong men so often without suspecting it, that when there comes one whom they do suspect it would be madness not to bet against him. True, he may die before he has outscreamed his opponents, but that has nothing to do with it. If his scream was well pitched it will sound clearer when he is dead. We do not know what death is. If we know so little about life which we have experienced, how shall we know about death which we have not—and in the nature of things never can? Everyone, as I said years ago in *Alps and Sanctuaries*, is an immortal to himself, for he cannot know that he is dead until he is dead, and when dead how can he know anything about anything? All we know is, that even the humblest dead may live long after all trace of the body has disappeared; we see them doing it in the bodies and memories of those that come after them; and not a few live so much longer and more effectually than is desirable, that it has been necessary to get rid of them by Act of Parliament. It is love that alone gives life, and the truest life is that which we live not in ourselves but vicariously in others, and with which we have no concern. Our concern is so to order ourselves that we may be of the number of them that enter into life—although we know it not.

Æschylus did so order himself; but his life is not of that inspiriting kind that can be won through fighting the good fight only—or being believed to have fought it. His voice is the echo of a drone, drone-begotten and drone-sustained.

It is not a tone that a man must utter or die—
nay, even though he die; and likely enough half
the allusions and hard passages in Æschylus of
which we can make neither head nor tail are in
reality only puffs of some of the literary leaders
of his time.

The lady above referred to told me more about
her parrots. She was like a Nasmyth's hammer
going slow—very gentle, but irresistible. She
always read the newspaper to them. What was
the use of having a newspaper if one did not read
it to one's parrots?

'And have you divined,' I asked, 'to which
side they incline in politics?'

'They do not like Mr. Gladstone,' was the
somewhat freezing answer: 'this is the only point
on which we disagree, for I adore him. Don't
ask more about this, it is a great grief to me.
I tell them everything,' she continued, 'and hide
no secret from them.'

'But can any parrot be trusted to keep a
secret?'

'Mine can.'

'And on Sundays do you give them the same
course of reading as on a week-day, or do you
make a difference?'

'On Sundays I always read them a genea-
logical chapter from the Old or New Testament,
for I can thus introduce their names without
profanity. I always keep tea by me in case they
should ask for it in the night, and I have an
Etna to warm it for them; they take milk and
sugar. The old white-headed clergyman came
to see them last night; it was very painful, for

Jocko reminded him so strongly of his late . . .'

I thought she was going to say 'wife,' but it proved to have been only of a parrot that he had once known and loved.

One evening she was in difficulties about the quarantine, which was enforced that year on the Italian frontier. The local doctor had gone down that morning to see the Italian doctor and arrange some details. 'Then, perhaps, my dear,' she said to her husband, 'he is the quarantine.' 'No, my love,' replied her husband. 'The quarantine is not a person, it is a place where they put people'; but she would not be comforted, and suspected the quarantine as an enemy that might at any moment pounce upon her and her parrots. So a lady told me once that she had been in like trouble about the anthem. She read in her Prayer Book that in choirs and places where they sing 'here followeth the anthem,' yet the person with this most mysteriously sounding name never did follow. They had a choir, and no one could say the church was not a place where they sang, for they did sing—both chants and hymns. Why, then, this persistent slackness on the part of the anthem, who at this juncture should follow her papa, the rector, into the reading-desk? No doubt he would come some day, and then what would he be like? Fair or dark? Tall or short? Would he be bald and wear spectacles like papa, would he be young and good-looking? Anyhow, there was something wrong, for it was announced that he would follow, and he never did follow; therefore there was no knowing what he might not do next.

I heard of the parrots a year or two later as giving lessons in Italian to an English maid. I do not know what their terms were. Alas! since then both they and their mistress have joined the majority. When the poor lady felt her end was near she desired (and the responsibility for this must rest with her, not me) that the birds might be destroyed, as fearing that they might come to be neglected, and knowing that they could never be loved again as she had loved them. On being told that all was over, she said, 'Thank you,' and immediately expired.

Reflecting in such random fashion, and strolling with no greater method, I worked my way back through Cheapside and found myself once more in front of Sweeting's window. Again the turtles attracted me. They were alive, and so far at any rate they agreed with me. Nay, they had eyes, mouths, legs, if not arms, and feet, so there was much in which we were both of a mind, but surely they must be mistaken in arming themselves so very heavily. Any creature on getting what the turtle aimed at would over-reach itself and be landed not in safety but annihilation. It should have no communion with the outside world at all, for death could creep in wherever the creature could creep out; and it must creep out somewhere if it was to hook on to outside things. What death can be more absolute than such absolute isolation? Perfect death, indeed if it were attainable (which it is not), is as near perfect security as we can reach, but it is not the kind of security aimed at by any animal that is at the pains of defending itself. For such want to have things both ways, desiring the livingness of life without its perils, and the safety of death without its deadness, and some of us do actually get this for a considerable time, but we do not get it by plating ourselves with armour as the turtle does. We tried this in the Middle Ages, and no longer mock ourselves with the weight of armour that our forefathers carried in battle. Indeed the more deadly the weapons of attack become the more we go into the fight slug-wise.

Slugs have ridden their contempt for defensive armour as much to death as the turtles their pursuit of it. They have hardly more than skin enough to hold themselves together; they court death every time they cross the road. Yet death comes not to them more than to the turtle, whose defences are so great that there is little left inside to be defended. Moreover, the slugs fare best in the long run, for turtles are dying out, while slugs are not, and there must be millions of slugs all the world over for every single turtle. Of the two vanities, therefore, that of the slug seems most substantial.

In either case the creature thinks itself safe, but is sure to be found out sooner or later; nor is it easy to explain this mockery save by reflecting that everything must have its meat in due season, and that meat can only be found for such a multitude of mouths by giving everything as meat in due season to something else. This is like the Kilkenny cats, or robbing Peter to pay Paul; but it is the way of the world, and as every animal must contribute in kind to the picnic of

the universe, one does not see what better
arrangement could be made than the providing
each race with a hereditary fallacy, which shall
in the end get it into a scrape, but which shall
generally stand the wear and tear of life for some
time. '*Do ut des*' is the writing on all flesh to him
that eats it; and no creature is dearer to itself
than it is to some other that would devour it.

Nor is there any statement or proposition more
invulnerable than living forms are. Propositions
prey upon and are grounded upon one another
just like living forms. They support one another
as plants and animals do; they are based ultimately on credit, or faith, rather than the cash of
irrefragable conviction. The whole universe is
carried on on the credit system, and if the mutual
confidence on which it is based were to collapse,
it must itself collapse immediately. Just or unjust, it lives by faith; it is based on vague and
impalpable opinion that by some inscrutable
process passes into will and action, and is made
manifest in matter and in flesh: it is meteoric—
suspended in mid-air; it is the baseless fabric of
a vision so vast, so vivid, and so gorgeous that
no base can seem more broad than such stupendous baselessness, and yet any man can bring it
about his ears by being over-curious; when faith
fails, a system based on faith fails also.

Whether the universe is really a paying concern, or whether it is an inflated bubble that must
burst sooner or later, this is another matter. If
people were to demand cash payment in irrefragable certainty for everything that they have
taken hitherto as paper money on the credit of

the bank of public opinion, is there money enough behind it all to stand so great a drain even on so great a reserve? Probably there is not, but happily there can be no such panic, for even though the cultured classes may do so, the uncultured are too dull to have brains enough to commit such stupendous folly. It takes a long course of academic training to educate a man up to the standard which he must reach before he can entertain such questions seriously, and by a merciful dispensation of Providence university training is almost as costly as it is unprofitable. The majority will thus be always unable to afford it, and will base their opinions on mother wit and current opinion rather than on demonstration.

So I turned my steps homewards; I saw a good many more things on my way home, but I was told that I was not to see more this time than I could get into twelve pages of the *Universal Review*; I must therefore reserve any remark which I think might perhaps entertain the reader for another occasion.

A MEDIEVAL GIRL SCHOOL

THIS last summer I revisited Oropa, near Biella, to see what connection I could find between the Oropa chapels and those at Varallo. I will take this opportunity of describing the chapels at Oropa, and more especially the remarkable fossil, or petrified girl school, commonly known as the *Dimora*, or Sojourn of the Virgin Mary in the Temple.

If I do not take these works so seriously as the reader may expect, let me beg him, before he blames me, to go to Oropa and see the originals for himself. Have the good people of Oropa themselves taken them very seriously? Are we in an atmosphere where we need be at much pains to speak with bated breath? We, as is well known, love to take even our pleasures sadly; the Italians take even their sadness *allegramente*, and combine devotion with amusement in a manner that we shall do well to study if not imitate. For this best agrees with what we gather to have been the custom of Christ himself, who, indeed, never speaks of austerity but to condemn it. If Christianity is to be a living faith, it must penetrate a man's whole life, so that he can no more rid himself of it than he can of his flesh and bones or of his breathing. The Christianity that can be taken up and laid down as if it were a watch or a book is Christianity in name only. The true Christian can no more part from Christ in mirth than in sorrow. And, after all, what is the essence of Christianity? What is the kernel of the nut? Surely common sense and cheerfulness, with unflinching opposition to the charlatanisms and Pharisaisms of a man's own times. The essence of Christianity lies neither in dogma, nor yet in abnormally holy life, but in faith in an unseen world, in doing one's duty, in speaking the truth, in finding the true life rather in others than in oneself, and in the certain hope that he who loses his life on these behalfs finds more than he has lost. What can Agnosticism do against such Christianity as this? I should be shocked

if anything I had ever written or shall ever write
should seem to make light of these things. I
should be shocked also if I did not know how to
be amused with things that amiable people
obviously intended to be amusing.

The reader may need to be reminded that
Oropa is among the somewhat infrequent sanctuaries at which the Madonna and infant Christ
are not white, but black. I shall return to this
peculiarity of Oropa later on, but will leave it
for the present. For the general characteristics
of the place I must refer the reader to my book
Alps and Sanctuaries. I propose to confine myself
here to the ten or a dozen chapels containing
life-sized terra-cotta figures, painted up to nature,
that form one of the main features of the place.
At a first glance, perhaps, all these chapels will
seem uninteresting; I venture to think, however,
that some, if not most of them, though falling a
good deal short of the best work at Varallo and
Crea, are still in their own way of considerable
importance. The first chapel with which we
need concern ourselves is numbered 4, and shows
the Conception of the Virgin Mary. It represents St. Anne as kneeling before a terrific dragon
or, as the Italians call it, 'insect,' about the size of
a Crystal Palace pleiosaur. This 'insect' is supposed to have just had its head badly crushed by
St. Anne, who seems to be begging its pardon.
The text 'Ipsa conteret caput tuum' is written
outside the chapel. The figures have no artistic
interest. As regards dragons being called insects,
the reader may perhaps remember that the island
of S. Giulio, in the Lago d'Orta, was infested

with *insetti*, which S. Giulio destroyed, and which appear, in a fresco underneath the church on the island, to have been monstrous and ferocious dragons; but I cannot remember whether their bodies are divided into three sections, and whether or no they have exactly six legs—without which, I am told, they cannot be true insects.

The fifth chapel represents the Birth of the Virgin. Having obtained permission to go inside it, I found the date 1715 cut large and deep on the back of one figure before baking, and I imagine that this date covers the whole. There is a Queen Anne feeling throughout the composition, and if we were told that the sculptor and Francis Bird, sculptor of the statue in front of St. Paul's Cathedral, had studied under the same master, we could very well believe it. The apartment in which the Virgin was born is spacious, and in striking contrast to the one in which she herself gave birth to the Redeemer. St. Anne occupies the centre of the composition, in an enormous bed; on her right there is a lady of the George Cruikshank style of beauty, and on the left an older person. Both are gesticulating and impressing upon St. Anne the enormous obligation she has just conferred upon mankind; they seem also to be imploring her not to overtax her strength, but, strange to say, they are giving her neither flowers nor anything to eat and drink. I know no other birth of the Virgin in which St. Anne wants so little keeping up.

I have explained in my book *Ex Voto*, but should perhaps repeat here, that the distinguishing characteristic of the Birth of the Virgin, as

rendered by Valsesian artists, is that St. Anne
always has eggs immediately after the infant is
born, and usually a good deal more, whereas the
Madonna never has anything to eat or drink.
The eggs are in accordance with a custom that
still prevails among the peasant classes in the
Valsesia, where women on giving birth to a child
generally are given a *sabaglione*—an egg beaten
up with a little wine, or rum, and sugar. East
of Milan the Virgin's mother does not have eggs,
and I suppose, from the absence of the eggs at
Oropa, that the custom above referred to does
not prevail in the Biellese district. The Virgin
also is invariably washed. St. John the Baptist,
when he is born at all, which is not very often,
is also washed; but I have not observed that
St. Elizabeth has anything like the attention
paid her that is given to St. Anne. What, however, is wanting here at Oropa in meat and drink
is made up in Cupids; they swarm like flies on
the walls, clouds, cornices, and capitals of
columns.

Against the right-hand wall are two lady-
helps, each warming a towel at a glowing fire,
to be ready against the baby should come out of
its bath; while in the right-hand foreground we
have the *levatrice*, who having discharged her
task, and being now so disposed, has removed the
bottle from the chimney-piece, and put it near
some bread, fruit and a chicken, over which she
is about to discuss the confinement with two
other gossips. The *levatrice* is a very characteristic figure, but the best in the chapel is the
one of the head-nurse, near the middle of the

composition; she has now the infant in full charge, and is showing it to St. Joachim, with an expression as though she were telling him that her husband was a merry man. I am afraid Shakespeare was dead before the sculptor was born, otherwise I should have felt certain that he had drawn Juliet's nurse from this figure. As for the little Virgin herself, I believe her to be a fine boy of about ten months old. Viewing the work as a whole, if I only felt more sure what artistic merit really is, I should say that, though the chapel cannot be rated very highly from some standpoints, there are others from which it may be praised warmly enough. It is innocent of anatomy-worship, free from affectation or swagger, and not devoid of a good deal of homely *naïveté*. It can no more be compared with Tabachetti or Donatello than Hogarth can with Rembrandt or Giovanni Bellini; but as it does not transcend the limitations of its age, so neither is it wanting in whatever merits that age possessed; and there is no age without merits of some kind. There is no inscription saying who made the figures, but tradition gives them to Pietro Aureggio Termine, of Biella, commonly called Aureggio. This is confirmed by their strong resemblance to those in the *Dimora* Chapel, in which there is an inscription that names Aureggio as the sculptor.

The sixth chapel deals with the Presentation of the Virgin in the Temple. The Virgin is very small, but it must be remembered that she is only seven years old, and she is not nearly so small as she is at Crea, where, though a life-sized figure is intended, the head is hardly bigger than an apple. She is rushing up the steps with open arms towards the High Priest, who is standing at the top. For her it is nothing alarming; it is the High Priest who appears frightened; but it will all come right in time. The Virgin seems to be saying, 'Why, don't you know me? I'm the Virgin Mary.' But the High Priest does not feel so sure about that, and will make further inquiries. The scene, which comprises some twenty figures, is animated enough, and though it hardly kindles enthusiasm, still does not fail to please. It looks as though of somewhat older date than the Birth of the Virgin chapel, and I should say shows more signs of direct Valsesian influence. In Marocco's book about Oropa it is ascribed to Aureggio, but I find it difficult to accept this.

The seventh, and in many respects most interesting chapel at Oropa, shows what is in reality a medieval Italian girl school, as nearly like the thing itself as the artist could make it; we are expected, however, to see in this the high-class kind of Girton College for young gentlewomen that was attached to the Temple at Jerusalem, under the direction of the Chief Priest's wife, or some one of his near female relatives. Here all well-to-do Jewish young women completed their education, and here accordingly we find the Virgin, whose parents desired she should shine in every accomplishment, and enjoy all the advantages their ample means commanded.

I have met with no traces of the Virgin during

the years between her Presentation in the Temple and her becoming head girl at Temple College. These years, we may be assured, can hardly have been other than eventful; but incidents, or bits of life, are like living forms—it is only here and there, as by rare chance, that one of them gets arrested and fossilised; the greater number disappear like the greater number of antediluvian molluscs, and no one can say why one of these flies, as it were, of life should get preserved in amber more than another. Talk, indeed, about luck and cunning; what a grain of sand as against a hundredweight is cunning's share here as against luck's. What moment could be more humdrum and unworthy of special record than the one chosen by the artist for the chapel we are considering? Why should this one get arrested in its flight and made immortal when so many worthier ones have perished? Yet preserved it assuredly is; it is as though some fairy's wand had struck the medieval Miss Pinkerton, Amelia Sedley, and others who do duty instead of the Hebrew originals. It has locked them up as sleeping beauties, whose charms all may look upon. Surely the hours are like the women grinding at the mill—the one is taken and the other left, and none can give the reason more than he can say why Gallio should have won immortality by caring for none of 'these things.'

It seems to me, moreover, that fairies have changed their practice now in the matter of sleeping beauties, much as shopkeepers have done in Regent Street. Formerly the shopkeeper used to shut up his goods behind strong shutters, so that no one might see them after closing hours. Now he leaves everything open to the eye and turns the gas on. So the fairies, who used to lock up their sleeping beauties in impenetrable thickets, now leave them in the most public places they can find, as knowing ʻhat they will there most certainly escape notice. Look at De Hooghe; look at *The Pilgrim's Progress*, or even Shakespeare himself—how long they slept unawakened, though they were in broad daylight and on the public thoroughfares all the time. Look at Tabachetti, and the masterpieces he left at Varallo. His figures there are exposed to the gaze of every passer-by; yet who heeds them? Who, save a very few, even know of their existence? Look again at Gaudenzio Ferrari, or the 'Danse des Paysans,' by Holbein, to which I ventured to call attention in the *Universal Review*. No, no; if a thing be in Central Africa, it is the glory of this age to find it out; so the fairies think it safer to conceal their *protégés* under a show of openness; for the schoolmaster is much abroad, and there is no hedge so thick or so thorny as the dulness of culture.

It may be, again, that ever so many years hence, when Mr. Darwin's earth-worms shall have buried Oropa hundreds of feet deep, someone sinking a well or making a railway-cutting will unearth these chapels, and will believe them to have been houses, and to contain the *exuviæ* of the living forms that tenanted them. In the meantime, however, let us return to a consideration of the chapel as it may now be seen by anyone who cares to pass that way.

The work consists of about forty figures in all, not counting Cupids, and is divided into four main divisions. First, there is the large public sitting-room or drawing-room of the College, where the elder young ladies are engaged in various elegant employments. Three, at a table to the left, are making a mitre for the Bishop, as may be seen from the model on the table. Some are merely spinning or about to spin. One young lady, sitting rather apart from the others, is doing an elaborate piece of needlework at a tambour-frame near the window; others are making lace or slippers, probably for the new curate; another is struggling with a letter, or perhaps a theme, which seems to be giving her a good deal of trouble, but which, when done, will, I am sure, be beautiful. One dear little girl is simply reading *Paul and Virginia* underneath the window, and is so concealed that I hardly think she can be seen from the outside at all, though from inside she is delightful; it was with great regret that I could not get her into any photograph. One most amiable young woman has got a child's head on her lap, the child having played itself to sleep. All are industriously and agreeably employed in some way or other; all are plump; all are nice-looking; there is not one Becky Sharp in the whole school; on the contrary, as in 'Pious Orgies,' all is pious—or sub-pious—and all, if not great, is at least eminently respectable. One feels that St. Joachim and St. Anne could not have chosen a school more judiciously, and that if one had a daughter oneself this is exactly where one would wish to place her. If there is a fault of any kind in the arrangements, it is that they do not keep cats enough. The place is overrun with mice, though what these can find to eat I know not. It occurs to me also that the young ladies might be kept a little more free of spiders' webs; but in all these chapels, bats, mice, and spiders are troublesome.

Off the main drawing-room on the side facing the window there is a daïs, which is approached by a large raised semicircular step, higher than the rest of the floor, but lower than the daïs itself. The daïs is, of course, reserved for the venerable Lady Principal and the under-mistresses, one of whom, by the way, is a little more *mondaine* than might have been expected, and is admiring herself in a looking-glass—unless, indeed, she is only looking to see if there is a spot of ink on her face. The Lady Principal is seated near a table, on which lie some books in expensive bindings, which I imagine to have been presented to her by the parents of pupils who were leaving school. One has given her a photographic album; another a large scrapbook, for illustrations of all kinds; a third volume has red edges, and is presumably of a devotional character. If I dared venture another criticism, I should say it would be better not to keep the ink-pot on the top of these books. The Lady Principal is being read to by the monitress for the week, whose duty it was to recite selected passages from the most approved Hebrew writers; she appears to be a good deal outraged, possibly at the faulty intonation of the reader, which she has long tried vainly to correct; or perhaps she has been hearing of the atrocious way in which her forefathers had treated the prophets, and is explaining to the young ladies how impossible it would be, in their own more enlightened age, for a prophet to fail of recognition.

On the half-daïs, as I suppose the large semi-circular step between the main room and the daïs should be called, we find, first, the monitress for the week, who stands up while she recites; and secondly, the Virgin herself, who is the only pupil allowed a seat so near to the august presence of the Lady Principal. She is ostensibly doing a piece of embroidery which is stretched on a cushion on her lap, but I should say that she was chiefly interested in the nearest of four pretty little Cupids, who are all trying to attract her attention, though they pay no court to any other young lady. I have sometimes wondered whether the obviously scandalised gesture of the Lady Principal might not be directed at these Cupids, rather than at anything the monitress may have been reading, for she would surely find them disquieting. Or she may be saying, 'Why, bless me! I do declare the Virgin has got another hamper, and St. Anne's cakes are always so terribly rich!' Certainly the hamper is there, close to the Virgin, and the Lady Principal's action may be well directed at it, but it may have been sent to some other young lady, and be put on the sub-daïs for public exhibition. It looks as if it might have come from Fortnum and Mason's, and I half expected to find a label, addressing it to 'The Virgin Mary, Temple College, Jerusalem,' but if ever there was one the

mice have long since eaten it. The Virgin herself
does not seem to care much about it, but if she
has a fault it is that she is generally a little
apathetic.

Whose the hamper was, however, is a point we
shall never now certainly determine, for the best
fossil is worse than the worst living form. Why,
alas! was not Mr. Edison alive when this chapel
was made? We might then have had a daily
phonographic recital of the conversation, and an
announcement might be put outside the chapels,
telling us at what hours the figures would speak.

On either side of the main room there are two
annexes opening out from it; these are reserved
chiefly for the younger children, some of whom,
I think, are little boys. In the left annex, behind
the ladies who are making a mitre, there is a child
who has got a cake, and another has some fruit—
possibly given them by the Virgin—and a third
child is begging for some of it. The light failed
so completely here that I was not able to photograph any of these figures. It was a dull September afternoon, and the clouds had settled thick
round the chapel, which is never very light, and
is nearly 4000 feet above the sea. I waited till
such twilight as made it hopeless that more detail
could be got—and a queer ghostly place enough
it was to wait in—but after giving the plate an
exposure of fifty minutes, I saw I could get no
more, and desisted.

These long photographic exposures have the
advantage that one is compelled to study a work
in detail through mere lack of other employment,
and that one can take one's notes in peace with-

out being tempted to hurry over them; but even so I continually find I have omitted to note, and have clean forgotten, much that I want later on.

In the other annex there are also one or two younger children, but it seems to have been set apart for conversation and relaxation more than any other part of the establishment.

I have already said that the work is signed by an inscription inside the chapel, to the effect that the sculptures are by Pietro Aureggio Termine di Biella. It will be seen that the young ladies are exceedingly like one another, and that the artist aimed at nothing more than a faithful rendering of the life of his own times. Let us be thankful that he aimed at nothing less. Perhaps his wife kept a girls' school; or he may have had a large family of fat, good-natured daughters, whose little ways he had studied attentively; at all events the work is full of spontaneous incident, and cannot fail to become more and more interesting as the age it renders falls farther back into the past. It is to be regretted that many artists, better-known men, have not been satisfied with the humbler ambitions of this most amiable and interesting sculptor. If he has left us no laboured life-studies, he has at least done something for us which we can find nowhere else, which we should be very sorry not to have, and the fidelity of which to Italian life at the beginning of the eighteenth century will not be disputed.

The eighth chapel is that of the *Sposalizio*, is certainly not by Aureggio, and I should say was mainly by the same sculptor who did the

Presentation in the Temple. On going inside I found the figures had come from more than one source; some of them are constructed so absolutely on Valsesian principles, as regards technique, that it may be assumed they came from Varallo. Each of these last figures is in three pieces, that are baked separately and cemented together afterwards, hence they are more easily transported; no more clay is used than is absolutely necessary; and the off-side of the figure is neglected; they will be found chiefly, if not entirely, at the top of the steps. The other figures are more solidly built, and do not remind me in their business features of anything in the Valsesia. There was a sculptor, Francesco Sala, of Locarno (doubtless the village a short distance below Varallo, and not the Locarno on the Lago Maggiore), who made designs for some of the Oropa chapels, and some of whose letters are still preserved, but whether the Valsesian figures in this present work are by him or not I cannot say.

The statues are twenty-five in number; I could find no date or signature; the work reminds me of Montrigone; several of the figures are not at all bad, and several have horsehair for hair, as at Varallo. The effect of the whole composition is better than we have a right to expect from any sculpture dating from the beginning of the eighteenth century.

The ninth chapel, the Annunciation, presents no feature of interest; nor yet does the tenth, the Visit of Mary to Elizabeth. The eleventh, the Nativity, though rather better, is still not remarkable.

The twelfth, the Purification, is absurdly bad, but I do not know whether the expression of strong personal dislike to the Virgin which the High Priest wears is intended as prophetic, or whether it is the result of incompetence, or whether it is merely a smile gone wrong in the baking. It is amusing to find Marocco, who has not been strict about archæological accuracy hitherto, complain here that there is an anachronism, inasmuch as some young ecclesiastics are dressed as they would be at present, and one of them actually carries a wax candle. This is not as it should be; in works like those at Oropa, where implicit reliance is justly placed on the earnest endeavours that have been so successfully made to thoroughly and carefully and patiently ensure the accuracy of the minutest details, it is a pity that even a single error should have escaped detection; this, however, has most unfortunately happened here, and Marocco feels it his duty to put us on our guard. He explains that the mistake arose from the sculptor's having taken both his general arrangement and his details from some picture of the fourteenth or fifteenth century, when the value of the strictest historical accuracy was not yet so fully understood.

It seems to me that in the matter of accuracy, priests and men of science whether lay or regular on the one hand, and plain people whether lay or regular on the other, are trying to play a different game, and fail to understand one another because they do not see that their objects are not the same. The cleric and the man of science (who is only the cleric in his latest development) are trying to develop a throat with two distinct passages—one that shall refuse to pass even the smallest gnat, and another that shall gracefully gulp even the largest camel; whereas we men of the street desire but one throat, and are content that this shall swallow nothing bigger than a pony. Everyone knows that there is no such effectual means of developing the power to swallow camels as incessant watchfulness for opportunities of straining at gnats, and this should explain many passages that puzzle us in the work both of our clerics and our scientists. I, not being a man of science, still continue to do what I said I did in *Alps and Sanctuaries*, and make it a rule to earnestly and patiently and carefully swallow a few of the smallest gnats I can find several times a day, as the best astringent for the throat I know of.

The thirteenth chapel is the Marriage Feast at Cana of Galilee. This is the best chapel as a work of art; indeed, it is the only one which can claim to be taken quite seriously. Not that all the figures are very good; those to the left of the composition are commonplace enough; nor are the Christ and the giver of the feast at all remarkable; but the ten or dozen figures of guests and attendants at the right-hand end of the work are as good as anything of their kind can be, and remind me so strongly of Tabachetti that I cannot doubt they were done by someone who was indirectly influenced by that great sculptor's work. It is not likely that Tabachetti was alive long after 1640, by which time he would have been about eighty years old; and the foundations of this chapel were not laid till about 1690; the statues are probably a few years later; they can hardly, therefore, be by one who had even studied under Tabachetti; but until I found out the dates, and went inside the chapel to see the way in which the figures had been constructed, I was inclined to think they might be by Tabachetti himself, of whom, indeed, they are not unworthy. On examining the figures I found them more heavily constructed than Tabachetti's are, with smaller holes for taking out superfluous clay, and more finished on the off-sides. Marocco says the sculptor is not known. I looked in vain for any date or signature. Possibly the right-hand figures (for the left-hand ones can hardly be by the same hand) may be by some sculptor from Crea, which is at no very great distance from Oropa, who was penetrated by Tabachetti's influence; but whether as regards action and concert with one another, or as regards excellence in detail, I do not see how anything can be more realistic, and yet more harmoniously composed. The placing of the musicians in a minstrels' gallery helps the effect; these musicians are six in number, and the other figures are twenty-three. Under the table, between Christ and the giver of the feast, there is a cat.

The fourteenth chapel, the Assumption of the Virgin Mary, is without interest.

The fifteenth, the Coronation of the Virgin, contains forty-six angels, twenty-six cherubs, fifty-six saints, the Holy Trinity, the Madonna herself, and twenty-four innocents, making 156 statues in all. Of these I am afraid there is not one of more than ordinary merit; the most interesting is a half-length nude life-study of Disma—the good thief. After what had been promised him it was impossible to exclude him, but it was felt that a half-length nude figure would be as much as he could reasonably expect.

Behind the sanctuary there is a semi-ruinous and wholly valueless work, which shows the finding of the black image, which is now in the church, but is only shown on great festivals.

This leads us to a consideration that I have delayed till now. The black image is the central feature of Oropa; it is the *raison d'être* of the whole place, and all else is a mere incrustation, so to speak, around it. According to this image, then, which was carved by St. Luke himself, and than which nothing can be better authenticated, both the Madonna and the infant Christ were as black as anything can be conceived. It is not likely that they were as black as they have been painted; no one yet ever was so black as that; yet, even allowing for some exaggeration on St. Luke's part, they must have been exceedingly black if the portrait is to be accepted; and uncompromisingly black they accordingly are on most of the wayside chapels for many a mile around Oropa. Yet in the chapels we have been hitherto considering—works in which, as we know, the most punctilious regard has been shown to accuracy—both the Virgin and Christ are uncompromisingly white. As in the shops under the Colonnade where devotional knick-knacks are sold, you can buy a black china image or a white one, whichever you like; so with the pictures—the black and white are placed side by side—*pagando il danaro si può scegliere*. It rests not with history or with the Church to say whether the Madonna and Child were black or white, but you may settle it for yourself, whichever way you please, or rather you are required, with the acquiescence of the Church, to hold that they were both black and white at one and the same time.

It cannot be maintained that the Church leaves the matter undecided, and by tolerating both types proclaims the question an open one, for she acquiesces in the portrait by St. Luke as genuine. How, then, justify the whiteness of the Holy Family in the chapels? If the portrait is not known as genuine, why set such a stumbling-block in our paths as to show us a black Madonna and a white one, both as historically accurate, within a few yards of one another?

I ask this not in mockery, but as knowing that the Church must have an explanation to give, if she would only give it, and as myself unable to find any, even the most far-fetched, that can bring what we see at Oropa, Loreto and elsewhere into harmony with modern conscience, either intellectual or ethical.

I see, indeed, from an interesting article in the *Atlantic Monthly* for September, 1889, entitled 'The Black Madonna of Loreto,' that black Madonnas were so frequent in ancient Christian art that 'some of the early writers of the Church felt obliged to account for it by explaining that the Virgin was of a very dark complexion, as might be proved by the verse of Canticles which says, "I am black, but comely, O ye daughters of Jerusalem." Others maintained that she became black during her sojourn in Egypt. . . . Priests, of to-day, say that extreme age and exposure to the smoke of countless altar-candles have caused that change in complexion which the more naïve fathers of the Church attributed to the power of an Egyptian sun'; but the writer ruthlessly disposes of this supposition by pointing out that in nearly all the instances of black Madonnas it is the flesh alone that is entirely black, the crimson of the lips, the white of the eyes, and the draperies having preserved their original colour. The authoress of the article (Mrs. Hilliard) goes on to tell us that Pausanias mentions two statues of the black Venus, and says that the oldest statue of Ceres among the Phigalenses was black. She adds that Minerva Aglaurus, the daughter of Cecrops, at Athens, was black; that Corinth had a black Venus, as also the Thespians; that the oracles of Dodona and Delphi were founded by black doves, the emissaries of Venus, and that the Isis Multimammia in the Capitol at Rome is black.

Sometimes I have asked myself whether the Church does not intend to suggest that the whole story falls outside the domain of history, and is to be held as the one great epos, or myth, common to all mankind; adaptable by each nation according to its own several needs; translatable, so to speak, into the facts of each individual nation, as the written word is translatable into its language, but appertaining to the realm of

the imagination rather than to that of the understanding, and precious for spiritual rather than
literal truths. More briefly, I have wondered
whether she may not intend that such details as
whether the Virgin was white or black are of
very little importance in comparison with the
basing of ethics on a story that shall appeal to
black races as well as to white ones.

If so, it is time we were made to understand
this more clearly. If the Church, whether of
Rome or England, would lean to some such view
as this—tainted though it be with mysticism—if
we could see either great branch of the Church
make a frank, authoritative attempt to bring its
teaching into greater harmony with the educated
understanding and conscience of the time,
instead of trying to fetter that understanding
with bonds that gall it daily more and more
profoundly; then I, for one, in view of the difficulty and graciousness of the task, and in view
of the great importance of historical continuity,
would gladly sink much of my own private
opinion as to the value of the Christian ideal,
and would gratefully help either Church or both,
according to the best of my very feeble ability.
On these terms, indeed, I could swallow not a
few camels myself cheerfully enough.

Can we, however, see any signs as though
either Rome or England will stir hand or foot to
meet us? Can any step be pointed to as though
either Church wished to make things easier for
men holding the opinions held by the late Mr.
Darwin, or by Mr. Herbert Spencer and Professor Huxley? How can those who accept

evolution with any thoroughness accept such doctrines as the Incarnation or the Redemption with any but a quasi-allegorical and poetical interpretation? Can we conceivably accept these doctrines in the literal sense in which the Church advances them? And can the leaders of the Church be blind to the resistlessness of the current that has set against those literal interpretations which she seems to hug more and more closely the more religious life is awakened at all? The clergyman is wanted as supplementing the doctor and the lawyer in all civilised communities; these three keep watch on one another, and prevent one another from becoming too powerful. I, who distrust the *doctrinaire* in science even more than the *doctrinaire* in religion, should view with dismay the abolition of the Church of England, as knowing that a blatant bastard science would instantly step into her shoes; but if some such deplorable consummation is to be avoided in England, it can only be through more evident leaning on the part of our clergy to such an interpretation of the Sacred History as the presence of a black and white Madonna almost side by side at Oropa appears to suggest.

I fear that in these last paragraphs I may have trenched on dangerous grounds, but it is not possible to go to such places as Oropa without asking oneself what they mean and involve. As for the average Italian pilgrims, they do not appear to give the matter so much as a thought. They love Oropa, and flock to it in thousands during the summer; the President of the Administration assured me that they lodged, after a fashion, as many as ten thousand pilgrims on the 15th of last August. It is astonishing how living the statues are to these people, and how the wicked are upbraided and the good applauded. At Varallo, since I took the photographs I published in my book *Ex Voto*, an angry pilgrim has smashed the nose of the dwarf in Tabachetti's Journey to Calvary, for no other reason than inability to restrain his indignation against one who was helping to inflict pain on Christ. It is the real hair and the painting up to nature that does it. Here at Oropa I found a paper on the floor of the *Sposalizio* Chapel, which ran as follows:—

'By the grace of God and the will of the administrative chapter of this sanctuary, there have come here to work ——, mason, —— —, carpenter, and —— —, plumber, all of Chiavazza, on the twenty-first day of January, 1886, full of cold (*pieni di freddo*).

'They write these two lines to record their visit. They pray the Blessed Virgin that she will maintain them safe and sound from everything equivocal that may befall them (*sempre sani e salvi da ogni equivoco li possa accadere*). Oh, farewell! We reverently salute all the present statues, and especially the Blessed Virgin, and the reader.'

Through the *Universal Review*, I suppose, all its readers are to consider themselves saluted; at any rate, these good fellows, in the effusiveness of their hearts, actually wrote the above in pencil. I was sorely tempted to steal it, but, after copying it, left it in the Chief Priest's hands instead.

Henry Austin Dobson

1840–1921

AN OLD LONDON BOOKSELLER

'Dec. 22. Mr. John Newbery, of St. Paul's churchyard, sincerely lamented by all who knew him.' These words, copied from the *Gentleman's Magazine* for 1767, record the death of one who, in his way, was an eighteenth-century notability. He belonged to the good old 'Keep-your-Shop-and-your-Shop-will-keep-you' class of tradesmen, who lived without pretence over their places of business, in the City, worked industriously during the week, marched off to St. Bride's or St. Dunstan's on Sunday morning with a crop-eared 'prentice in the rear to carry the great gilt Bible, and jogged away in crowded chaises of summer afternoons to eat tarts at Highgate or drink tea out of china in the Long Room at Bagnigge Wells. In due time they made their 'plumbs'; sent their sons to St. Paul's or Merchant Taylors', sometimes even to Oxford or Cambridge; and finally left their portraits to posterity in the becoming and worshipful garb of Sheriffs or Common-councilmen. Unfortunately for this paper, there is no such limner's likeness of 'honest John Newbery.' Yet we are not wholly without details as to his character and personal appearance. That 'glorious pillar of unshaken orthodoxy,' Dr. Primrose, formerly of Wakefield, for whom, as all the world knows, he had published a pamphlet 'against the Deuterogamists of the age,' describes him as a red-faced good-natured little man, who was always in a hurry. 'He was no sooner alighted,' says the worthy Vicar, 'but he was in haste to be gone; for he was ever on business of the utmost importance.' 'Mr. Idler' confirms this indication. 'When he enters a house, his first declaration is, that he cannot sit down; and so short are his visits, that he seldom appears to have come for any other reason but to say, He must go.' It is not difficult to fill in the outline of Johnson and Goldsmith. 'The philanthropic bookseller in St. Paul's church-yard' was plainly a bustling, multifarious, and not unkindly personage, essentially commercial, essentially enterprising, rigorously exacting his money's worth of work, keeping prudent record of all casual cash advances, but, on the whole, not unbeneficent in his business fashion to the needy brethren of the pen by whom he was surrounded. Many of John Newbery's guineas passed to Johnson, to Goldsmith, to poor mad Christopher Smart, who married his step-daughter. As Johnson implies, it is not impossible that he finally fell a victim to that unreasoning mental activity which left him always struggling hopelessly with more schemes and proposals than one man could possibly manage. His wig must often have been awry, and his spectacles mislaid, in that perpetual journey from pillar to post which ultimately landed him, at the comparatively early age of fifty-four, in his grave at Waltham St. Lawrence.

It was at Waltham St. Lawrence, a quiet little
Berkshire village, whose churchyard is dotted
with the tombs of earlier Newberys, that he had
been born. His father, a small farmer, destined
him for his own calling. But, like Gay, it was
not John Newbery's fate 'to brighten plough-
shares in paternal land.' He passed early into the
service of a 'merchant,' otherwise a printer and
newspaper proprietor, at Reading, managing
so well that, when his employer died, he was
left a co-legatee in the business. Thereupon,
being a resolute man, he did better still, and
married his master's widow, who had three
children. Even this succeeded; upon which,
progressing always in prosperity, he began to
think of starting in London. Before doing so,
he made a tour in the provinces. Of this expedition there exists a curious record in the shape of
an unprinted journal, throwing much light upon
modes of travelling in those early coaching days,
when the unfortunate outside passenger (like
Pastor Moritz in a later paper) had to choose
between being jolted to death in the basket, or
clinging like a fly to the slippery top of the
vehicle. The majority of the entries are merely
matter of business—titles for new books, recipes
for diet-drinks, shrewd trade maxims, and the
like. But here and there the writer intersperses
notes of general interest—on Dick Turpin the
highwayman, or Lady Godiva and peeping Tom,
and (more than once) upon that 'curious and
very useful machine,' the Ducking-Stool for
scolds, a 'plan of which instrument (he says) he
shall procure and transplant to Berkshire for the

good of his native county.' His business at
Reading was as miscellaneous as his memoran-
dum book, and he seems to have dealt in all
kinds of goods. About 1744 he removed to
London, opening a shop at the sign of the 'Bible
and Crown,' near Devereux Court, without
Temple Bar, together with a branch establishment at the Royal Exchange. To this Johnson
probably refers when he says: 'He has one
habitation near Bow Church, and another about
a mile distant. By this ingenious distribution of
himself between two houses, he has contrived to
be found at neither.' From the 'Bible and
Crown' which had been his old Reading sign,
he moved a year later to the 'Bible and Sun' in
St. Paul's Churchyard. This continued to be
his headquarters until his death. Gradually his
indiscriminate activities narrowed themselves to
two distinct branches of business, in these days
incongruous enough—the sale of books and the
sale of patent medicines. While at Reading, he
had become part owner, among other things, of
Dr. Hooper's Female Pills; and soon after his
settlement in London, he acquired the sole
management of a more famous panacea, Dr.
James's Fever Powders, which had in their time
an extraordinary vogue. According to Mrs.
Delany, the King dosed the Princess Elizabeth
with them. Gray and Cowper both believed in
their efficacy; and Horace Walpole declared he
should take them if the house were on fire.
Fielding specially praises them in 'Amelia,'
affirming that in almost any country but England
they would have brought 'public Honours and

Rewards' to his 'worthy and ingenious Friend Dr. *James*'; while Goldsmith may be said to have laid down his life for them. With the sale of these and kindred specifics, John Newbery alternated his unwearied speculations as a bookseller. He was at the back of Smollett's venture of the *British Magazine;* it was for his *Universal Chronicle* that Johnson wrote his 'Idler' and quizzed his proprietor as 'Jack Whirler'; he was the publisher of Goldsmith's 'Traveller' and 'Citizen of the World'; and he probably found part of the historical sixty guineas which somebody paid for the 'Vicar of Wakefield.' He died at Canbury or Canonbury House, Islington, in the still-existent Tower of which he was an occasional resident. Indeed, it is more than probable that he was at one time the responsible landlord of that favourite retiring place for literary men—a retiring place not without its exceptional advantages, if we are to believe last-century advertisements, which, in addition to a natural cold bath, speak of 'a superlative Room, furnish'd for a single Person, or two Gentlemen, having a Prospect into five Counties [*longos prospicit agros!*], and the use of a good Garden and Summer-House.' Besides this there were traditions of Prior Bolton and Anne of Cleves, of Bacon and Elizabeth, of Sir John Spencer and William Feilding, Earl of Denbigh (the novelist's grand-uncle), which should certainly have figured in any schedule of attractions, and must naturally have been interesting to the Smarts and Hills and Woodfalls and Goldsmiths who afterwards inhabited the old ivy-clad Tower.

Newbery's epitaph in the churchyard of his native village lays its main stress upon his connection with Dr. James's nostrum; and it was doubtless to this and the other patent medicines with which he was connected that he owed the material part of his prosperity. Yet it is not now upon the celebrated 'Arquebusade Water' (dear to Lady Mary Coke), or the far-famed 'Cephalic Snuff,' or the incomparable 'Beaume de Vie,' once so familiar in eighteenth-century advertisements, that he bases his individual claim to the gratitude of posterity. It is, to quote his biographer, Mr. Welsh, as 'the first bookseller who made the issue of books, specially intended for children, a business of any importance'; as the publisher of 'The Renowned History of Giles Gingerbread: a little Boy who lived upon Learning,' of 'Mrs. Margery Two-Shoes' (afterward Lady Jones), of the redoubtable 'Tommy Trip and his dog Jouler,' of the 'Lilliputian Magazine,' and of numbers of other tiny masterpieces in that flowered and gilt Dutch paper of which the art has been lost, that he is best remembered. Concerning these commendable little treatises, with their matter-of-fact title-pages and their artless appeal to all little Masters and Misses 'who are good, or intend to be good,' there are varying opinions. Dr. Johnson, according to Mrs. Thrale, thought them too childish for their purpose. He preferred the 'Seven Champions,' or 'Parisenus and Parismenus.' 'Babies,' he said in his legislative way, 'do not want to hear about babies. They like to be told of giants and castles, and of somewhat which can stretch and stimulate their

little minds.' 'Remember always,' he added, 'that
the parents buy the books, and that the children
never read them.' Yet it is claimed for Robert
Southey that in Newbery's 'delectable histories'
he found just that very stimulus which made him
a life-long book-lover; and it is characteristic of
Charles Lamb (a better judge of children's literature than Johnson) that he puts forward these
particular publications against the Barbaulds
and Trimmers ('those blights and blasts of all
that is human in man and child'), as presenting
the very quality which Johnson desired, the
'beautiful interest in wild tales, which made the
child a man, while all the time he suspected
himself to be no bigger than a child.' 'Think
what you would have been now,' he writes to
Coleridge of 'Goody Two-Shoes,' 'if instead of
being fed with tales and old wives' fables in
childhood, you had been crammed with geo-
graphy and natural history!'

The authorship of these 'classics of the nursery'
is an old battle ground. Newbery, it is alleged,
wrote some of them himself. He was (says Dr.
Primrose when he met him) 'at that time actually
compiling materials for the history of one Mr.
Thomas Trip,' and if this can hardly be accepted
as proof positive, it may be safely asserted that to
Newbery's business instincts are due those ingenious references to his different wares and
publications which crop up so unexpectedly in
the course of the narrative. For example, in
'Goody Two-Shoes' we are told that the heroine's
father 'died miserably' because he was 'seized
with a violent Fever in a place where Dr. *James's*

Powder was not to be had'! But who were Newbery's assistant authors? Giles and Griffith
Jones, say some; Oliver Goldsmith, say others.
With respect to the last-named no particular
testimony seems to be forthcoming beyond his
known relations to the publisher, and the so-
called 'evidence of style.' In the absence of con-
firmatory details the former is worthless; and
the latter is often entirely misleading. Without
going back to the time-honoured case of Erasmus
and Scaliger's oration, two modern instances of
this may be cited. Mr. Thackeray, says Mr.
Forster, claimed the 'Pleasant and Delightful
History of Thomas Hickathrift' for Henry Fielding. But both Mr. Forster and Mr. Thackeray
should have remembered that their common
acquaintance, Mr. Isaac Bickerstaff, of the
Tatler, had written of Hickathrift as a chap-
book when Fielding was a baby. In the same
way 'Tommy Trip' has, by no mean judges,
been attributed to Goldsmith upon the strength
of the following quatrain:—

> Three children sliding on the ice
>   Upon a summer's day,
> As it fell out they all fell in,
>   The rest they ran away.

Alas! and alas! for the 'evidence of style.' Not
only had these identical lines been turned into
Latin in the *Gentleman's Magazine* for July, 1754,
when Goldsmith was still studying medicine at
Leyden; but they are quoted at p. 30 of 'The
Character of Richard St[ee]le, Esq.'; by 'Toby,
Abel's Kinsman,' which was issued by 'J. Mor-
phew, near Stationer's Hall' as far back as the

month of November, 1713. As a matter of fact, they are much older still, being affirmed by Chambers in his excellent 'Book of Days' to be, in their first form, part of a long and rambling story in doggerel rhyme dating from the early part of the Civil Wars, which is to be found at the end of a little old book entitled 'The Loves of Hero and Leander,' 12mo, London, 1653, and 1677.

George Saintsbury

1845–1933

THACKERAY: A POSTSCRIPT

No survey of the work of a great writer on the present scale—especially no survey of work so shot and mottled with personal colour as Thackeray's —would be complete without some remarks, fuller and rather wider-ranging than those in the first of these Introductions,[1] on his personality. I never knew him—I am not aware that I ever even saw him, though I was much in and about Kensington from 1850 to his death. But I have since known many people who did know him; and for the last twenty years the infallible search-light of private letters, published by this person and that, has been more and more freely turned upon him. Now this is even of more value than the later spoken testimony of third parties.

It is well known that this last was not in-variably favourable to Thackeray. Those who loved him loved him very much. But his daughter—and if, as Miss Rossetti says, 'There is no friend like a sister,' there certainly appears to be, despite the experience of Servius Tullius and Lear, no such loyal defender as a daughter —herself says, 'I suppose some people disliked my father.' They certainly did; and what is more, not a few of those who actually liked him,

[1] [In vol. i of the Oxford Thackeray.]

seem to have done so with grudging and 'by allowance.' It has even been said to a '*wash* neophyte' who expressed sorrow that he had *not* known the object of his admiration, 'You are much better off as you are,' or words to that effect. The 'rubs' seem to have been taken in various places. The 'bitterness' of which Mr. John Blackwood speaks in an excellent testimony after Thackeray's death, seems to have been one great occasion. His contemporaries (except intimate friends of more than usual wit, like Mr. Venables) do not seem to have detected the 'sentimentalism' which has been a later reproach. But even they appear to have been sometimes offended by his 'infatuations' (as they called them) for particular persons, and by his (as it seems to me) delightful interest in wine and dinners and harmless pleasures of various kinds. The fools of a certain type thought him not sober and serious enough—too fond of puns and misspellings and high jinks in life and literature. The fools of another were offended by his occasional severities of speech and outbreaks of temper. In fact, as he never suffered any kind of fool gladly, so neither did any kind of fool suffer him without a certain discomfort. Now, most of us contain something of some kind of fool.

Yet he has given a very sufficient key to his character in all his work, at least from the 'Hoggarty Diamond' onwards, while his letters not merely supply the key, but open the lock, and display, with hardly its most secret drawers excepted, the whole cabinet. To expound Thackeray fully would be to write a 'New

Anatomy of Melancholy.' The causes of his melancholia were, no doubt, to some extent external. He was an instance of the not very uncommon combination of great capacity for work with a most profound loathing of compulsory work; and, partly by his own faults and follies, but much more, it would seem, by the faults and follies of others, he was at the very outset deprived of the income which would have made it possible for him to work or not, as he pleased. This was very likely our gain; but he would have been less than human if he had thought it his. He had singular ill-luck in his first attempts at making literature a profession—the branches broke under him, and the steps crumbled, as they do in a bad dream. He attained domestic happiness, only to lose it by a worse stroke than that of Death itself. For years even after this, he had not only the trial—how trying to an intensely nervous nature those who do not understand can never be made to understand—of picking up a livelihood from day to day, from hand to mouth, by bits and scraps and orts—but two great aggravations of this trial. He must have known that he was not doing himself full justice; he must have known that others were not doing him even the justice that he deserved. He was one of the greatest men of letters in Europe—with Tennyson and Carlyle he made up the trinity of greatest men of letters in England. And in 1845—on the eve of 'Vanity Fair,' and after half a dozen things which, however imperfectly accomplished, were works of genius, if ever such works were—Macvey Napier,

an official steward and inspector of literature,
made quite sincere, polite, and respectable inquiries as to who Mr. Thackeray was. When he
did achieve, he must have felt to the full Johnson's famous sentence to Chesterfield. It was
late; he was alone; and he was weary. Nor,
though nobody was ever further from Wer-
therism or Byronism or any other of the numerous
cosmopolitan and polyglot synonyms for 'pose,'
does he ever seem to have recovered, save in fits
and glimpses, the 'joy of living.' Though the
last three or four years of his life, at least, were
certainly passed in something like a Land of
Beulah, he never seems to have clung to life, or
shrunk from death, in the very slightest degree.
Except in the case of actual saints and martyrs,
and of sufferers from some great bodily or mental
agony, I never remember reading about any one
so little 'loath to depart' as Thackeray.

This could not come from, though it might be
encouraged by, merely external causes of the
kind mentioned—and it certainly did not. That
Thackeray was, by nature, one of Aristotle's
σφόδρα μελαγχολικοί there can be not the slightest
doubt. The obviously autobiographical passages
in 'Pendennis' and 'The Virginians' would be
enough, if the whole context of the 'Works' were
not more than enough. And the conviction is
driven home by all sorts of curious by-evidence.
It is the sense of *proximus ardet*—the terror of the
misanthropy into which melancholy so easily
slips—which makes him such a hanging judge
to Swift. The celebrated 'cynicism' is the harder,
and the equally celebrated 'sentimentality' the

more melting mood of this melancholy.[1] The puns and the cacographies, the little gastronomical diversions, and the flittings to Brighton and Paris, are its palliatives and its allopathic drugs. And in the higher ranges of humour it supplies exactly that tendency to 'feel in earnest while thinking in jest' which is perhaps the only approach to a satisfactory definition of humour itself, and which is due to a friend and house-inmate of his own, Miss Anne Evans, who had the living embodiment of it often before her.

It is not mere paradox to say that this temperament is less difficult to live constantly with (though it may be that too if it lives with the wrong people) than to live with, or to meet, occasionally. For it is essentially a temperament of moods; and the Goddess of Chance cannot be trusted always or often to adjust these moods to other people's at the particular time. But assuredly it is not necessarily, or even probably, an unloving, and it should not be an unloved one. To Thackeray's good qualities almost every page of his works—certainly nine hundred and ninety-nine pages out of a thousand—will bear witness; and the witness is confirmed externally. 'Kind' is the adjective most frequently used of him by those who knew him best. His generosity is unquestionable; and there is absolutely no trace of 'bad blood' in him, though he certainly

---

[1] It is probably not worth while to say any more about these two silly 'tickets.' If, when the literary cant of the day on the whole turns to sentimentalism, a man is accused of being a cynic, and if, when it turns to antisentimentalism, he is accused of being a sentimentalist, it is pretty certain that *omne tulit punctum*.

did, at a bad time of journalism, acquire some of its bad habits, and was long before he got rid of them. His utterances on religion (at least ecclesiastical religion) and politics are sometimes rather trying, not because of their purport, but because of a certain irresponsible and amateurish character about them which makes one wish that, knowing so little about these matters, he had held his tongue.[1] When you have, comparatively late in life, to borrow a Bible from the Carlyles in order to read (apparently for the first time) the Books of Joshua and Judges, it would surely be wise to let your opinions on Theodicy mature a little.

But contrasts are of the essence of the melancholious temperament, and occasional irreverences — mostly ignorances likewise — of expression do not interfere with the fact of the immense reverence which was the citadel of Thackeray's mind, and the vantage-ground of his outlook on life. For here there was no ignorance, but, on the contrary, an astonishing and miraculous knowledge. And such reverence, with such knowledge, saves at once satire from being mere snarl or mere sniggle, and sentiment from being mere sentimentality. When they put some of our modern analysts above him, it makes me think of a story told in somebody's 'Memoirs' — of an amateur in mechanics who used to carry

---

[1] 'It is very well known that religion and politics are perfectly understood by everybody; as they require neither study nor experience,' says Chesterfield with admirable gravity—availing himself, it is true, of an earlier utterance of Swift's, but pointing and polishing it.

some half-finished brass-work in his pocket, and take it out to file at odd moments, thereby setting his friends' teeth not a little on edge. Thackeray does not do this; he only gives you the perfectly finished and infallible watch. When they say, 'Oh! but Balzac?' the answer is quite easy. Balzac's men and women are what Frenchmen and Frenchwomen would or would not like to be, or what they think they ought or ought not to be: Thackeray's men and women are what Englishmen and Englishwomen are. Nor is there any mere insularity; for exceedingly cool admirers of his—or rather scarcely admirers of his at all—have admitted that if there is a perfect sketch of a 'foreigner' anywhere in the whole literature of Europe, that sketch is Paul de Florac. In fact, there is something uncanny in his perfect mastery of humanity.

The two most famous of the unfavourable judgments[1] passed on him by men who may count as his peers in the wide sense are Carlyle's, that he was 'not a strong soul,' and Matthew Arnold's, that he was not a great writer. They require somewhat different treatment. The first

---

[1] Of the accusation of another distinguished but exceedingly uncritical contemporary—that Thackeray is a 'meat-fly' who settles on and disgusts us with life—it can hardly be necessary to take serious notice. But I think I have seen a variant and probably a derivative of this complaint, which is even more curious if less extravagant—that the author of 'Vanity Fair' 'makes us discontented with ourselves.' Now one had thought that to do this was to confer about the highest benefit possible. At any rate the person who wishes to be self-satisfied may be left to his desires, which are extremely likely to be granted, in spite of the teasing teeth of any troublesome Titmarsh.

cannot be met with a simple contradiction.
Carlyle's judgments, splenetic and one-sided as
they often are, seldom or never can be so met.
In a certain sense Thackeray was no more a
strong man than the Sage of Chelsea himself—it
may be even less. There was nothing still or
stoical about him. But perhaps we are rather
in need of a moral Longinus to point out that
strength is not mere solidity or stolidity, not
mere absence of weakness. And the concomitant
allowance 'big, fierce, weeping,' is remarkable,
for it at least excludes littleness, and cowardice,
and Voltairean snigger. Moreover, it has to be
remembered that this character was written
ten years before Thackeray's death; and when,
though his fame was made, his fortune, such as
it was to be, was still only beginning. Yet the
chief demurrer to this judgment must always be
that already advanced. Is mere absence of
emotion, not merely a good thing, but *the* good
thing? If it be, we must no doubt rule Thackeray
out of the strengths of England. He will find
himself in the company, for instance, of Swift,
of Johnson, of Burke, of Nelson, not to mention
his critic. It is just possible to imagine worse
company.

As to the other complaint of his not being a
great writer, I think we may, without any dis-
respect to its author, pass it by somewhat summarily. Mr. Arnold was in many ways different
from Thackeray—in none, perhaps, more different than in his attitude to contemporaries, which
was nearly always grudging, though I do not believe that this was due to any want of generosity.

It is almost enough first to ask in what canon of greatness Thackeray is disqualified, and when the canon is produced to disqualify it at once as an inevitable consequence of its operation. It hardly matters whether we take 'writer' in its more limited sense as concerning 'style' or in its wider as extending to invention or choice of subject and to application of treatment. If fertility that is inexhaustible and variety that is infinite; if phrase that is at once utterly personal to the user and utterly suitable to the subject— if these things, and many others which have been pointed out, will not make a great writer, why, perhaps Thackeray is not one. But in that case one is driven to borrow from Miss Carolina Wilhelmina Amelia Skeggs, and ask where a great writer is to be found?

I remember having, some twenty years ago, delight of battle for at least an hour by, and not far from, Kensington clock, on the subject of Thackeray, with the late Mr. Henley. At last, *à propos* of exactly what I have forgotten, I happened to say, 'And this, you see, is because he was such a gentleman.' 'No,' said Henley, 'it is because he was such a genius.' 'Well,' I said, 'my dear Henley, suppose we put it, that it is because he was such a genius who was also such a gentleman.' So we laughed, and shook hands, and parted. And really I am inclined to think that these words were, and are, 'the conclusion of the whole matter' about Thackeray.

Archibald Philip Primrose, Lord Rosebery

1847–1929

EPSOM

WHEN I first came to live at Epsom, a quarter
of a century ago, it was a little sleepy town, surrounded by long stretches of down and common.
Its perennial slumber was broken twice a year by
race meetings, when the followers and camp
followers of the Turf stormed the neighbourhood
during a few agitated days, then struck their
tents and left the town, sodden and exhausted.
Thereafter the calm recommenced, and the inhabitants could saunter over miles of open turf
to breathe the purest air in England. But the
memory of those six days of carnival kept off the
speculative builder and his serious clients. Thus
the town remained rural and old-fashioned. Now
Now all that is changed. The clients of the
builder have reconsidered their objections, and
so he has come and cut into the lanes and hedges.
A gaunt asylum shrouds the misery of hundreds
or thousands of the mad patients of London.
One or two commons are enclosed. The stray
hedges of greenery, which were the heritage of
the wayfarer, are being gradually fenced in. A
new railroad, traversing a rural desert, lands its
stray passengers on to a belated bull-ring, which

tops the downs with its aggressive bulk. It is all,
I suppose, necessary, nay inevitable. But these
changes have killed the old Epsom. The new
Epsom is only a fragment of the past, and only
a fragment of the future.

Long ago, Epsom was fashionable. Charles
the Second raced here and played bowls here.
Prince George of Denmark, the husband of
Queen Anne, came here and drank the waters.
Frederick Prince of Wales lived here, enjoyed
hawking on the downs, and, it is said, fought a
chimney-sweep, sustaining defeat. But the
glorious epoch of Epsom seems to have ended
with the seventeenth century. The stay of
Frederick Prince of Wales at Epsom was in its
unfashionable days; perhaps he only came to
court obscurity when in conflict with his father.
It is difficult indeed to ascertain when he was
at Epsom, in spite of the strong local tradition
and the statement of Horace Walpole that he
actually owned Durdans. Probably he went on
a visit to Lord Guilford, who did own Durdans,
and who was a Lord of his Bedchamber. But
in any case the chalybeate or cathartic glories
of Epsom had then passed away.

When and whence were those glories? It
appears that in the later years of Queen Elizabeth the waters had been obscurely, indeed
parochially, drunk; and in the middle of the
seventeenth century foreigners were said to come
from abroad for that purpose. It was, however,
the demolition of the neighbouring Palace of
Nonsuch which launched Epsom on its brief
career as a watering-place; for the great structure

furnished much building material, and so was a quarry out of which were erected dwellings in a sumptuous style, new to the country village. This was in 1670, for in that year Charles II had given Nonsuch to Barbara Villiers, who lost no time in converting it into cash.

Our local historian, Mr. Pownall, who published his little book in 1825, lingers fondly over those glorious times. 'Soon after the improvements made by Mr. Parkhurst at the Wells (about 1690), the village was enlarged to a considerable extent. It became the centre of fashion, several houses were erected for lodgings, and yet the place would not contain all the visitors, many of whom were obliged to seek for accommodation in the neighbouring villages. Taverns, at that time reputed to be the largest in England, were opened; sedan chairs and numbered coaches attended. There was a public breakfast, with dancing and music, every morning at the Wells. There was also a ring, as in Hyde Park; and on the downs, races were held daily at noon; with cudgelling and wrestling matches, foot races, etc., in the afternoon. The evenings were usually spent in private parties, assemblies, or cards; and we may add, that neither Bath nor Tunbridge ever boasted of more noble visitors than Epsom, or exceeded it in splendour, at the time we are describing.'

In spite of this glowing description, I am inclined to doubt whether Epsom was ever fashionable in the sense in which that epithet is applied to Tunbridge Wells or Bath. It was probably the haunt rather of the middle classes than of noble visitors. That at least is the impression left by Shadwell's coarse comedy. It may be noted, too, that a great number of letters from great people were dated from Bath, but few or none from Epsom. The houses of Bath, too, are redolent with the tradition of sublime names. There are scarcely any such at Epsom. Lord Berkeley, no doubt, had his house and entertained his friends. We have a glimpse of Lord Buckhurst and Sir Charles Sedley flirting with Nell Gwynne in the High Street. Lord Baltimore led a debauched life at Woodcote. Lord Lyttelton closed a debauched life at Pit Place. But these noble names almost exhaust the record. And the visitors to the town who believed in the virtue of the waters, while they were cured at least as much by air, abstinence, exercise, and a healing faith, as by the merits of the well, were, it may be surmised, in the main what were called 'cits.' This does not imply that they were not as gay and as profitable as the gouty statesmen and nobles who sought health and gambling tables elsewhere.

In spite of Prince George of Denmark, the decline of Epsom began, we are told by our historian, in 1704. The 'knavery of an apothecary' was, it appears, sufficient to put an end to our career of brilliancy. This miscreant bought land, sank a well, erected ballrooms, gambling rooms and a pump. Shops, too, 'for milliners, jewellers, and toymen,' and a bowling green were there. His advertisements were indeed alluring. There was a 'variety of rafling shops, attended every day by a fine consort of musick';

there were cock-fights and horse-races, there were also empty shops for 'a bookseller, pictures, a haberdasher of hats, shoemaker, fishmonger and butcher, with conveniences for several other trades.' The centre of these attractions he called the New Wells. Where this guilty paradise was situated I do not know, but as a source of health it was deceptive. 'The water of the New Wells did not possess any virtue, and consequently those who drank it did not derive any benefit therefrom.' So sighs Pownall, but as nothing was charged for the waters, it may perhaps be said that their want of quality constituted no direct fraud on the public. Worse than all, the old and virtuous wells, full of healing, 'grew into unmerited disrepute, for want of a distinction.' Still in all this, though there may have been folly and presumption, there was no actual iniquity. The crime of the man of medicine remains to be told. He procured a lease of the Old Wells and locked them up till he died in 1727. Are there any waters in the world which could triumph over treatment of this kind?

Toland, who wrote in 1711, under the hollow and glittering reign of the wicked apothecary, penned a glowing description. And yet, though the scene that he describes is brilliant and animated, within four years of this period Epsom was, according to Pownall, gradually deserted owing to the 'knavish tricks' of the spurious healer.

In 1720 there was another brief spell of prosperity, not of the surest, when the South Sea Bubble for a time filled Epsom with its train of speculators and adventurers: 'alchemists, Dutchmen, Germans, Jews,' and 'gaming with every other description of profligacy and vice, prevailed to an enormous extent.' And at that period, several large houses were erected, 'amongst them that of Baron Swasso.'

Who Baron Swasso may have been we cannot guess—though his name rings like that of a possible alchemist—but at any rate he did not arrest the decadence of Epsom. The South Sea Bubble burst and Epsom fell once more. In 1736 the celebrated 'Female Bone-setter,' a Mrs. Mapp, gave us a temporary glamour of popularity, though it was but a flicker. The neighbouring gentry, however, continued their patronage, and every Monday in the summer they 'came to the Wells and had a public breakfast with music, dancing, and cards until about three o'clock.' There is a pathetic advertisement in 1754, quite in the modern indirect style, which aims at stimulating this fleeting fashion.

'EPSOM OLD WELL. The gentlemen and ladies who did me the honour to breakfast at this place last Monday morning have signified their pleasure of breakfasting here every Monday during the Season; I take this opportunity to return my unfeigned thanks for the favour of so genteel an appearance, and humbly hope for the continuance of the same, which will lay under the greatest obligation their most humble servant JANE HAWKINS. Note. The Purging waters of this place are in excellent order.'

But even this genteel appearance and the attractions mentioned in the Note failed to

stimulate the flagging repute of the faded watering-place, and Epsom 'became (as it now remains) a populous, wealthy and respectable
village, without retaining any of its former
dissipated and vicious sources of amusing.'

The vogue of Bath and of sea-bathing gave
Epsom the final death-stroke as a health resort;
'the modern delightful practice of sea-bathing,'
as Pownall forgivingly calls it. When people
began to bathe in the sea, they indeed seem to
have become demoralised. 'The well is preserved . . . but is now only visited occasionally
by strangers who, not having faith in the mineral
waters, after drinking them a few times, come to
the erroneous conclusion that there is no virtue
in them.'

There is one further flash of fashion to be
recorded. Some of the emigrants of the French
Revolution lit upon this peaceful neighbourhood
as a haven of refuge. One group settled at
Juniper Hall, whose secular and majestic cedars
at the foot of Boxhill still refresh the traveller's
eye. Here there resided Talleyrand and Madame
de Staël, the Duc de Montmorency, and M. de
Jaucourt, and M. D'Arblay, who was courting
Fanny Burney. At West Humble were the De
Broglies. Another young couple came straight
from the church in which they were married to
Epsom. Their name was de Gontout, and she was
destined to end as Duchesse de Gontout, Gover-
ness of the Children of France. They were
delighted with Epsom, where they inhabited a
little house, 'close to the race-course, surrounded
by charming country-houses. We learned later

that our arrival had excited a sensation among
the inhabitants of these pretty houses, who were
curious to see the French people who had
escaped from the disasters of their country, and
in the evening peered through our window-
blinds to see us.' The Duchess goes on to
describe the races, where the English, she says,
lose their habitual phlegm, become active and
gay, betting with vivacity and tumult. But this
little flock of fugitives soon dispersed again,
leaving the faint aroma of a pleasant tradition.

Still, though the waters failed us, a miracle yet
remained to be wrought on behalf of Epsom. In
the last quarter of the eighteenth century a
roystering party at a neighbouring country-
house founded two races, in two successive years,
one for three-year-old colts and fillies, the other
for three-year-old fillies, and named them gratefully after their host and his house—the Derby
and the Oaks. Seldom has a carouse had a more
permanent effect. Up to that time Epsom had
enjoyed little more than the ordinary races of a
market-town. The great Eclipse, himself, who
long lived in Epsom, had run there in some
obscurity. But now horses, some of them unworthy to draw him in a post-chaise, were to
earn immortality by winning on Epsom Downs
before hundreds of thousands of spectators.
Parliament was to adjourn during the ensuing
century, not without debate, to watch the
struggle. Ministers and ex-Ministers would ride
or drive down to the famous race; and in white
hats with blue veils discuss the prospects of their
favourites. Political leaders would give vent to

splendid groans when they realised that they had sold the winner. In the midst of the Crimean War the result of the Derby was to be recorded in General Orders. Crowds would assemble in London, and from London to Epsom to watch the still greater crowds returning from the contest. For a week Epsom would reek of racing. During that period the eyes of the sporting section of the civilised world would be turned on the little Surrey town. Many indeed, who were in no respect sporting, became sporting for that occasion.

It is much the same now. The Olympian dust is the same, and is still scattered by the flying horses. The world still admires—not perhaps with so concentrated a gaze. And all this excitement, enthusiasm, triumph, whatever you may call it, Epsom and the universe perhaps owe to an extra magnum of Lord Derby's choice claret, or a superfluous bottle of Lord Derby's curious port.

For two weeks, then, or a part of them, Epsom races and revels; and recovers during the remaining fifty. The recovery is less sweet than it was, for what was once rural is now suburban. But Nature, happily, as we know, is not easily expelled. There are still common land and down, still stately trees and vernal blossom, the nightingales still sing, though it may be to an asylum, the air is still racy and clear.

The time may come when this can no longer be said, when each available inch will be covered by brick or stucco, and when that which cannot be built upon, the still sacred commons, will be surrounded by dun streets of whitey-brown houses. Then will be the moment for the resident, who remembers and respects old, or even recent Epsom, to 'twitch his mantle blue' and betake himself with his goods and chattels 'to fresh woods and pastures new.'

Alice Meynell

1847–1922

THE POINT OF HONOUR

Not without significance is the Spanish nationality of Velasquez. In Spain was the Point put upon Honour; and Velasquez was the first Impressionist. As an Impressionist he claimed, implicitly if not explicitly, a whole series of delicate trusts in his trustworthiness; he made an appeal to the confidence of his peers; he relied on his own candour, and asked that the candid should rely upon him; he kept the chastity of art when other masters were content with its honesty, and when others saved artistic conscience he safeguarded the point of honour. Contemporary masters more or less proved their position, and convinced the world by something of demonstration; the first Impressionist simply asked that his word should be accepted. To those who would not take his word he offers no bond. To those who will, he grants the distinction of a share in his responsibility.

Somewhat unrefined, in comparison with his lofty and simple claim to be believed on a suggestion, is the commoner painter's production of his credentials, his appeal to the sanctions of ordinary experience, his self-defence against the suspicion of making irresponsible mysteries in art. 'You can see for yourself,' the lesser man

seems to say to the world, 'thus things are, and
I render them in such manner that your intelligence may be satisfied.' This is an appeal to
average experience—at the best the cumulative
experience; and with the average, or with the
sum, art cannot deal without derogation. The
Spaniard seems to say: 'Thus things are in my
pictorial sight. Trust me, I apprehend them so.'
We are not excluded from his counsels, but we
are asked to attribute a certain authority to him,
master of the craft as he is, master of that art of
seeing pictorially which is the beginning and not
far from the end—not far short of the whole—
of the art of painting. So little indeed are we
shut out from the mysteries of a great Impressionist's impression that Velasquez requires us
to be in some degree his colleagues. Thus may
each of us to whom he appeals take praise from
the praised: he leaves my educated eyes to do a
little of the work. He respects my responsibility
no less—though he respects it less explicitly—
than I do his. What he allows me would not be
granted by a meaner master. If he does not hold
himself bound to prove his own truth, he returns
thanks for my trust. It is as though he used his
countrymen's courteous hyperbole and called
his house my own. In a sense of the most noble
hostship he does me the honours of his picture.

Because Impressionism with all its extreme—
let us hope its ultimate—derivatives is so free,
therefore is it doubly bound. Because there is
none to arraign it, it is a thousand times responsible. To undertake this art for the sake of its
privileges without confessing its obligations—or

at least without confessing them up to the point
of honour—is to take a vulgar freedom: to see
immunities precisely where there are duties, and
an advantage where there is a bond. A very
mob of men have taken Impressionism upon
themselves, in several forms and under a succession of names, in this our later day. It is against
all probabilities that more than a few among
these have within them the point of honour. In
their galleries we are beset with a dim distrust.
And to distrust is more humiliating than to
be distrusted. How many of these landscape-
painters, deliberately rash, are painting the truth
of their own impressions? An ethical question
as to loyalty is easily answered; truth and falsehood as to fact are, happily for the intelligence
of the common conscience, not hard to divide.
But when the *dubium* concerns not fact but artistic
truth, can the many be sure that their sensitiveness, their candour, their scruple, their delicate
equipoise of perceptions, the vigilance of their
apprehension, are enough? Now Impressionists
have told us things as to their impressions—as
to the effect of things upon the temperament of
this man and upon the mood of that—which
should not be asserted except on the artistic point
of honour. The majority can tell ordinary truth,
but should not trust themselves for truth extraordinary. They can face the general judgment,
but they should hesitate to produce work that
appeals to the last judgment, which is the judgment within. There is too much reason to divine
that a certain number of those who aspire to
differ from the greatest of masters have no tem-

peraments worth speaking of, no point of view worth seizing, no vigilance worth awaiting, no mood worth waylaying. And to be, *de parti pris*, an Impressionist without these! O Velasquez! Nor is literature quite free from a like reproach in her own things. An author, here and there, will make as though he had a word worth hearing—nay, worth overhearing—a word that seeks to withdraw even while it is uttered; and yet what it seems to dissemble is all too probably a platitude. But obviously, literature is not—as is the craft and mystery of painting—so at the mercy of a half-imposture, so guarded by unprovable honour. For the art of painting is reserved that shadowy risk, that undefined salvation. If the artistic temperament—tedious word!—with all its grotesque privileges, becomes yet more common than it is, there will be yet less responsibility; for the point of honour is the simple secret of the few.

MRS. JOHNSON

This paper shall not be headed 'Tetty.' What may be a graceful enough freedom with the wives of other men shall be prohibited in the case of Johnson's, she with whose name no writer until now has scrupled to take freedoms whereto all graces were lacking. 'Tetty' it should not be, if for no other reason, for this—that the chance of writing 'Tetty' as a title is a kind of facile literary opportunity; it shall be denied. The Essay owes thus much amends of deliberate care to Dr. Johnson's wife. But, indeed, the reason is graver. What wish would he have had but that the language in the making whereof he took no ignoble part should somewhere, at some time, treat his only friend with ordinary honour?

Men who would trust Dr. Johnson with their orthodoxy, with their vocabulary, and with the most intimate vanity of their human wishes, refuse, with every mark of insolence, to trust him in regard to his wife. On that one point no reverence is paid to him, no deference, no respect, not so much as the credit due to our common sanity. Yet he is not reviled on account of his Thrale—nor, indeed, is his Thrale now seriously reproached for her Piozzi. It is true that Macaulay, preparing himself and his reader 'in his well-known way' (as a rustic of Mr. Hardy's might have it) for the recital of her second marriage, says that it would have been well if she had been laid beside the kind and generous Thrale when, in the prime of her life, he died. But Macaulay has not left us heirs to his indignation. His well-known way was to exhaust those possibilities of effect in which the commonplace is so rich. And he was permitted to point his paragraphs as he would, not only by calling Mrs. Thrale's attachment to her second husband 'a degrading passion,' but by summoning a chorus of 'all London' to the same purpose. She fled, he tells us, from the laughter and hisses of her countrymen and countrywomen to a land where she was unknown. Thus when Macaulay chastises Mrs. Elizabeth Porter for marrying Johnson, he is not inconsistent, for he pursues

Mrs. Thrale with equal rigour for her audacity in keeping gaiety and grace in her mind and manners longer than Macaulay liked to see such ornaments added to the charm of twice 'married brows.'

It is not so with succeeding essayists. One of these minor biographers is so gentle as to call the attachment of Mrs. Thrale and Piozzi 'a mutual affection.' He adds, 'No one who has had some experience of life will be inclined to condemn Mrs. Thrale.' But there is no such courtesy, even from him, for Mrs. Johnson. Neither to him nor to any other writer has it yet occurred that if England loves her great Englishman's memory, she owes not only courtesy, but gratitude, to the only woman who loved him while there was yet time.

Not a thought of that debt has stayed the alacrity with which a caricature has been acclaimed as the only possible portrait of Mrs. Johnson. Garrick's school reminiscences would probably have made a much more charming woman grotesque. Garrick is welcome to his remembrances; we may even reserve for ourselves the liberty of envying those who heard him. But honest laughter should not fall into that tone of common antithesis which seems to say, 'See what are the absurdities of the great! Such is life! On this one point we, even we, are wiser than Dr. Johnson—we know how grotesque was his wife. We know something of the privacies of her toilet-table. We are able to compare her figure with the figures we, unlike him in his youth, have had the opportunity of admiring—

the figures of the well-bred and well-dressed.' It is a sorry success to be able to say so much.

But in fact such a triumph belongs to no man. When Samuel Johnson, at twenty-six, married his wife, he gave the dull an advantage over himself which none but the dullest will take. He chose, for love, a woman who had the wit to admire him at first meeting, and in spite of first sight. 'That,' she said to her daughter, 'is the most sensible man I ever met.' He was penniless. She had what was no mean portion for those times and those conditions; and, granted that she was affected, and provincial, and short, and all the rest with which she is charged, she was probably not without suitors; nor do her defects or faults seem to have been those of an unadmired or neglected woman. Next, let us remember what was the aspect of Johnson's form and face, even in his twenties, and how little he could have touched the senses of a widow fond of externals. This one loved him, accepted him, made him happy, gave to one of the noblest of all English hearts the one love of its sombre life. And English literature has had no better phrase for her than Macaulay's—'She accepted, with a readiness which did her little honour, the addresses of a suitor who might have been her son.'

Her readiness did her incalculable honour. But it is at least worth remembering that Johnson had first done her incalculable honour. No one has given to man or woman the right to judge as to the worthiness of her who received it. The meanest man is generally allowed his own counsel as to his own wife; one of the greatest of men has been denied it. 'The lover,' says Macaulay, 'continued to be under the illusions of the wedding day till the lady died.' What is so graciously said is not enough. He was under those 'illusions' until he too died, when he had long passed her latest age, and was therefore able to set right that balance of years which has so much irritated the impertinent. Johnson passed from this life twelve years older than she, and so for twelve years his constant eyes had to turn backwards to dwell upon her. Time gave him a younger wife.

And here I will put into Mrs. Johnson's mouth, that mouth to which no one else has ever attributed any beautiful sayings, the words of Marceline Desbordes-Valmore to the young husband she loved: 'Older than thou! Let me never see thou knowest it. Forget it! I will remember it, to die before thy death.'

Macaulay, in his unerring effectiveness, uses Johnson's short sight for an added affront to Mrs. Johnson. The bridegroom was too weak of eyesight 'to distinguish ceruse from natural bloom.' Nevertheless, he saw well enough, when he was old, to distinguish Mrs. Thrale's dresses. He reproved her for wearing a dark dress; it was unsuitable, he said, for her size; a little creature should show gay colours 'like an insect.' We are not called upon to admire his wife; why, then, our taste being thus uncompromised, do we not suffer him to admire her? It is the most gratuitous kind of intrusion. Moreover, the biographers are eager to permit that touch of romance and grace in his relations to Mrs. Thrale, which they officially deny in the case of Mrs. Johnson. But the difference is all on the other side. He would not have bidden his wife dress like an insect. Mrs. Thrale was to him 'the first of womankind' only because his wife was dead.

Beauclerc, we learn, was wont to cap Garrick's mimicry of Johnson's love-making by repeating the words of Johnson himself in after-years—'It was a love-match on both sides.' And obviously he was as strange a lover as they said. Who doubted it? Was there any other woman in England to give such a suitor the opportunity of an eternal love? 'A life radically wretched,' was the life of this master of Letters; but she, who has received nothing in return except ignominy from these unthankful Letters, had been alone to make it otherwise. Well for him that he married so young as to earn the ridicule of all the biographers in England; for by doing so he, most happily, possessed his wife for nearly twenty years. I have called her his only friend. So indeed she was, though he had followers, disciples, rivals, competitors, and companions, many degrees of admirers, a biographer, a patron, and a public. He had also the houseful of sad old women who quarrelled under his beneficent protection. But what friend had he? He was 'solitary' from the day she died.

Let us consider under what solemn conditions and in what immortal phrase the word 'solitary' stands. He wrote it, all Englishmen know where. He wrote it in the hour of that melancholy triumph when he had been at last set free from

the dependence upon hope. He hoped no more,
and he needed not to hope. The 'notice' of Lord
Chesterfield had been too long deferred; it was
granted at last, when it was a flattery which
Johnson's court of friends would applaud. But
not for their sake was it welcome. To no living
ear would he bring it and report it with delight.

He was indifferent, he was known. The
sensitiveness to pleasure was gone, and the
sensitiveness to pain, slights, and neglect would
thenceforth be suffered to rest; no man in England
would put that to proof again. No man in England, did I say? But, indeed, that is not so. No
slight to him, to his person, or to his fame could
have had power to cause him pain more sensibly
than the customary, habitual, ready-made ridicule that has been cast by posterity upon her
whom he loved for twenty years, prayed for
during thirty-two years more, who satisfied one
of the saddest human hearts, but to whom the
world, assiduous to admire him, hardly accords
human dignity. He wrote praises of her manners
and of her person for her tomb. But her epitaph,
that does not name her, is in the greatest of
English prose. What was favour to him? 'I am
indifferent. . . . I am known. . . . I am solitary,
and cannot impart it.'

Sir Edmund Gosse

1849–1928

WALT WHITMAN

I

FATIMA was permitted, nay encouraged, to make use of all the rooms, so elegantly and commodiously furnished, in Bluebeard Castle, with one exception. It was in vain that the housemaid and the cook pointed out to her that each of the ladies who had preceded her as a tenant had smuggled herself into that one forbidden chamber and had never come out again. Their sad experience was thrown away upon Fatima, who penetrated the fatal apartment and became an object of melancholy derision. The little room called 'Walt Whitman,' in the castle of literature, reminds one of that in which the relics of Bluebeard's levity were stored. We all know that discomfort and perplexity await us there, that nobody ever came back from it with an intelligible message, that it is piled with the bones of critics; yet such is the perversity of the analytic mind, that each one of us, sooner or later, finds himself peeping through the keyhole and fumbling at the lock.

As the latest of these imprudent explorers, I stand a moment with the handle in my hand and essay a defence of those whose skeletons will presently be discovered. Was it their fault? Was their failure not rather due to a sort of magic that hangs over the place? To drop metaphor, I am sadly conscious that, after reading what a great many people of authority and of assumption have written about Whitman—reading it, too, in a humble spirit—though I have been stimulated and entertained, I have not been at all instructed. Pleasant light, of course, has been thrown on the critics themselves and on their various peculiarities. But upon Whitman, upon the place he holds in literature and life, upon the questions, what he was and why he was, surely very little. To me, at least, after all the oceans of talk, after all the extravagant eulogy, all the mad vituperation, he remains perfectly cryptic and opaque. I find no reason given by these authorities why he should have made his appearance, or what his appearance signifies. I am told that he is abysmal, putrid, glorious, universal and contemptible. I like these excellent adjectives, but I cannot see how to apply them to Whitman. Yet, like a boy at a shooting-gallery, I cannot go home till I, too, have had my six shots at this running-deer.

On the main divisions of literature it seems that a critic should have not merely a firm opinion, but sound argument to back that opinion. It is a piglarlicky mind that is satisfied with saying, 'I like you, Dr. Fell, the reason why I cannot tell.' Analysis is the art of telling the reason why. But still more feeble and slovenly is the criticism that has to say, 'I liked Dr. Fell yesterday and I don't like him to-day, but I can give no reason.' The shrine of Walt Whitman, however, is strewn around with remarks of this kind. Poor Mr. Swinburne has been cruelly laughed at for calling him a 'strong-winged soul, with prophetic lips hot with the blood-beats of song,' and yet a drunken apple-woman reeling in a gutter. But he is not alone in this inconsistency. Almost every competent writer who has attempted to give an estimate of Whitman has tumbled about in the same extraordinary way. Something mephitic breathes from this strange personality, something that maddens the judgment until the wisest lose their self-control.

Therefore, I propound a theory. It is this, that there is no real Walt Whitman, that is to say, that he cannot be taken as any other figure in literature is taken, as an entity of positive value and defined characteristics, as, for instance, we take the life and writings of Racine, or of Keats, or of Jeremy Taylor, including the style with the substance, the teaching with the idiosyncrasy. In these ordinary cases the worth and specific weight of the man are not greatly affected by our attitude towards him. An atheist or a quaker may contemplate the writings of the Bishop of Down without sympathy; that does not prevent the *Holy Dying* from presenting, even to the mind of such an opponent, certain defined features which are unmodified by like or dislike. This is true of any fresh or vivid talent which may have appeared among us yesterday. But I contend that it is not true of Whitman. Whitman is mere *bathybius*; he is literature in the condition of protoplasm—an intellectual organism so simple that it takes the instant impression of whatever mood approaches it. Hence the critic who touches Whitman is immediately confronted with his own image stamped upon that viscid and tenacious surface. He finds, not what Whitman has to give, but what he himself has brought. And when, in quite another mood, he comes again to Whitman, he finds that other self of his own stamped upon the provoking protoplasm.

If this theory is allowed a moment's consideration, it cannot, I think, but tend to be accepted. It accounts for all the difficulties in the criticism of Whitman. It shows us why Robert Louis Stevenson has found a Stevenson in *Leaves of Grass*, and John Addington Symonds a Symonds. It explains why Emerson considered the book 'the most extraordinary piece of wit and wisdom that America has yet [in 1855] produced'; why Thoreau thought all the sermons ever preached not equal to it for divinity; why Italian *dilettanti* and Scandinavian gymnasts, anarchists and parsons and champions of women's rights, the most opposite and incongruous types, have the habit of taking Whitman to their hearts for a little while and then flinging him away from them in abhorrence, and, perhaps, of drawing him to them again with passion. This last, however, I think occurs more rarely. Almost every sensitive and natural person has gone through a period of fierce Whitmanomania; but it is a disease which rarely afflicts the same patient more than once. It is, in fact, a sort of highly-irritated egotism come to a head, and people are almost always better after it.

Unless we adopt some such theory as this, it is difficult to account in any way for the persistent influences of Walt Whitman's writings. They have now lasted about forty years, and show no sign whatever of losing their vitality. Nobody is able to analyse their charm, yet the charm is undeniable. They present no salient features, such as have been observed in all other literature, from Homer and David down to the latest generation. They offer a sort of Plymouth Brethrenism of form, a negation of all the laws and ritual of literature. As a book, to be a living book, must contain a vigorous and appropriate arrangement of words, this one solitary feature occurs in *Leaves of Grass*. I think it is not to be denied by any candid critic, however inimical, that passages of extreme verbal felicity are to be found frequently scattered over the pages of Whitman's rhapsodies. But, this one concession made to form, there is no other. Not merely are rhythm and metre conspicuously absent, but composition, evolution, vertebration of style, even syntax and the limits of the English tongue, are disregarded. Every reader who comes to Whitman starts upon an expedition to the virgin forest. He must take his conveniences with him. He will make of the excursion what his own spirit dictates. There are solitudes, fresh air, rough landscape, and a well of water, but if he wishes to enjoy the latter he must bring his own cup with him. When people are still young and like roughing it, they appreciate a picnic into

Whitman-land, but it is not meant for those who choose to see their intellectual comforts round them.

II

In the early and middle years of his life, Whitman was obscure and rarely visited. When he grew old, pilgrims not unfrequently took scrip and staff, and set out to worship him. Several accounts of his appearance and mode of address on these occasions have been published, and if I add one more it must be my excuse that the visit to be described was not undertaken in the customary spirit. All other accounts, so far as I know, of interviews with Whitman have been written by disciples who approached the shrine adoring and ready to be dazzled. The visitor whose experience—and it was a very delightful one —is now to be chronicled, started under what was, perhaps, the disadvantage of being very unwilling to go; at least, it will be admitted that the tribute —for tribute it has to be—is all the more sincere.

When I was in Boston, in the winter of 1884, I received a note from Whitman asking me not to leave America without coming to see him. My first instinct was promptly to decline the invitation. Camden, New Jersey, was a very long way off. But better counsels prevailed; curiosity and civility combined to draw me, and I wrote to him that I would come. It would be fatuous to mention all this, if it were not that I particularly wish to bring out the peculiar magic of the old man, acting, not on a disciple, but on a stiff-necked and froward unbeliever.

To reach Camden, one must arrive at Philadelphia, where I put up on the 2nd of January, 1885, ready to pass over into New Jersey next morning. I took the hall-porter of the hotel into my confidence, and asked if he had ever heard of Mr. Whitman. Oh, yes, they all knew 'Walt,' he said; on fine days he used to cross over on the ferry and take the tram into Philadelphia. He liked to stroll about in Chestnut Street and look at the people, and if you smiled at him he would smile back again; everybody knew 'Walt.' In the North, I had been told that he was almost bedridden, in consequence of an attack of paralysis. This seemed inconsistent with wandering round Philadelphia.

The distance being considerable, I started early on the 3rd, crossed the broad Delaware River, where blocks of ice bumped and crackled around us, and saw the flat shores of New Jersey expanding in front, raked by the broad morning light. I was put ashore in a crude and apparently uninhabited village, grim with that concentrated ugliness that only an American township in the depth of winter can display. Nobody to ask the way, or next to nobody. I wandered aimlessly about, and was just ready to give all I possessed to be back again in New York, when I discovered that I was opposite No. 328 Mickle Street, and that on a minute brass plate was engraved 'W. Whitman.' I knocked at this dreary little two-storey tenement house, and wondered what was going to happen. A melancholy woman opened the door; it was too late now to go away. But before I could speak, a large figure, hobbling down the stairs, called out in a cheery voice, 'Is that my friend?' Suddenly, by I know not what magnetic charm, all wiredrawn literary reservations faded out of being, and one's only sensation was of gratified satisfaction at being the 'friend' of this very nice old gentleman.

There was a good deal of greeting on the stairs, and then the host, moving actively, though clumsily, and with a stick, advanced to his own dwelling-room on the first storey. The opening impression was, as the closing one would be, of extreme simplicity. A large room, without carpet on the scrubbed planks, a small bedstead, a little round stove with a stack-pipe in the middle of the room, one chair—that was all the furniture. On the walls and in the fireplace such a miserable wall-paper—tinted, with a spot—as one sees in the bedrooms of labourers' cottages; no pictures hung in the room, but pegs and shelves loaded with objects. Various boxes lay about, and one huge clamped trunk, and heaps, mountains of papers in a wild confusion, swept up here and there into stacks and peaks; but all the room, and the old man himself, clean in the highest degree, raised to the nth power of stainlessness, scoured and scrubbed to such a pitch that dirt seemed defied for all remaining time. Whitman, in particular, in his suit of hodden grey and shirt thrown wide open at the throat, his grey hair and whiter beard voluminously flowing, seemed positively blanched with cleanliness; the whole man sand-white with spotlessness like a deal table that has grown old under the scrubbing-brush.

Whitman sat down in the one chair with a small poker in his hand and spent much of his leisure in feeding and irritating the stove. I cleared some papers away from off a box and sat opposite to him. When he was not actively engaged upon the stove his steady attention was fixed upon his visitor, and I had a perfect opportunity of forming a mental picture of him. He sat with a very curious pose of the head thrown backward, as if resting it one vertebra lower down the spinal column than other people do, and thus tilting his face a little upwards. With his head so poised and the whole man fixed in contemplation of the interlocutor, he seemed to pass into a state of absolute passivity, waiting for remarks or incidents, the glassy eyes half closed, the large knotted hands spread out before him. So he would remain, immovable for a quarter of an hour at a time, even the action of speech betraying no movement, the lips hidden under a cascade of beard. If it be true that all remarkable human beings resemble animals, then Walt Whitman was like a cat—a great old grey Angora Tom, alert in repose, serenely blinking under his combed waves of hair, with eyes inscrutably dreaming.

His talk was elemental, like his writings. It had none of the usual ornaments or irritants of conversation. It welled out naturally, or stopped; it was innocent of every species of rhetoric or epigram. It was the perfectly simple utterance of unaffected urbanity. So, I imagine, an Oriental sage would talk, in a low uniform tone, without any excitement or haste, without emphasis, in a land where time and flurry were unknown. Whitman sat there with his great head tilted back, smiling serenely, and he talked about himself. He mentioned his poverty, which was patent, and his paralysis; those were the two burdens beneath which he crouched, like Issachar; he seemed to be quite at home with both of them, and scarcely heeded them. I think I asked leave to move my box, for the light began to pour in at the great uncurtained window; and then Whitman said that someone had promised him a gift of curtains, but he was not eager for them, he thought they 'kept out some of the light.' Light and air, that was all he wanted; and through the winter he sat there patiently waiting for the air and light of summer, when he would hobble out again and bask his body in a shallow creek he knew 'back of Camden.' Meanwhile he waited, waited with infinite patience, uncomplaining, thinking about the sand, and the thin hot layer of water over it, in that shy New Jersey creek. And he winked away in silence, while I thought of the Indian poet Valmiki, when, in a trance of voluptuous abstraction, he sat under the fig-tree and was slowly eaten of ants.

In the bareness of Whitman's great double room only two objects suggested art in any way, but each of these was appropriate. One was a print of a Red Indian, given him, he told me, by Catlin; it had inspired the passage about 'the red aborigines' in *Starting from Paumanok.* The other—positively the sole and only thing that redeemed the bareness of the back-room where Whitman's bound works were stored—was a photograph of a very handsome young man in a boat, sculling. I asked him about this portrait and he said several notable things in consequence. He explained, first of all, that this was one of his greatest friends, a professional oarsman from Canada, a well-known sporting character. He continued, that these were the people he liked best, athletes who had a business in the open air; that those were the plainest and most affectionate of men, those who lived in the light and air and had to study to keep their bodies clean and fresh and ruddy; that his soul went out to such people, and that they were strangely drawn to him, so that at the lowest ebb of his fortunes, when the world reviled him and ridiculed him most, fortunate men of this kind, highly prosperous as gymnasts or runners, had sought him out and had been friendly to him. 'And now,' he went on, 'I only wait for the spring, to hobble out with my staff into the woods, and when I can sit all day long close to a set of woodmen at their work, I am perfectly happy, for something of their life mixes with the smell of the chopped timber, and it passes into my veins and I am old and ill no longer.' I think these were his precise words, and they struck me more than anything else that he said throughout that long and pleasant day I spent with him.

It might be supposed, and I think that even admirers have said, that Whitman had no humour. But that seemed to me not quite correct. No boisterous humour, truly, but a gentle sort of sly fun, something like Tennyson's, he certainly showed. For example, he told me of some tribute from India, and added, with a twinkling smile, 'You see, I "sound my barbaric yawp over the roofs of the world." ' But this was rare: mostly he seemed dwelling in a vague pastoral past life, the lovely days when he was young, and went about with 'the boys' in the sun. He read me many things; a new 'poem,' intoning the long irregular lines of it not very distinctly; and a preface to some new edition. All this has left, I confess, a dim impression, swallowed up in the serene self-unconsciousness, the sweet, dignified urbanity, the feline immobility.

As I passed from the little house and stood in dull, deserted Mickle Street once more, my heart was full of affection for this beautiful old man, who had just said in his calm accents, 'Good-bye, my friend!' I felt that the experience of the day was embalmed by something that a great poet had written long ago, but I could not find what it was till we started once more to cross the frosty Delaware; then it came to me, and I knew that when Shelley spoke of

> *Peace within and calm around,*
> *And that content, surpassing wealth,*
> *The sage in meditation found,*
> *And walk'd with inward glory crown'd,*

he had been prophesying of Walt Whitman, nor shall I ever read those lines again without thinking of the old rhapsodist in his empty room, glorified by patience and philosophy.

And so an unbeliever went to see Walt Whitman, and was captivated without being converted.

III

It is related of the great Condé that, at the opening of his last campaign, sunken in melancholy, half maddened with fatigue and the dog-star heat of summer, having reached at length the cool meadows in front of the Abbey of St. Antoine, he suddenly leaped from his horse, flung away his arms and his clothing, and rolled stark-naked in the grass under a group of trees. Having taken this bath amidst his astonished officers, he rose smiling and calm, permitted himself to be dressed and armed anew, and rode to battle with all his accustomed resolution. The instinct which this anecdote illustrates lies deep down in human nature, and the more we are muffled up in social conventions the more we occasionally long for a whimsical return to nudity. If a writer is strong enough, from one cause or another, to strip the clothing off from civilisation, that writer is sure of a welcome from thousands of over-civilised readers.

Now the central feature of the writings of Walt Whitman is their nakedness. In saying this I do not refer to half-a-dozen phrases, which might with ease be eliminated, that have thrown Mrs. Grundy into fits. No responsible criticism will make a man stand or fall by what are simply examples of the carrying of a theory to excess. But of the theory itself I speak, and it is one of uncompromising openness. It is a defence of bare human nature, stripped, not merely of all its trappings and badges, but even of those garments which are universally held necessary to keep the cold away. In so many of his writings, and particularly, of course, in the *Discours* of 1750, Rousseau undertook the defence of social nudity. He called upon his world, which prided itself so much upon its elegance, to divest the body politic of all its robes. He declared that while Nature has made man happy and virtuous, society it is that renders him miserable and depraved, therefore let him get rid of social conventions and roll naked in the grass under the elm-trees. The invitation, as I have said, is one which never lacks acceptance, and Rousseau was followed into the forest by a multitude.

If Walt Whitman goes further than Rousseau, it merely is that he is more elementary. The temperament of the American is in every direction less complex. He has none of the restless intellectual vivacity, none of the fire, none of the passionate hatred of iniquity which mark the French philosopher. With Walt Whitman a coarse simplicity suffices, a certain blunt and determined negation of artificiality of every kind. He is, roughly speaking, a keenly observant and sentient being, without thought, without selection, without intensity, egged on by his nervous system to a revelation of himself. He records his own sensations one after another, careful only to present them in veracious form, without drapery or rhetoric. His charm for others is precisely this, that he observes so closely, and records so great a multitude of observations, and presents them with so complete an absence of prejudice, that any person who approaches his writings with an unbiassed mind must discover in them a reflection of some part of himself. This I believe to be the secret of the extraordinary attraction which these rhapsodical utterances have for most emotional persons at one crisis or another in their life's development. But I think criticism ought to be able to distinguish between the semi-hysterical pleasure of self-recognition and the sober and legitimate delights of literature.

The works of Walt Whitman cover a great many pages, but the texture of them is anything but subtle. When once the mind perceives what it is that Whitman says, it is found that he repeats himself over and over again, and that all his 'gospel' (as the odious modern cant puts it) is capable of being strained into very narrow limits. One 'poem' contains at least the germ of all the sheaves and sheaves of writing that Whitman published. There is not one aspect of his nature which is not stated, or more than broadly hinted at, in the single piece which he named after himself, 'Walt Whitman.' It was appropriately named, for an unclothing of himself, an invitation to all the world to come and prove that, stripped of his clothes, he was exactly like everybody else, was the essence of his religion, his philosophy, and his poetry.

It is not unfair to concentrate attention on the section of sixty pages which bears the name 'Walt Whitman' in the volume of his collected writings. It is very interesting reading. No truly candid person meeting with it for the first time, and not previously prejudiced against it, could but be struck with its felicities of diction and its air of uncontrolled sincerity. A young man of generous impulses could scarcely, I think, read it and not fall under the spell of its sympathetic illusions. It contains unusually many of those happy phrases which are, I contend, the sole purely literary possession of Whitman. It contains dozens of those closely-packed lines in each of which Whitman contrives to concentrate a whole picture of some action or condition of Nature. It contains, perhaps, the finest, certainly the most captivating, of all Whitman's natural apostrophes:

Press close, bare-bosom'd night. Press close, magnetic,
    nourishing night!
Night of south winds! night of the large few stars!
Still, nodding night! mad, naked summer night!
Smile, O voluptuous, cool-breath'd earth!
Earth of the slumbering and liquid trees!
Earth of departed sunset! earth of the mountains, misty-topt!
Earth of the vitreous pour of the full moon, just tinged with
    blue!
Earth of shine and dark, mottling the tide of the river!
Earth of the limpid grey of clouds, brighter and clearer for
    my sake!
Far-swooping, elbow'd earth! rich, apple-blossom'd earth!
Smile, for your lover comes!

All this represents the best side of the author; but 'Walt Whitman' exhibits his bad sides as well—his brutality, mis-styling itself openness, his toleration of the ugly and the forbidden, his terrible laxity of thought and fatuity of judgment.

If he studies 'Walt Whitman' carefully, a reader of middle life will probably come to the conclusion that the best way to classify the wholly anomalous and irregular writer who produced it is to place him by himself as a maker of poems in solution. I am inclined to admit that in Walt Whitman we have just missed receiving from the New World one of the greatest of modern poets, but that we have missed it must at the same time be acknowledged. To be a poet it is not necessary to be a consistent and original thinker, with an elaborately-balanced system of ethics. The absence of intellectual quality, the superabundance of the emotional, the objective, the pictorial, are no reasons for undervaluing Whitman's imagination. But there is one condition which distinguishes art from mere amorphous expression; that condition is the result of a process through which the vague and engaging observations of Whitman never passed. He felt acutely and accurately, his imagination was purged of external impurities, he lay spread abroad in a condition of literary solution. But there he remained, an expanse of crystallisable substances, waiting for the structural change that never came; rich above almost all his coevals in the properties of poetry, and yet, for want of a definite shape and fixity, doomed to sit for ever apart from the company of the Poets.

Augustine Birrell

1850–1933

THE HOUSE OF COMMONS

A Lecture delivered at the Cowdenbeath (Fifeshire)
Literary Society on Oct. 15, 1896.

THERE is a story told of an ancient dandy in London who, taking, one sunny afternoon, his accustomed stroll down Bond Street, met an acquaintance hurrying in the direction of Westminster. 'Whither away so fast this hot day?' murmured the dandy. 'To the House of Commons,' cried his strenuous friend, brushing past him. 'What!' said the dandy, with a yawn, 'does that go on still?' Yes; the House of Commons still goes on, still attracts an enormous, some think an inordinate, amount of public attention. What are called 'politics' occupy in Great Britain a curiously prominent place. Literature, art, science, are avenues to a fame more enduring, more agreeable, more personally attractive than that which awaits at the end of his career the once prominent party politician. Yet with us a party leader looms more largely in the public mind, excites more curiosity, than almost any other description of mortal. He often appears where he would not seem to have any particular business. If a bust is to be unveiled of a man of letters, if a public eulogium is to be pronounced on a man of science, if the health is to be proposed of a painter or an actor, or if some distinguished foreigner is to be feasted, the astute managers of the function, anxious to draw a crowd, and to make the thing a success, try, in the first instance, at all events, to secure the presence of Mr. Balfour, or Lord Rosebery, or Lord Salisbury, or Mr. Chamberlain, rather than of Lord Kelvin or Mr. Leslie Stephen. The fact is that politicians, and particularly the heroes of the House of Commons, the gladiators of politics, share in the country some of the popularity which naturally belongs to famous jockeys, which once belonged to the heroes of the prize ring. It is more difficult to explain this than to understand it. Our party strife, our Parliamentary contests, have long presented many of the features of a sport. When Mr. Gladstone declared in the House of Commons, with an irresistible twinkle of the eye, that he was an 'old Parliamentary hand,' the House was convulsed with laughter, and the next morning the whole country chuckled with delight. We all liked to think that our leading statesman was not only full of enthusiasm and zeal, but also a wily old fellow, who knew a thing or two better than his neighbours. I have always thought the instantaneous popularity of this remark of Mr. Gladstone's illustrates very well the curiously mixed feelings we entertain towards those great Parliamentary chieftains who have made their reputations on the floor of the House of Commons. There is nothing noble or exalted in the history of the House of Commons. Indeed, a devil's advocate, had he the requisite talent, could easily deliver an oration as long and as eloquent as any of Burke's or Sheridan's, taking as his subject the stupidity, cowardice, and, until quite recent times, the corruption of the House of Commons. I confess I cannot call to mind a single occasion in its long and remarkable history when the House of Commons, as a whole, played a part either obviously heroic or conspicuously wise; but we all of us can recall hundreds of occasions when, heroism and wisdom being greatly needed, the House of Commons exhibited either selfish indifference, crass ignorance, or the vulgarest passion. Nor can it honestly be said that our Parliamentary heroes have been the noblest of our race. Among great ministers, Sir Robert Walpole had good sense; Lord North, a kind heart; the elder Pitt, a high spirit; his son, a lofty nature; Peel, a sense of duty; Lord John Russell, a dauntless courage; Disraeli, patience to wait; but for no one of these distinguished men is it possible to have any very warm personal regard. If you turn to men who have never been powerful Ministers, the language of eulogy is perhaps a little easier. Edmund Burke, alone of Parliamentary orators, lives on in his speeches, full as they are of wisdom and humanity; through the too fierce argumentations of Charles James Fox, that great man with a marred career, there always glowed a furious something which warms my heart to its innermost depth. John Bright is a great Parliamentary figure, though many of his speeches lack a 'gracious somewhat.' Richard Cobden's oratory possessed one unique quality: it almost persuaded his political opponents that he was right and they were wrong. Among the many brilliant lawyers who have, like birds of passage, flitted through the House of Commons usually on their way to what they thought to be better things, I know but one of whom I could honestly say, 'May my soul be with his!' I refer to Sir Samuel Romilly, the very perfection in my eyes of a lawyer, a gentleman, and a member of Parliament, whose pure figure stands out in the frieze of our Parliamentary history like the figure of Apollo amongst a herd of satyrs and goats. And he, in a fit of depression, made an end of himself.

No, the charm—the undeniable charm; the strength—the unquestioned strength; the utility —of the House of Commons do not depend upon the nobility of the characters of either its leaders or its rank and file; nor on its insight into affairs —its capacity to read the signs of the times, its moral force, still less its spiritual depth; but because it has always somehow or other, both before Reform Bills and after Reform Bills, represented truthfully and forcefully, not the best sense of the wisest people, not the loftiest aspirations of the noblest people, but the primary instincts, the rooted habits of a mixed race of men and women destined in the strange providence of God to play a great part in the history of the world. A zealous philanthropy may well turn pale at the history of the House of Commons which, all through the eighteenth century, tolerated with fearful composure the infamies of the slave trade, the horrors of our gaols, the barbarity of our criminal code, the savagery of the press-gang, the heathenism of the multitude, the condition of things in our mines. The eager reformer must blush as he reads of our Parliamentary representation—of rotten boroughs, of deserted villages with two members, and of Manchester with none. The financial purist must shudder as he studies the Civil List, and ponders over the pensions and sinecures which spread corruption broadcast through the land. It is true enough, and yet the fact remains, that all this time the British nation was stumbling and groaning along the path which has floated the Union Jack in every quarter of the globe. I do not know that it can be said the House of Commons did much to assist the action of this drama; but, at all events, it did not succeed in frustrating it.

However, my object to-night is to say something about the House of Commons as it exists at present, and as it strikes the humble individual who has sat in it for seven years as your representative. Well, first of all I am a Scottish member, and as a Scottish member one's attitude to the House of Commons is not a little that of an outsider. Scotland has nothing to do with the early history of the English Parliament. Until 1707 you had a Parliament of your own, with Lords and Commons sitting all together cheek by jowl. A great economy of time, for, as Andrew Fairservice in *Rob Roy* puts it, there was no need then for Lords and Commons to have their havers twice over. There is no need to be ashamed of the old Scots Parliament. It passed laws of unrivalled brevity and perfect intelligibility, a now lost art. Scotland owes more to its old Parliament than it yet does to the United Parliament. If you seek a record of its labours you will find one in an essay penned sixty years ago by a Scotch Tory, the very man who wrote a history of Europe in twenty volumes, to prove that Heaven was always on the side of the Tories.[1]

The old Scots Parliament met for the last time on March 25, 1707. Unions are never popular. The Union of England and Scotland was undoubtedly most unpopular. One member for Fifeshire voted for it, and two against it. I wonder which way I should have voted. Cupar, Burntisland, Kinghorn, Dunfermline, Inverkeithing, and Queensferry voted Aye; but St. Andrews, Dysart, Kirkcaldy, Pittenweem, voted No. The first article of the Treaty for Union, which involved the rest, was carried by 116 votes against 83; and then, as Lord Seafield said, 'There was the end of an auld sang'; but some day—who knows?—the auld sang may be set to a new tune. But this much is certain—the new tune will in no way affect the loyalty of Scotsmen to the Union of the two countries. But for that Union Scotland would not stand where she does in the eyes of the world. What Scotland wanted, what Scotland standing alone could never have had, was a theatre wide enough for the energy of her sons. A country so small, so barren, could never have supplied such a theatre. Scotsmen must have taken service abroad, and spent their lives fighting other men's battles, or

[1] Alison's *Essays*, vol. i.

building up other men's fortunes. United with South Britain she has been able to play a glorious part both at home and abroad, and this she has done without losing either her Scottish character or her Scottish accent. Still, the fact remains that the seventy-two members from Scotland preserve a character of their own among the 590 representatives from England, Wales, and Ireland. This must be so. Scotch law is very different from English law. We have in Scotland our own laws and our own judicature. A Scotsman cannot be sued in an English court unless he is snapped with a writ whilst sojourning in that strange land. Scotland has her own religion; for, though I am far from saying that traces of a common Christianity may not be found lurking both in Presbyterianism and Episcopacy, still, speaking as a Parliament man, the religions of the two countries may be considered as distinct. In England, those who do not believe in the Divine authority of Episcopacy, who deny either the validity of the orders of the Episcopalian clergy or that there are such things as holy orders at all, who repudiate the sacramentarian system, and hate the pretensions of a priesthood, are engaged in a daily, bitter strife with the Church party, with which Scotland has as yet no concern. The educational system is different. Here you have universal School Boards, and pay an allegiance—sometimes real, sometimes formal —to a Catechism which, though often supposed to be the most Scotch thing in existence, was, as a matter of fact, compiled in England by Englishmen. In England School Boards are far from universal, and clerically conducted schools provide the education of half the school-going population. The Scottish system of local government is different in important respects from the English. For example, your Parish Councils administer the Poor Law; in England they do not. Your rating system is different. Here the rate is divided between the owner and the occupier; in England the occupier pays the whole rate. All these differences invite different treatment—there have to be English Bills and Scotch Bills; and though some Scotch members may honestly try to understand English Bills, I never knew an English member, unless he was by birth a Scotsman, who ever took, or pretended to take, the least trouble to understand a Scotch Bill. They vote if they happen to be in the House whilst Scotch business is being discussed, but they vote as they are told by their party managers. It follows, as I say, from this that a Scotch member surveys the House of Commons somewhat as an outsider.

The great characteristic of the House of Commons is that it is a deliberative and consultative chamber, meeting together for the purposes of framing laws (if it considers any new laws necessary) which are to bind the whole nation, and of criticising the Executive. It does not meet for the purpose of oratory, or to strengthen party organisation, but to frame laws of universal obligation and to find fault with or support Ministers. This at once gets rid of the platform orator, and establishes the difference between public meetings and the House of Commons.

It is no discredit to the public meeting or to the House of Commons to say that what will find favour with the one excites the disgust of the other, for the two have little in common. The object of a speaker at a public meeting is to excite enthusiasm and to spread his faith; but in the House of Commons his object is to remove objections, to state propositions in a way least likely to make reply easy, to show that a scheme is practicable and free from particular injustices, to handle figures with dexterity, and to avoid empty phraseology. There is nothing the House of Commons hates more than to be reminded of the purgatorial flames through which each member has had to pass in order to take his seat by the side of the Speaker; and therefore it is that the utterance in all innocence, by some new member of either party, of the cries and watchwords with which he was accustomed to enliven his electioneering speeches never fails to excite the angry groans of his opponents and the sarcastic smiles of his friends. Nor is there anything dishonest in this. There is a time for all things, and the House of Commons is before everything a deliberative and consultative assembly. Another marked characteristic of the House of Commons is its total indifference to outside reputations or great fortunes. Local magnates, manufacturers whose chimneys blacken a whole countryside, merchants whose ships plough the broad and narrow seas, speculators in cotton and in sugar, mayors and provosts whose portraits adorn town halls, whose names are household words in their own districts, lawyers so eminent that they will not open their mouths in the courts for less than a hundred guineas, need not hope to be received by the House of Commons otherwise than with languid indifference. If they prove to be bores, so much the worse; if they prove not to be bores, so much the better. If they push themselves to the front, it will be by Parliamentary methods; if they remain insignificant, it is only what was to be expected. Never was an assembly so free from all taint of mercenariness as the House of Commons. It does not care a snap of its finger whether the income of a new member is £100,000 a year or £3 a week—whether his father was a duke or a blacksmith; its only concern with him is that, if he has anything to say, he may say it, and that if he has nothing to say, he will say nothing.

The House of Commons is often said to be a place of great good-fellowship. Within certain necessarily restricted limits it is. It is difficult to maintain aloofness. You may find yourself serving on a Committee alongside some one whose public utterances or party intrigues you have always regarded with aversion; but it may easily be that you agree with him, not, it may be, as to the Government of Ireland or the sacred principles of Free Trade, but as to the prudence or folly of a particular line of railway, or the necessity of a new water-supply for some large town. You hob-a-nob at luncheon, you grumble together over your dinner, you lament the spread of football clubs and brass bands in your respective constituencies; you criticise your leaders, and are soon quite at home in the society of the very man you thought you detested. There is nothing like a common topic to break the ice, and two members of Parliament have always something to talk about. But farther than this it is hard to go. The House is too large. Amongst an assembly of 670 men well on in life the hand of Death is always busy. Vacancies occur with startling regularity. The only uncertainty is, who is to drop out of the ranks. 'Death of a Member of Parliament' is a common announcement on the placards of the evening papers; and then the thriftiest of Scotch members fumbles for his bawbee, buys the paper, stops under the next lamp-post to see who it is who has gone, whose figure will no more be seen in the Tea-room and the Lobby. Whoever it is, big man or little, a silent member or a talkative one, a wise man or a fool, his place will soon be filled up, and his party Whip will be heard moving for a new writ to issue for the Borough of Small-Talk in the place of Jeremiah Jones, deceased. 'Poor Jones!' we all say; 'not a bad fellow, Jones; I suppose Brown will get the seat this time.'

I know no place where the great truth that no man is necessary is brought home to the mind so remorselessly, and yet so refreshingly, as the House of Commons. Over even the greatest reputations it closes with barely a bubble. And yet the vanity of politicians is enormous. Lord Melbourne, you will remember, when asked his opinion of men, replied, with his accustomed expletive, which I omit as unfit for the polite ear of Cowdenbeath, 'Good fellows, very good fellows, but vain, very vain.'

There is a great deal of vanity, both expressed and concealed, in the House of Commons. I often wonder why, for I cannot imagine a place where men so habitually disregard each other's feelings, so openly trample on each other's egotisms. You rise to address the House. The Speaker calls on you by name. You begin your speech. Hardly are you through with the first sentence when your oldest friend, your college chum, the man you have appointed guardian of your infant children, rises in his place, gives you a stony stare, and, seizing his hat in his hand, ostentatiously walks out of the House, as much as to say, 'I can stand many things, but not this.'

Whilst speaking in the House I have never failed to notice one man, at all events, who was paying me the compliment of the closest attention, who never took his eyes off me, who hung upon my words, on whom everything I was saying seemed to be making the greatest impression. In my early days I used to address myself to this man, and try my best to make my discourse worthy of his attention; but sad experience has taught me that this solitary auditor is not in the least interested either in me or in my speech, and that the only reason why he listens so intently and eyes me so closely is because he has made up his mind to follow me, and is eager to leap to his feet, in the hope of catching the Speaker's eye, the very moment I sit down. Yet, for all this, vanity thrives in the House—though what it feeds on I cannot say. We are all anxious to exaggerate our own importance, and desperately anxious to make reputations for ourselves and

to have our names associated with some subject
—to pose as its patron and friend. On great
Parliamentary nights these vanities, from which
even our leaders are not wholly exempt, are very
conspicuous. On such occasions the House of
Commons has reminded me of a great drying-
ground, where all the clothes of a neighbourhood may be seen fluttering in a gale of wind.
There are night-gowns and shirts and petticoats
so distended and distorted by the breeze as to
seem the garments of a race of giants, rather
than of poor mortal man; even the stockings of
some slim maiden, when puffed out by the law-
less wind, assume dropsical proportions. But the
wind sinks, having done its task, and then the
matter-of-fact washerwoman unpegs the garments, sprinkles them with water, and ruthlessly
passes over them her flat-irons, and, lo and
behold! these giant's robes are reduced to their
familiar, domestic, and insignificant proportions.

A marked characteristic of the House of Commons is its generosity. We have heard far too
much lately of contending jealousies. The only
thing the House is really jealous of is its own
reputation. If a member, no matter who he is,
or where he sits, or what he says, makes a good
speech and creates a powerful impression, nobody is more delighted, more expansively and
effusively delighted, than Sir William Harcourt.
On such occasions he glows with generosity. And
this is equally true of Mr. Balfour, and indeed
of the whole House, which invariably welcomes
talent and rejoices over growing reputations.

Members of Parliament may be divided into

two classes: Front Bench men and Back Bench men. The former are those who fill or have filled posts in an Administration, and they sit either on the Government Bench or on the Front Opposition Bench. These personages enjoy certain privileges, and the most obvious of these privileges is that they speak with a table in front of them, whereby they are enabled cunningly to conceal their notes. Now, the private or Back Bench member has no place in which to conceal his notes, save his hat, a structure ill-fitted for the purpose. Another of the privileges of a Front Bench man is that he has, or is supposed to have, a right of intervention in debate just when he chooses. This is an enormous advantage. Just consider the unhappy fate of a private member who is anxious to speak during an important debate. He prepares his speech, and comes down to the House with it concealed about his person. He bides his time; an excellent opportunity occurs; nobody has as yet said what he is going to say; he rises in his place; but, alas! fifteen other members with fifteen other speeches in their pockets rise too, and the Speaker calls on one of them, and down falls our unhappy member, to wait another opportunity. This may happen frequently, and often does happen fifteen or sixteen times. He has to sit still and hear other men mangle his arguments, quote his quotations. Night follows night, and the speech remains undelivered, festering in his brain, polluting his mind. At last he gets his chance—the Speaker calls out his name; but by this time he has got sick of the subject—it has grown weary, stale, flat, and unprofitable. He has lost his interest, and soon loses the thread of his discourse; he flounders and flops, has recourse to his hat, repeats himself, grows hot and uncomfortable, forgets his best points, and finally sits down dejected, discouraged, disappointed. And all the time his wife is in the Ladies' Gallery gnashing her teeth at the poor figure he is cutting! No wonder he hates the Front Bench man. But there are gradations in the Front Bench. Between the leaders of the House, who bag all the best moments, and the humble Under Secretary or Civil Lord there is a great gulf fixed. These latter gentry are not allowed to speak at all, except on matters relating to their departments, or when they are told off to speak by the leader. Nothing is more amusing than to notice the entire eclipse of some notorious chatterbox who has been given some minor post in an Administration. Before he took office he was chirping on every bough; hardly a night passed but his sweet voice was to be heard. After he has taken office he frequently has to hold his tongue for a whole session. Poor fellow! he will sometimes buttonhole you in the Lobby, and almost tearfully complain of the irksomeness of office, and tell you how he longs for the hour of emancipation, when once more his voice, like that of the turtle, shall be heard in the land. If you gently remind him of the salary he draws, and hint that it may be some consolation even for silence, ten to one he walks away in a huff, and attributes your innocent remarks to jealousy. Between the Front Bench and the Back Bench there has

always been a feud. Front Bench men of the first
rank are too apt, so it is said, to regard the
House of Commons as a show run for their
benefit, to look upon themselves as a race of
actor-managers who arrange the playbill, and
divide all the best parts among themselves. The
traditions of Parliament foster this idea. But the
Back Bench men are not always in the mood
to submit to be for ever either the audience or
the supernumeraries, and whenever they get
the chance of asserting themselves against their
leaders they take it. But in public they seldom
get the chance, so they have to content themselves with being as disagreeable in private as
they possibly can. What I think is a just complaint, frequently made by Back Benchers, relates to the habit Parliamentary leaders of late
have greatly indulged in, of occupying an enormous amount of time abusing one another for
past inconsistencies of conduct. These amenities,
sometimes called *tu quoques*, or 'You are another,'
are infinitely wearisome, and proceed upon the
mistaken assumption that the House of Commons greatly concerns itself with the political
reputation of its leaders. It does nothing of the
sort. What it wants is leaders who can make
business go, who will show sport, and lead their
hounds across a good line of country.

As a Back Benchman, the only real complaint
I have to make is of the woeful waste of time.
One goes down to the House every day—Satur-
days and Wednesdays excepted—at 4 o'clock,
and you are supposed to remain there till midnight. On Wednesdays the House meets at 12

and adjourns at 5.30. What do we do all this
time? To be interested in everything that is
going on is flatly impossible. A quantity of the
business is of a local character, dealing with
places and schemes of which we know and can
know nothing. Then there are terribly protracted debates on the second readings of Bills,
occasionally interesting, but necessarily full of
repetitions. I do not well see how this is to be
prevented; but it is a shocking infliction. The
Committee stage of a Bill you have really mastered
is interesting and instructive, but even this stage
is too protracted; and then comes a later stage
—the report stage—when a great deal is said all
over again; and even this is frequently followed
by a debate on the third reading. Of course,
you are not in the House all the time. There is
the Library, the Tea-room, and the Smoking-
room, where you may play chess and draughts,
but no other game whatsoever. But nobody does
anything vehemently. An air of languor per-
vades the whole place. Listlessness abounds.
Members stroll from one room to another, turn
over the newspapers, and yawn in each other's
faces. In the summer months, the Terrace by
the riverside has been recently converted into a
kind of watering-place. From five o'clock to
seven it is crowded with fine ladies and country
cousins, drinking tea and devouring strawberries.
Occasionally some Parliamentary person of importance will choose to stalk by, and even—such
is the affability of true greatness—have a cup of
tea with a party of friends. A poorer way of
killing time has not, I think, yet been discovered;

but it is a convincing proof of the *ennui* of Parliamentary life.

The great problem of Ministers is the reform of the rules of the House of Commons—how to make the House at once a deliberative and yet a business-like assembly.

And yet men do not willingly strike off the chains of this slavery. A private member of Parliament nowadays gets nothing, neither pudding nor praise, in exchange for his time and his money. Patronage he has absolutely none—not a single place, even in the Post-Office, to give away. Nor has he a single privilege that I am aware of. His routine duties on committees are onerous, nor are his opportunities of making speeches, if he wishes to do so, otherwise than few and far between. His leaders treat him with frigid civility, and nobody cares for a letter from him unless it encloses a postal order for at least ten shillings. And yet the labour of winning a seat and of retaining a seat is very great; nor is the expense insignificant.

When one thinks of all the different ways of spending £700, a Parliamentary election does not obviously strike you as being one of the most delightful. It may be said you have the opportunity of legislating on your own account. You may bring in a Bill of your own, and have the satisfaction of hearing it read a third time. Hardly is this true. In former days some of the most useful laws in the Statute Book were pioneered through the House by private members. But now, so greedy have Governments become, that they take nearly all the time available for legislative purposes, and, unless the private member gets the first place in the ballot, he has not a chance of carrying any measure through if it excites the least opposition. But when all is said and done, the House of Commons is a fascinating place. It has one great passion, one genuine feeling, and that is, to represent and give practical expression to the mind of the whole nation. It has no prejudices in this matter, for it has no existence independent of its creators. It has nothing to do with the choice of its component parts. The constituencies may send up whom they choose, but these persons, when they do come up, must not expect to be hailed as 'Saviours of Society.' No; they must be content to be parts of a whole, to give and take, to hear their pet creeds, faiths, and fancies, rudely questioned, tested, and weighed. A great nation will never consent to be dominated either by a sect or by an interest. And yet, if the House of Commons has a leaning to any particular class of member —which by rights it ought to have—it is for an increased direct representation of the wage-earning community. I hope such representatives may be forthcoming in greater numbers as time goes on. But if they are to do any good in the House of Commons, they must go there, not as conquering heroes to whom the unknown future belongs, but as Britons anxious to contribute out of their special knowledge, from their hived experience, to the collective wisdom of the nation; they must be willing to learn as well as to teach, to increase the stock of their information, to acknowledge mistakes, to widen their views; and, above all, must they recognise that the mighty river of our national existence, if it is to continue to flow as triumphantly as before, must continue to be fed by many tributary streams.

There are, I know, those who affect to believe that representative assemblies do not stand where they did, and that the day of their doom is not far distant. I see no reason to believe anything of the kind, for, scan the horizon as you may, you cannot discover what there is to take their place. We have no mind for military despotisms, even if we had a military hero. Nor are we disposed to believe in the superior wisdom of that so-called statesmanship which is manufactured in Government offices. Better by far the occasional mistakes of a free people and a popular assembly than the deadly and persistent errors of diplomatists and hereditary statesmen. The House of Commons will, I cannot doubt, be still going on when the twentieth century breathes its last. Change it will know, and reform; but, founded as it is upon a rational and manly system of representation, why should it not always continue to reflect, cautiously but truthfully, the mind and will of the British people?

R. B. Cunninghame Graham

1852–1936

WITH THE NORTH-EAST WIND

A NORTH-EAST haar had hung the city with a
pall of grey. It gave an air of hardness to the
stone-built houses, blending them with the stone-
paved streets, till you could scarce see where the
houses ended and the street began. A thin grey
dust hung in the air. It coloured everything,
and people's faces all looked pinched with the
first touch of autumn cold. The wind, boisterous
and gusty, whisked the soot-grimed city leaves
about in the high suburb at the foot of a long
range of hills, making one think it would be easy
to have done with life on such an uncongenial
day. Tramways were packed with people of the
working class, all of them of the alert, quick-
witted type only to be seen in the great city on
the Clyde, in all our Empire, and comparable
alone to the dwellers in Chicago for dry vivacity.

By the air they wore of chastened pleasure, all
those who knew them saw that they were intent
upon a funeral. To serious-minded men such as
they are, for all their quickness, nothing is so
soul-filling, for it is of the nature of a fact that
no one can deny. A wedding has its possibilities,
for it may lead to children, or divorce, but funerals
are in another category. At them the Scottish
people is at its best, for never more than then

does the deep underlying tenderness peep through the hardness of the rind. On foot and in the tramways, but most especially on foot, converged long lines of men and women, though fewer women, for the national prejudice that in years gone by thought it not decent for a wife to follow to the grave her husband's coffin, still holds a little in the north. Yet there was something in the crowd that showed it was to attend no common funeral, that they were 'stepping west.' No one wore black, except a minister or two, who looked a little like the belated rook you sometimes see amongst a flock of seagulls, in that vast ocean of grey tweed.

They tramped along, the whistling north-east wind pinching their features, making their eyes run, and as they went, almost unconsciously they fell into procession, for beyond the tramway line, a country lane that had not quite put on the graces of a street, though straggling houses were dotted here and there along it, received the crowd and marshalled it, as it were mechanically, without volition of its own. Kept in between the walls, and blocked in front by the hearse and long procession of the mourning-coaches, the people slowly surged along. The greater portion of the crowd were townsmen, but there were miners washed and in their Sunday best. Their faces showed the blue marks of healed-up scars into which coal dust or gunpowder had become tattooed, scars gained in the battle of their lives down in the pits, remembrances of falls of rock or of occasions when the mine had 'fired upon them.'

Many had known Keir Hardie in his youth, had 'wrocht wi' him out-by,' at Blantyre, at Hamilton, in Ayrshire, and all of them had heard him speak a hundred times. Even to those who had not heard him, his name was as a household word. Miners predominated, but men of every trade were there. Many were members of that black-coated proletariat, whose narrow circumstances and daily struggle for appearances make their life harder to them than is the life of any working man before he has had to dye his hair. Women tramped, too, for the dead leader had been a champion of their sex. They all respected him, loving him with that half-contemptuous gratitude that women often show to men who make the 'woman question' the object of their lives.

After the Scottish fashion at a funeral, greetings were freely passed, and Reid, who hadna' seen his friend Mackinder since the time of the Mid-Lanark fight, greeted him with 'Ye mind when first Keir Hardie was puttin' up for Parliament,' and wrung his hand, hardened in the mine, with one as hardened, and instantly began to recall elections of the past.

'Ye mind yon Wishaw meeting?'

'Aye, ou aye; ye mean when a' they Irish wouldna' hear John Ferguson. Man, he almost grat after the meeting aboot it.'

'Aye, but they gied Hardie himself a maist respectful hearing . . . aye, ou aye.'

Others remembered him a boy, and others in his home at Cumnock, but all spoke of him with affection, holding him as something of their own, apart from other politicians, almost apart from men.

Old comrades who had been with him either at this election or that meeting, had helped or had intended to have helped at the crises of his life, fought their old battles over, as they tramped along, all shivering in the wind.

The procession reached a long dip in the road, and the head of it, full half a mile away, could be seen gathered round the hearse, outside the chapel of the crematorium, whose ominous tall chimney, through which the ashes, and perchance the souls of thousands have escaped towards some empyrean or another, towered up starkly. At last all had arrived, and the small open space was crowded, the hearse and carriages appearing stuck amongst the people, like raisins in a cake, so thick they pressed upon them. The chapel, differing from the ordinary chapel of the faiths as much as does a motor driver from a cabman, had an air as of modernity about it, which contrasted strangely with the ordinary looking crowd, the adjacent hills, the decent mourning coaches and the black-coated undertakers who bore the coffin up the steps. Outside, the wind whistled and swayed the soot-stained trees about; but inside the chapel the heat was stifling.

When all was duly done, and long exordiums passed upon the man who in his life had been the target for the abuse of Press and pulpit, the coffin slid away to its appointed place. One thought one heard the roaring of the flames, and somehow missed the familiar lowering of the

body . . . earth to earth . . . to which the centuries of use and wont have made us all familiar,
though dust to dust in this case was the more
appropriate.

In either case, the book is closed for ever, and
the familiar face is seen no more.

So, standing just outside the chapel in the
cold, waiting till all the usual greetings had been
exchanged, I fell a-musing on the man whom I
had known so well. I saw him as he was thirty
years ago, outlined against a bing or standing
in a quarry in some mining village, and heard
his once familiar address of 'Men.' He used no
other in those days, to the immense disgust of
legislators and other worthy but unimaginative
men whom he might chance to meet. About
him seemed to stand a shadowy band, most of
whom now are dead or lost to view, or have
gone under in the fight.

John Ferguson was there, the old-time Irish
leader, the friend of Davitt and of Butt. Tall
and erect he stood, dressed in his long frock-coat,
his roll of papers in one hand, and with the other
stuck into his breast, with all the air of being the
last Roman left alive. Tom Mann, with his
black hair, his flashing eyes, and his tumultuous
speech peppered with expletives. Beside him,
Sandy Haddow, of Parkhead, massive and Doric
in his speech, with a grey woollen comforter
rolled round his neck, and hands like panels of
a door. Champion, pale, slight, and interesting,
still the artillery officer, in spite of Socialism.
John Burns; and Small, the miners' agent, with
his close brown beard and taste for literature.

Smillie stood near, he of the seven elections, and then check weigher at a pit, either at Cadzow or Larkhall. There, too, was silver-tongued Shaw Maxwell and Chisholm Robertson, looking out darkly on the world through tinted spectacles; with him Bruce Glasier, girt with a red sash and with an aureole of fair curly hair around his head, half poet and half revolutionary.

They were all young and ardent, and as I mused upon them and their fate, and upon those of them who have gone down into the oblivion that waits for those who live before their time, I shivered in the wind.

Had he, too, lived in vain, he whose scant ashes were no doubt by this time all collected in an urn, and did they really represent all that remained of him?

Standing amongst the band of shadowy comrades I had known, I saw him, simple and yet with something of the prophet in his air, and something of the seer. Effective and yet ineffectual, something there was about him that attracted little children to him, and I should think lost dogs. He made mistakes, but then those who make no mistakes seldom make anything. His life was one long battle, so it seemed to me that it was fitting that at his funeral the north-east wind should howl amongst the trees, tossing and twisting them as he himself was twisted and storm-tossed in his tempestuous passage through the world.

As the crowd moved away, and in the hearse and mourning-coaches the spavined horses limped slowly down the road, a gleam of sunshine, such as had shone too little in his life, lighted up everything.

The swaying trees and dark, grey houses of the ugly suburb of the town were all transfigured for a moment. The chapel door was closed, and from the chimney of the crematorium a faint blue smoke was issuing, which, by degrees, faded into the atmosphere, just as the soul, for all I know, may melt into the air.

When the last stragglers had gone, and bits of paper scurried uneasily along before the wind, the world seemed empty, with nothing friendly in it, but the shoulder of Ben Lomond peeping out shyly over the Kilpatrick Hills.

SET FREE

A FINE, persistent rain had filled the streets with mud. It lay so thickly that it seemed as if black snow had fallen, and from the pools which had collected here and there upon its surface the passing carriages were reflected, as by a mirage, distorted in the glare of the electric light. The passers-by had all a look of ghosts in the thick foggy air. Rain trickled from their hats and umbrellas, and mud and water oozed beneath their tread. The thoroughfares were blocked in places with cabs all full of people going off upon their holiday, for it was Christmas week. Bells were heard fitfully, calling the faithful to the churches to prepare to celebrate the birth of Him who died upon the Cross to bring peace to the earth.

The trees which overhang the roadway by the park dropped inky showers upon the tramps sleeping or talking on the seats. The drops splashed on the stones and on the cross-board of the rest for porters' burdens which still survives, a relic of the past, between the cast-iron lamp-posts with their bright globes of light. Here and there at the corners of the streets that lead down to the artery between the parks stood women dressed fashionably, wearing large hats with ostrich feathers. True that their numbers were diminished, for an orgasm of virtue had recently swept over those who rule, and had decreed Vice should do homage to her twin-sister Virtue, but only on the sly. Still, they were there to show how much had been achieved for women by our faith, in the last thousand years. Policemen stood about upon their beats, stout and well-fed, looking with scorn if a tax-payer in a threadbare coat passed by them, and ever ready after the fashion of the world, to aid the rich, the strong, and those who did not need their help, and spurn the miserable.

During the week the churches had been thronged with worshippers. Some went to pray, others resorted to the fane from custom, and again, some from a vague feeling that religion was a bulwark reared in defence of property in seasons of unrest, though this of course they had not reasoned out, but felt instinctively, just as a man fears danger in the night upon a lonely road. Hymns had been sung and sermons preached inculcating goodwill, peace, charity and forbearance to the weak. Yet London was as pitiless as ever, and the strong pushed the weak down in the gutter, actually and in the moral sphere. Women were downtrodden, except they happened to be rich, though men talked chivalrously whilst not refraining for an instant to take advantage of the power that law and nature placed within their reach. The animal creation seemed to have been devised by God to bring out all that was most base in man. If they were tame and looked to him as man, in theory, looks toward his God, he worked them pitilessly. Their loves, their preferences, their simple joys, attachments to the places where they had first seen the light and frisked beside their mothers in the fields, were all uncared for, even were subjects for derision or for mirth, if they were marked at all. If, on the other hand, they were of those, winged or four-footed, who had never bowed the knee or drooped the wing to man's domination, their treatment was still worse. They had no rights, except of being killed at proper seasons, which were contrived so artfully that but a bare three months of the whole year was left unstained with blood. Woods in their thickest depths witnessed their agony. Deep in the corries of the hills, in fields, in rivers, on the land, the sea, and in the bowels of the earth they left their fellows, dumb, stricken, wretched, and died silently, wondering perhaps what crimes they had committed in their lives so innocent and pure. No one commiserated them, for they were clearly sent into the world as living targets to improve man's power of shooting, or to be chased and torn to pieces in order to draw out the highest feelings of his self-esteem and give him opportunities to say, as their eyes glazed in death, 'There is one flesh of man, and yet another of the beasts, all glory to His name.'

Through the soft rain the roar of the great city rose, though dulled and deadened, still menacing and terrible, as if the worst of human passions, as always happens in a crowd, had got the upper hand, and were astir to wreak themselves on any object ready to their hand. Machines ran to and fro, noisy and sending forth mephitic fumes, and seeming somehow as if they were the masters, and the pale men who drove them only slaves of the great forces they had brought into their lives. They swerved and skated, bearing their fill of trembling passengers, and making every living thing give them the road on pain of muti-lated limbs or death as horrible as by the car of some great idol in the East. No car of Jugger-naut was half so terrible, and as they took their passage through the streets men shrank into the second place and seemed but to exist on suffer-ance, as tenders of machines.

Still, it was Christmas week, and the glad tidings preached so long ago, so fitted for the quiet ways and pastoral existence of those who heard them first, so strangely incongruous with us of modern times, were still supposed to animate men's minds. The night wore on, and through the sordid rows of stuccoed houses the interminable file of cabs, of carriages and motor omni-buses, still took its course, and trains of market-carts drawn by small puffing engines began to pass along the street. In them, high in the air, lying upon the heaped-up vegetables or seated on the backboard clinging by one arm to the chain, boys slumbered, their heads swaying and wagging to and fro as the carts rumbled on the stones. Then the carts disappeared, and the remaining traffic increased its speed in the half-empty streets, the drivers, anxious to get home, shaving each other's wheels in haste or carelessness. Round coffee-stalls stood groups of people in the flaring light of naphtha-lamps—soldiers, a man in evening dress, a street-walker or two, and some of those strange, hardly human-looking hags who only seem to rise from the recesses of the night, and with the dawn retreat into some Malebolge of the slums. The time and place had broken down all barriers of caste and they stood laughing at obscenities, primitive and crude, such as have drawn the laughter of mankind from the beginning of the world.

In the great open space between the junction of the parks, where on one side the hospital frowns on the paltry Græco-Cockney sham triumphal arch, just underneath the monolith from which the bronze Iron Duke looks down upon the statues of the men he qualified as 'blackguards' in his life, a little crowd surrounded something lying on the ground. A covered van, battered and shabby, stood, with a broken shaft. Under the wheels the mud was stained with a dark patch already turning black, and the smashed shaft was spotted here and there with blood. A heap of broken harness lay in a pile, and near it on its side a horse with a leg broken by a motor omnibus. His coat was dank with sweat, and his lean sides were raw in places with the harness, that he would wear no more. His neck was galled with the wet collar which was thrown upon the pile of harness, its flannel lining stained with the matter of the sores which scarcely healed before work opened them again. The horse's yellow teeth, which his lips, open in his agony, disclosed, showed that he was old and that his martyrdom was not of yesterday. His breath came painfully and his thin flanks heaved like a wheezy bellows in a smithy, and now and then one of his legs contracted and was drawn up to his belly and then extended slowly till the shoe clanked upon the ground. The broken leg, limp and bedaubed in mud, looked like a sausage badly filled, and the protruding splinter of the bone showed whitely through the skin.

The little crowd stood gazing at him as he lay, not without sympathy, but dully, as if they too were over-driven in their lives.

Then came a policeman who, after listening to the deposition of the owner of the horse, took out a little book, and having written in it briskly with a stumpy pencil, returned it to his pocket with an air of having done his duty and passed on upon his way.

The electric lamps flared on the scene. In the deserted park the wind amongst the trees murmured a threnody, and on the road the dying horse lay as a rock sticks up, just in the tideway of a harbour, thin, dirty, overworked, castrated, underfed, familiar from his youth with blows and with ill-treatment, but now about to be set free.

W. H. Hudson

1841–1922

THE SAMPHIRE GATHERER

At sunset, when the strong wind from the sea
was beginning to feel cold, I stood on the top of
the sand-hill looking down at an old woman
hurrying about over the low damp ground beneath—a bit of sea-flat divided from the sea by
the ridge of sand; and I wondered at her, because
her figure was that of a feeble old woman, yet
she moved—I had almost said flitted—over that
damp level ground in a surprisingly swift light
manner, pausing at intervals to stoop and gather
something from the surface. But I couldn't see
her distinctly enough to satisfy myself: the sun
was sinking below the horizon, and that dimness
in the air and coldness in the wind at day's
decline, when the year too was declining, made
all objects look dim. Going down to her I found
that she was old, with thin grey hair on an uncovered head, a lean dark face with regular
features and grey eyes that were not old and
looked steadily at mine, affecting me with a
sudden mysterious sadness. For they were unsmiling eyes and themselves expressed an un-
utterable sadness, as it appeared to me at the
first swift glance; or perhaps not that, as it presently seemed, but a shadowy something which
sadness had left in them, when all pleasure and

all interest in life forsook her, with all affections, and she no longer cherished either memories or hopes. This may be nothing but conjecture or fancy, but if she had been a visitor from another world she could not have seemed more strange to me.

I asked her what she was doing there so late in the day, and she answered in a quiet even voice which had a shadow in it too, that she was gathering samphire of that kind which grows on the flat saltings and has a dull green leek-like fleshy leaf. At this season, she informed me, it was fit for gathering to pickle and put by for use during the year. She carried a pail to put it in, and a table-knife in her hand to dig the plants up by the roots, and she also had an old sack in which she put every dry stick and chip of wood she came across. She added that she had gathered samphire at this same spot every August end for very many years.

I prolonged the conversation, questioning her and listening with affected interest to her mechanical answers, while trying to fathom those unsmiling, unearthly eyes that looked so steadily at mine.

And presently, as we talked, a babble of human voices reached our ears, and half turning we saw the crowd, or rather procession, of golfers coming from the golf-house by the links where they had been drinking tea. Ladies and gentlemen players, forty or more of them, following in a loose line, in couples and small groups, on their way to the Golfers' Hotel, a little further up the coast; a remarkably good-looking lot with well-fed happy faces, well dressed and in a merry mood, all freely talking and laughing. Some were staying at the hotel, and for the others a score or so of motor-cars were standing before its gates to take them inland to their homes, or to houses where they were staying.

We suspended the conversation while they were passing us, within three yards of where we stood, and as they passed the story of the links where they had been amusing themselves since luncheon-time came into my mind. The land there was owned by an old, an ancient, family; they had occupied it, so it is said, since the Conquest; but the head of the house was now poor, having no house property in London, no coal mines in Wales, no income from any other source than the land, the twenty or thirty thousand acres let for farming. Even so he would not have been poor, strictly speaking, but for the sons, who preferred a life of pleasure in town, where they probably had private establishments of their own. At all events they kept race-horses, and had their cars, and lived in the best clubs, and year by year the patient old father was called upon to discharge their debts of honour. It was a painful position for so estimable a man to be placed in, and he was much pitied by his friends and neighbours, who regarded him as a worthy representative of the best and oldest family in the county. But he was compelled to do what he could to make both ends meet, and one of the little things he did was to establish golf-links over a mile or so of sand-hills, lying between the ancient coast village and the sea, and to build and run a Golfers' Hotel in order to attract visitors from all parts. In this way, incidentally, the villagers were cut off from their old direct way to the sea and deprived of those barren dunes, which were their open space and recreation ground and had stood them in the place of a common for long centuries. They were warned off and told that they must use a path to the beach which took them over half a mile from the village. And they had been very humble and obedient and had made no complaint. Indeed, the agent had assured them that they had every reason to be grateful to the overlord, since in return for that trivial inconvenience they had been put to they would have the golfers there, and there would be employment for some of the village boys as caddies. Nevertheless, I had discovered that they were not grateful but considered that an injustice had been done to them, and it rankled in their hearts.

I remembered all this while the golfers were streaming by, and wondered if this poor woman did not, like her fellow-villagers, cherish a secret bitterness against those who had deprived them of the use of the dunes where for generations they had been accustomed to walk or sit or lie on the loose yellow sands among the barren grasses, and had also cut off their direct way to the sea where they went daily in search of bits of firewood and whatever else the waves threw up which would be a help to them in their poor lives.

If it be so, I thought, some change will surely come into those unchanging eyes at the sight of all these merry, happy golfers on their way to their hotel and their cars and luxurious homes.

But though I watched her face closely there was no change, no faintest trace of ill-feeling or feeling of any kind; only that same shadow which had been there was there still, and her fixed eyes were like those of a captive bird or animal, that gaze at us, yet seem not to see us but to look through and beyond us. And it was the same when they had all gone by and we finished our talk and I put money in her hand; she thanked me without a smile, in the same quiet even tone of voice in which she had replied to my question about the samphire.

I went up once more to the top of the ridge, and looking down saw her again as I had seen her at first, only dimmer, swiftly, lightly moving or flitting moth-like or ghost-like over the low flat salting, still gathering samphire in the cold wind, and the thought that came to me was that I was looking at and had been interviewing a being that was very like a ghost, or in any case a soul, a something which could not be described, like certain atmospheric effects in earth and water and sky which are ignored by the land-scape painter. To protect himself he cultivates what is called the 'sloth of the eye': he thrusts his fingers into his ears, so to speak, not to hear that mocking voice that follows and mocks him with his miserable limitations. He who seeks to convey his impressions with a pen is almost as badly off: the most he can do in such instances as the one related, is to endeavour to convey the emotion evoked by what he has witnessed.

Let me then take the case of the man who has

trained his eyes, or rather whose vision has unconsciously trained itself, to look at every face he meets, to find in most cases something, however little, of the person's inner life. Such a man could hardly walk the length of the Strand and Fleet Street or of Oxford Street without being startled at the sight of a face which haunts him with its tragedy, its mystery, the strange things it has half revealed. But it does not haunt him long; another arresting face follows, and then another, and the impressions all fade and vanish from the memory in a little while. But from time to time, at long intervals, once perhaps in a lustrum, he will encounter a face that will not cease to haunt him, whose vivid impression will not fade for years. It was a face and eyes of that kind which I met in the samphire gatherer on that cold evening; but the mystery of it is a mystery still.

HER OWN VILLAGE

ONE afternoon when cycling among the limestone hills of Derbyshire I came to an unlovely dreary-looking little village named Chilmorton. It was an exceptionally hot June day and I was consumed with thirst: never had I wanted tea so badly. Small gritstone-built houses and cottages of a somewhat sordid aspect stood on either side of the street, but there was no shop of any kind and not a living creature could I see. It was like a village of the dead or sleeping. At the top of the street I came to the church standing in the middle of its churchyard with the public-house for nearest neighbour. Here there was life. Going in I found it the most squalid and evil-smelling village pub I had ever entered. Half a dozen grimy-looking labourers were drinking at the bar, and the landlord was like them in appearance, with his dirty shirt-front open to give his patrons a view of his hairy sweating chest. I asked him to get me tea. 'Tea!' he shouted, staring at me as if I had insulted him; 'there's no tea here!' A little frightened at his aggressive manner I then meekly asked for soda-water, which he gave me, and it was warm and tasted like a decoction of mouldy straw. After taking a sip and paying for it I went to look at the church, which I was astonished to find open.

It was a relief to be in that cool, twilight, not unbeautiful interior after my day in the burning sun.

After resting and taking a look round I became interested in watching and listening to the talk of two other visitors who had come in before me. One was a slim, rather lean brown-skinned woman, still young but with the incipient crow's-feet, the lines on the forehead, the dusty-looking dark hair, and other signs of time and toil which almost invariably appear in the country labourer's wife before she attains to middle age. She was dressed in a black gown, presumably her best although it was getting a little rusty. Her companion was a fat, red-cheeked young girl in a towny costume, a straw hat decorated with bright flowers and ribbons, and a string of big coloured beads about her neck.

In a few minutes they went out, and when

going by me I had a good look at the woman's face, for it was turned towards me with an eager questioning look in her dark eyes and a very friendly smile on her lips. What was the attraction I suddenly found in that sunburnt face?— what did it say to me or remind me of?—what did it suggest?

I followed them out to where they were standing talking among the gravestones, and sitting down on a tomb near them spoke to the woman. She responded readily enough, apparently pleased to have someone to talk to, and pretty soon began to tell me the history of their lives. She told me that Chilmorton was her native place, but that she had been absent from it many many years. She knew just how many years because her child was only six months old when she left and was now fourteen though she looked more. She was such a big girl! Then her man took them to his native place in Staffordshire, where they had lived ever since. But their girl didn't live with them now. An aunt, a sister of her husband, had taken her to the town where she lived, and was having her taught at a private school. As soon as she left school her aunt hoped to get her a place in a draper's shop. For a long time past she had wanted to show her daughter her native place, but had never been able to manage it because it was so far to come and they didn't have much money to spend; but now at last she had brought her and was showing her everything.

Glancing at the girl who stood listening, but with no sign of interest in her face, I remarked

that her daughter would perhaps hardly think
the journey had been worth taking.

'Why do you say that?' she quickly demanded.

'Oh, well,' I replied, 'because Chilmorton
can't have much to interest a girl living in a
town.' Then I foolishly went on to say what I
thought of Chilmorton. The musty taste of that
warm soda-water was still in my mouth and made
me use some pretty strong words.

At that she flared up and desired me to know
that in spite of what I thought of it Chilmorton
was the sweetest, dearest village in England;
that she was born there and hoped to be buried
in its churchyard where her parents were lying,
and her grandparents and many others of her
family. She was thirty-six years old now, she
said, and would perhaps live to be an old woman,
but it would make her miserable for all the rest
of her life if she thought she would have to lie in
the earth at a distance from Chilmorton.

During this speech I began to think of the
soft reply it would now be necessary for me to
make, when, having finished speaking, she called
sharply to her daughter, 'Come, we've others to
see yet,' and, followed by the girl, walked briskly
away without so much as a good-bye, or even a
glance!

Oh, you poor foolish woman, thought I; why
take it to heart like that! and I was sorry and
laughed a little as I went back down the street.

It was beginning to wake up now! A man in
his shirt-sleeves and without a hat, a big angry
man, was furiously hunting a rebellious pig all
round a small field adjoining a cottage, trying

to corner it; he swore and shouted, and out of the
cottage came a frowsy-looking girl in a ragged
gown with her hair hanging all over her face, to
help him with the pig. A little further on I
caught sight of yet another human being, a tall
gaunt old woman in cap and shawl, who came
out of a cottage and moved feebly towards a pile
of faggots a few yards from the door. Just as she
got to the pile I passed, and she slowly turned
and gazed at me out of her dim old eyes. Her
wrinkled face was the colour of ashes and was
like the face of a corpse, still bearing on it the
marks of suffering endured for many miserable
years. And these three were the only inhabitants
I saw on my way down the street.

At the end of the village the street broadened
to a clean white road with high ancient hedge-
row elms on either side, their upper branches
meeting and forming a green canopy over it. As
soon as I got to the trees I stopped and dis-
mounted to enjoy the delightful sensation the
shade produced: there out of its power I could
best appreciate the sun shining in splendour on
the wide green hilly earth and in the green
translucent foliage above my head. In the upper
branches a blackbird was trolling out his music
in his usual careless leisurely manner; when I
stopped under it the singing was suspended for
half a minute or so, then resumed, but in a lower
key, which made it seem softer, sweeter, inex-
pressibly beautiful.

There are beautiful moments in our converse
with nature when all the avenues by which
nature comes to our souls seem one, when hear-

ing and seeing and smelling and feeling are one
sense, when the sweet sound that falls from a
bird is but the blue of heaven, the green of earth,
and the golden sunshine made audible.

Such a moment was mine as I stood under the
elms listening to the blackbird. And looking back
up the village street I thought of the woman in
the churchyard, her sun-parched eager face, her
questioning eyes and friendly smile: what was
the secret of its attraction?—what did that face
say to me or remind me of?—what did it suggest?

Now it was plain enough. She was still a child
at heart, in spite of those marks of time and toil
on her countenance, still full of wonder and
delight at this wonderful world of Chilmorton
set amidst its lime-stone hills, under the wide
blue sky—this poor squalid little village where
I couldn't get a cup of tea!

It was the child surviving in her which had
attracted and puzzled me; it does not often shine
through the dulling veil of years so brightly.
And as she now appeared to me as a child in
heart I could picture her as a child in years, in
her little cotton frock and thin bare legs, a
sun-burnt little girl of eight, with the wide-eyed,
eager, half-shy, half-trustful look, asking you, as
the child ever asks, what you think?—what you
feel? It was a wonderful world, and the world
was the village, its streets of gritstone houses,
the people living in them, the comedies and
tragedies of their lives and deaths, and burials
in the churchyard with grass and flowers to
grow over them by-and-by. And the church;—

I think its interior must have seemed vaster, more beautiful and sublime to her wondering little soul than the greatest cathedral can be to us. I think that our admiration for the loveliest blooms—the orchids and roses and chrysanthemums at our great annual shows—is a poor languid feeling compared to what she experienced at the sight of any common flower of the field. Best of all perhaps were the elms at the village end, those mighty rough-barked trees that had their tops 'so close against the sky.' And I think that when a blackbird chanced to sing in the upper branches it was as if some angelic being had dropped down out of the sky into that green translucent cloud of leaves, and seeing the child's eager face looking up had sung a little song of his own celestial country to please her.

William Paton Ker

1855–1923

ROMANTIC FALLACIES

THE title is not quite accurate: the fallacies of which I am to speak are not in Romance itself so much as in those who talk about it. 'Romance' is a dangerous word, and it is time that certain technical misuses of the name 'romantic' should be discouraged.

Mr. William Gilpin in his very pleasant Scotch tour[1] points out what he regards as a popular error in the indiscriminate use of the word 'picturesque' when what is really meant is 'romantic':

'On the right of the Pentland hills arises Arthur's seat: a rock which hangs over Edinburgh of peculiar appearance, romantic but not picturesque.' (i, p. 53.)

'A nearer approach did not give us a more pleasing idea of the environs of Edinburgh. We had always heard it represented as one of the most picturesque towns in Britain; but people often consider *romantic* and *picturesque* as synonyms. Arthur's seat, which is still the principal object, appears still as odd, misshapen and uncouth as before. . . . The

---

[1] Observations relative chiefly to picturesque beauty, made in the year 1776, on several parts of Great Britain, particularly the Highlands of Scotland. (Published 1789.)

town and castle indeed on the left make some amends, and are happily introduced.' (i, p. 59.)

He does not explain what he means by 'romantic,' but we can guess from his example. There must be something strange or curious hindering or thwarting the lines of pure harmonious beauty.

Sydney Smith perhaps may supply an example of the confusion indicated by Gilpin. Sir Walter Scott quotes an illustration from Sydney Smith's famous lectures on Moral Philosophy at the Royal Institution. To show the difference between the Beautiful and the Picturesque he gave his audience this: 'the Rector's horse is beautiful, the Curate's is picturesque.' If he had studied Gilpin more carefully, he would have said romantic.

It may be worth noticing here, whether it is relevant or not, that Gilpin gives the highest praise to the landscape that Scott loved as well as any in the world, the view of the Tweed from Fernielee, and that his pure taste in pictures is not so strict and pedantic as to refuse acknowledgment of what is added to the spirit of landscape by the charm of associations. He is in a land of romance, by the fabled flood, and he knows the power of songs to quicken the eye. But he does not use the word romantic where we should think it fitting enough: he has another meaning, another use for it. Gilpin will be mentioned again, but for the present I leave him, and come to part of the main business of this discourse. I would ask whether the Romantic revival and the Romantic age of poetry have not been overworked by critics and historians.

'The Romantic Movement in English Poetry' is the title of a book by Mr. Arthur Symons which ought to be better known, a book in which a poet reviews and judges all the poets of the great age, including many minor names, such as William Gifford and Robert Pollok, which are not there for praise. Now in this most lively and significant work, after the introduction, the idea of the Romantic movement scarcely shows itself at all; and the preface deals summarily with it, thus:

> 'The word "romantic" I think defines more clearly than any other what we find most characteristic in the renewal of poetry after its long banishment. The great poets of every age but the eighteenth have been romantic: what are Chaucer, Shakespeare and Coleridge if not romantic?'

Again, in the introduction:

> 'What is really meant by all these phrases and by the name of the romantic movement is simply the reawakening of the imagination, a reawakening to a sense of beauty and strangeness in natural things, and in all the impulses of the mind and the senses.'

If this is what romantic movement means, what are we to do as historians or critics when we come to inquire about things or poems that are indeed romantic? For the sake of the language and the dictionary, ought we not to make a stand, and say that romance has meanings of its own, that 'romantic' is too narrow a term for Chaucer and Shakespeare and a sense of beauty and strangeness in natural things and in all the impulses of the mind and the senses?

We may note that 'classic' and 'romantic' are found together in Thomas Warton on Dante, 'this wonderful compound of classical and romantic fancy.'

Byron observes that people are beginning to speak of classic and romantic as opposites, and he read the early version of Stendhal's essay on Racine and Shakespeare, which is the programme of the great French contest between the old and the new school of drama.

The French romantics of the 1820's took their name from the German romantic school of a generation earlier. The Germans began the mischief, though they are not to blame for our mistaken adoption of their label.

In Germany first and then in France, 'romantic school' had a definite meaning and justification, such as 'romantic revival' has not in this country. The romantic school of the Schlegels, of Jean Paul Richter, Tieck, and the rest, for whom Carlyle worked so hard to get them accepted in England, was a natural product of Germany, where all literature was founded on criticism and self-conscious following of some or another model or ideal. German literature after its old glory in the time of the Minnesingers had fallen away behind the rest of Christendom; it missed the Italian and the French renaissance, Petrarch, Ariosto, and Ronsard, and when it started again in the seventeenth century it had to learn its art of verse from the Netherlands and everything possible from France. Its greatest masters, Lessing and Goethe, are critics and theorists. The romantic school meant a new theory, a new policy, following on many older. But in England, where momentous and fertile imitations and adaptations had been accomplished in the sixteenth century by Wyatt and Surrey, Spenser and Marlowe, where so many forms of art had become traditional, there was no call for a romantic school—a self-conscious militant group —at the beginning of the nineteenth century, and *romantic* is a very partial and not very significant name for what really happened in the great revival of imagination.

Likewise in France in the day of *Hernani*, which Byron did not live to see, the factions classical and romantic had a meaning unlike anything that those badges could denote in England. The contest, as we know from the Memoirs of Alexandre Dumas and other historians, was an actual battle for the theatres. In England who are there to compare with the classical partisans of the old style of drama in France? Byron counts up the names of those who are to be trusted to maintain the right:

'The disciples of Pope were Johnson, Goldsmith, Rogers, Campbell, Crabbe, Gifford, Mathias, Hayley, and the author of the *Paradise of Coquettes*, to whom may be added Richards, Heber, Wrangham, Bland, Hodgson, Merivale, and others who have not had their full fame. . . .'

As fighting men these are not to be compared with the French classical party, and there never was, and could not be, in England anything like the battle for which Victor Hugo gave his Spanish watchword *hierro* in 1830. If there was an English classical school, Byron was its principal advocate: one need say no more to show how different the conditions were in England and in France.

Romantic is a bad name for the poetry of the nineteenth century because it sets you looking for a common quality when you ought to be reading or remembering individual poems, and understanding the law of their being, to which end the romantic idea will not always help you much. But romantic does mean something, and there was a romantic movement, which might be interesting to trace and follow from its beginnings in the seventeenth century. Dryden gives it a name: 'the fairy way of writing'; Hurd names it: 'a world of fine fabling.' You can see it in the twin towers of All Souls, early eighteenth-century romantic art. Compare the towers with the outside of the Library: that also is eighteenth-century Gothic, but that is not romantic, like the towers. The library, outside, is sober imitation of the fifteenth century in the chapel opposite, not much exaggerating nor attempting any new effect. The towers are a romantic dream: look and see how the proportions of the windows are drawn out, intended to be sublime. Then go and look at the Library inside, that most perfect work of true and sound imagination in the eighteenth century. The towers are of the same date, but their romantic spirit is not allowed to distract the artist when he sees his way to nobler rhythms and harmonies.

Oxford, if not the original home of the romantic movement, has at any rate contributed largely, and was early in giving its help. Not only by its refusal to break absolutely with the Gothic tradition in architecture, but in literature also it showed the way to get new corn out of old fields.

'Romantic' implies reminiscence: it means at first the sort of thing that is found in books of chivalry, or in the *Arcadia*, or in the *Grand Cyrus*. Hence the romantic schools have always depended more or less on the past; their life is in

> beauty, making beautiful old rhyme,
> In praise of ladies dead and lovely knights.

It is a commonplace of literary history that between 1760 and 1770 Percy's *Reliques* and Macpherson's *Ossian* and Chatterton's *Rowley Poems* made all the difference. But it is not generally remembered that reliques of ancient poetry began to be studied, and were made available for the reading public and all youthful poets, long before.

In the philological series of the Clarendon Press there is no more entertaining and spirited work than the edition of 'Christ's Kirk on the Green,' brought out by E. G. in 1691.

Edmund Gibson of Queen's was then not yet Bishop of London, but he had begun the studies which led later to his edition of the Saxon Chronicle, and with the help of the Press and all

its founts he was able to publish this specimen
of Scottish poetry:

> In Scotland was there never seen
> Sic dancing and deray,
> Neither at Falkland on the Green
> Nor Peebles to the play.

The commentary, which is the work of a
scholar, is made as imposing as possible with
Gothic, Anglo-Saxon, and Icelandic, each in its
appropriate type, including, if I am not mistaken, one fount which Franciscus Junius had
brought back from Sweden and presented to the
University.

The same founts are used in a much larger
work which was preparing at the same time,
Hickes's *Thesaurus*, in three large volumes, containing everything wanted for a foundation in
Germanic philology. In this vast medley Hickes
included, immediately after the Anglo-Saxon
poem of the *Fight at Finnesburh*, the Icelandic
poem of the *Sword of Angantyr*. Hervor at her
father's grave calling upon him to give her
the sword Tyrfing, the invincible, the accursed
sword. The mystery and terror of a haunted
twilight, between the worlds of life and death,
that is what the poem is, and something more;
the stress of human wills and passions, a high
spirit of honour. There is nothing finer, in its
way. And it was not left to philologers in the
folio volume of Hickes's *Thesaurus*. By some un-
explained and very amazing chance, this piece
of Germanic philology was excerpted roughly
and bodily out of the *Thesaurus*, and printed in

one of the volumes of a new and amplified edition of Dryden's *Poetical Miscellany*. Percy translated the poem later, and Lewis made use of it for a tale of wonder, and the Sword of Angantyr is one of the *Poèmes barbares* of Leconte de Lisle. And, as I have said, it was a philological publication of this University which first discovered this magic song more than 200 years ago.

I will not say much about the mediæval studies of Thomas Warton; what he did for history and scholarship and a fresh understanding of the Middle Ages and of Spenser and Milton as well is now continually more and more appreciated. He owed much to his father, Thomas Warton the elder, his ancestor in the chair of Poetry; something doubtless to his brother Joseph, who, with less taste for exploration in old romance, had a more secure and original judgment in modern poetry. With Thomas Warton the romantic revival or movement, or whatever it be called, is well on its way, and it is recognised by Dr. Johnson as something of a danger and a provocation:

> Wheresoe'er I turn my view
> All is strange, yet nothing new,
> Endless labour all day long,
> Endless labour to be wrong,
> Phrase that time has flung away,
> Uncouth words in disarray,
> Trick'd in antique ruff and bonnet,
> Ode and elegy and sonnet.

Johnson was provoked at Warton's excesses in Old English poetry. Warton and Johnson were friends all the same, and we may digress here to think of them on the road home to Oxford from Elsfield, Warton quickening too much for Johnson, and Johnson calling out '*sufflamina*' (put on your break chain).

There is nothing in mediæval philology that is essentially dangerous to a classical mind. The most absurd and pedantic railer at Shakespeare, the determined advocate of the dramatic unities, Thomas Rymer, was one of the pioneers, for England, in the old poetry of Provence. It would have been well, anyhow it would have been pleasant, if he had had more followers and earlier, to discover what beauty there is in the Provençal lyric, from which all modern verse is derived, to perceive how little the poetry of Bernart de Ventadorn needs any allowance on the score of time or circumstance; with what pride and confidence the Provençal poets may claim to have their work tested by as severe a standard as you please.

This really is where the romantic fallacy, or a fallacy about romance, has done most harm. Once the contrast of classical and romantic has been imposed on the mind, the reader of mediæval verse thinks romantically, and sees his authors quaintly doing quaint things in old-fashioned rhyme. It would not be difficult to find two or three Provençal lyrics of the twelfth century perfect in rhythm and measure under the same rules of art as Gray or Wordsworth, complete and rounded also in their poetical argument. A truer sense of classical poetry and some further study of the Middle Ages might have brought out the classical quality of Provençal and German lyric ages before Dante and Petrarch.

Addison on *Chevy Chase* is a very striking example of what might have been done with more research in olden treasures of poetry. When we talk of romantic revival, let us remember *Chevy Chase*, and how Addison read and praised the old ballad for its classic quality, its sincerity, its sense of proportion, how he used the old ballad to threaten and cow our little Gothic artists, the trifling conceited poets of his day. Dryden, twelve years earlier, in the Preface to the *Fables*, had given another example of the same sort of independent judgment, when he praised Chaucer for his truth of imagination, and blamed Ovid for his trifling ornament.

There was a romantic movement, then, which began before the eighteenth century, and it can be traced, and it is not altogether dull work tracing it. It does not come all from philology, or all from the Middle Ages—some of it comes from the Hebrides, and a man from Sussex writes an ode on the *Superstitions of the Highlands*. The Hebrides always tell in poetry: there was a happy false reading of their name: strictly they ought to be 'Ebudes,' but 'Ebudes' will not do in poetry, any more than 'Ioua insula,' which is the true Latin for Icolmcille, can compete in verse or prose with 'Iona.'

Milton began in *Lycidas*:

Whether beyond the stormy Hebrides,
Where thou perchance under the whelming tide
Visit'st the bottom of the monstrous world.

Thomson took it up in the *Castle of Indolence*, the most purely romantic poem before the *Ancient Mariner:*

> Or as some shepherd of the Hebrid isles,
> Placed far amid the melancholy main.

And Collins comes after with his *Ode*. It might have been well if more had been learned for modern fancy-work from Skye or Jura; the fairy mythology of the Western Islands is not false, like much of the conventional literary fairy tales. Shakespeare is responsible, through Drayton and Herrick, for much artificial prettiness in a kingdom of Oberon utterly different from the sombre, splendid region, underground, within the hill. Thomson in the *Castle of Indolence* and Collins in his *Ode* escape the literary convention of pert tripping fairies and dapper elves. Collins is not always safe: in his finest poem there are elves who sleep in flowers the day.

Nothing is more significant for the progress of the romantic movement and its danger, and the escape of true poetic imagination from the danger, than the stanza which Collins struck out, and the stanza that took its place in the second version of the *Ode to Evening:*

1747.

> Then let me rove some wild and heathy scene,
> Or find some ruin midst its dreary dells,
>   Whose walls more awful nod
>   By thy religious gleams.

1748 (*Dodsley*).

> Then lead, calm votaress, where some sheety lake
> Cheers the lone heath, or some time-hallowed pile,
>   Or upland fallows grey
>   Reflect its last cool gleam.

In the second version, besides the true personification in 'votaress,' who is from Milton's *Maske*, there is the fresh vision and understanding of the effect of a surface of water in twilight, when all the land round it is dark, and in place of the conventional ruin that 'nods,' there is the old building, church or castle, dimly seen as part of the evening light along with the large bulging hillside. If you look into it, you will see at once that the water is to the west, the 'time-hallowed pile' to the east, and all this is given in the fewest words, and with no vanity or insistence on the accurate rendering. The romantic fallacy is cleared away, and its place is taken in a different mode of vision and of poetry.

The progress of poetry in the eighteenth century, as later, as now, is not controlled by influences or fashions that can be called either romantic or the opposite. Romantic or classical may denote fashions of the reading public or of pedantic criticism, but the hope of poetry is simply in new minds free to choose their own way. The comparative blankness of the eighteenth century, the richness of the new age that followed, was not due to fashion or programme. All the difference was made by the birth of two or three infants in the early seventies. Wordsworth, Scott, and Coleridge, and a few more a little later, Byron, Shelley, and Keats. Their success did not come from a general tide of thought—their wits would have succeeded whatever the fashion of the time might be. 'Romantic revival' and other such terms are well enough for the general history of culture, 'typical developments'; but such terms may prevent you from understanding what William Wordsworth was thinking when he wrote the *Ode to Duty*, or the *Poem on Rob Roy's Grave*, what possessed the mind of Shelley to bring out his tragedy of *The Cenci*.

One of our own poets in this College, a quondam Fellow, Dr. Edward Young, not very thoroughly successful himself as a poet, was able at the age of seventy-five to write a piece of good advice to young adventurers in poetry, an essay rather glorious in its style, and I think sound in its judgment, a letter to the author of 'Sir Charles Grandison,' in 1759, which really adds something more to that wonderful year—the year of Quebec and Minden and so many other victories, also of Goldsmith's tract on the 'Present State of Polite Learning in Europe,' a gloomy prospect of blight and decay.

Young had written a *Poem on the Last Day* more absurd in places than any other composition on that dangerous theme: Satires, which were only not good enough to compete with Pope. Zanga in the *Revenge* long held the stage and deserved all he got: a most dexterous adaptation of Iago to a plot more simple and for certain purposes more telling than Shakespeare's; nearer the concentrated effect of Victor

Hugo. Then the *Night Thoughts;* the work of a man growing old, still ready for new experiments, and carrying this well through, in a fresh sort of blank verse, not that of the eighteenth-century Miltonic tradition, not like Thomson's *Seasons,* but drier, keener; and, for matter, discoursing on life and death with a more personal touch than was common. Young's letter on original composition is not meant to help any active project of his own. It is a free survey of the state of poetry, and a call for fresh and original work, for narrative poetry not delayed with ornament, for tragedy with a heart in it. A very remarkable thing, as was said at the time, to have been written by an old man.

Young does not give any particular prescription how the thing is to be done, except that he finds fault with Pope's use of rhyme for epic: a curious point when it is compared with Goldsmith's perpetual hatred of blank verse, first stated in his tract of this same year, where he finds English poetry far gone in decrepitude: 'the affected security of our odes, the tuneless flow of our blank verse.'

Young simply says, do not imitate; be original; be individual. Young is hard on Dryden, but what he says may be edifying apart from the question of Dryden's fame:

'Dryden had a great but a general capacity; and as for a general genius, there is no such thing in nature. A genius implies the rays of the mind concenter'd, and determined to some particular point; when they are scattered widely, they act feebly, and strike not with sufficient force to fire, or dissolve, the heart.'

I take this, and the whole of Young's 'Conjectures on Original Composition,' as a denial and refusal of any programme, prescription, rule, school, faction, influence, or agency, except what may be found or chosen by the poet himself when he bends his mind to his work. One thing I would note particularly, one reason for his hopeful spirit. Writing to the author of 'Sir Charles Grandison,' he tells him that:

'A friend of mine has obeyed that injunction [to make original use of his talent] and with a genius as well *moral* as *original* (to speak in bold terms) has cast out evil spirits; has made a convert to virtue of a species of composition once most its foe.'

His friend Mr. Richardson has reclaimed the novel, and we may allow some credit to the spirit of the age for that event: the novelists had given a good example to the poets; they had shown them, as the old song says, 'there's gear to win ye never saw.' And the new age came: Young was writing in the year that Burns was born.

By making too much of the name 'romantic' the critics and historians have troubled the study of poetry in two ways. They have made it harder to seize what was airy and evanescent already, those strange flowers of poetry that seem to live almost without any ground or substance, especially in the ballads. What am I thinking of? Such things as the ballad refrains 'by the bonny

mill-dams o' Binnorie,' and in the cruel story of
the robbers:

> He has killed this maid and has laid her by,
> For to bear the red rose company.

I am thinking of the Spanish ballad of the Count
Arnaldos, and the mariner's song from the
strange galley, and the Icelandic ballad of
Tristram:

> Isolt goes from the sea inland,
>   The street was long,
> And ever she heard the bells ringing
>   The goodly song.
>
> Isolt went from the sea inland,
>   The way was straight,
> And ever she heard the bells ringing
>   As she came thereat.
>
> Then she spake, the fair Isolt,
>   From over the foam,
> Nay, but Tristram should not die
>   When I come home.
>
> Out on the floor the priests were standing
>   With tapers fair,
> Queen Isolt came where Tristram lay,
>   And knelt there.
>
> To many a man in the world is given
>   Sorrow and pain,
> The Queen knelt down and died there, Isolt,
>   Where he lay slain.
>
> Out on the floor the priests they stood,
>   Their dirges said,
> The bells of gold were rung for Isolt
>   And Tristram dead.

> *(Nothing for them was shapen but to sunder.)*

I think also of many things in Greek and Latin poetry, of Pindar's vision, East of the Sun, West of the Moon; of Milanion in Propertius, a love-lorn wanderer among the rocks of Arcadia. There is no end, fortunately, to those recollections, though no more need be said about them now.

Joseph Conrad

1857–1924

ALPHONSE DAUDET

1898

IT is sweet to talk decorously of the dead who are part of our past, our indisputable possession. One must admit regretfully that to-day is but a scramble, that to-morrow may never come; it is only the precious yesterday that cannot be taken away from us. A gift from the dead, great and little, it makes life supportable, it almost makes one believe in a benevolent scheme of creation. And some kind of belief is very necessary. But the real knowledge of matters infinitely more profound than any conceivable scheme of creation is with the dead alone. That is why our talk about them should be as decorous as their silence. Their generosity and their discretion deserve nothing less at our hands; and they, who belong already to the unchangeable, would probably disdain to claim more than this from a mankind that changes its loves and its hates about every twenty-five years—at the coming of every new and wiser generation.

One of the most generous of the dead is Daudet, who, with a prodigality approaching magnificence, gave himself up to us without reserve in his work, with all his qualities and all his faults. Neither his qualities nor his faults were great, though they were by no means imperceptible. It is only his generosity that is out of the common. What strikes one most in his work is the disinterestedness of the toiler. With more talent than many bigger men, he did not preach about himself, he did not attempt to persuade mankind into a belief of his own greatness. He never posed as a scientist or as a seer, not even as a prophet; and he neglected his interests to the point of never propounding a theory for the purpose of giving a tremendous significance to his art, alone of all things, in a world that, by some strange oversight, has not been supplied with an obvious meaning. Neither did he affect a passive attitude before the spectacle of life, an attitude which in gods—and in a rare mortal here and there—may appear godlike, but assumed by some men, causes one, very unwillingly, to think of the melancholy quietude of an ape. He was not the wearisome expounder of this or that theory, here to-day and spurned to-morrow. He was not a great artist, he was not an artist at all, if you like—but he was Alphonse Daudet, a man as naïvely clear, honest, and vibrating as the sunshine of his native land; that regrettably undiscriminating sunshine which matures grapes and pumpkins alike, and cannot, of course, obtain the commendation of the very select who look at life from under a parasol.

Naturally, being a man from the South, he had a rather outspoken belief in himself, but his small distinction, worth many a greater, was in not being in bondage to some vanishing creed. He was a worker who could not compel the admiration of the few, but who deserved the affection of the many; and he may be spoken of with tenderness and regret, for he is not immortal—he is only dead. During his life the simple man whose business it ought to have been to climb, in the name of Art, some elevation or other, was content to remain below, on the plain, amongst his creations, and take an eager part in those disasters, weaknesses, and joys which are tragic enough in their droll way, but are by no means so momentous and profound as some writers—probably for the sake of Art—would like to make us believe. There is, when one thinks of it, a considerable want of candour in the august view of life. Without doubt a cautious reticence on the subject, or even a delicately false suggestion thrown out in that direction is, in a way, praiseworthy, since it helps to uphold the dignity of man—a matter of great importance, as any one can see; still one cannot help feeling that a certain amount of sincerity would not be wholly blamable. To state, then, with studied moderation a belief that in unfortunate moments of lucidity is irresistibly borne in upon most of us—the blind agitation caused mostly by hunger and complicated by love and ferocity does not deserve either by its beauty, or its morality, or its possible results, the artistic fuss made over it. It may be consoling—for human folly is very *bizarre*—but it is scarcely honest to shout at those who struggle drowning in an insignificant pool: You are indeed admirable and great to be the victims of such a profound, of such a terrible ocean!

And Daudet was honest; perhaps because he knew no better—but he was very honest. If he saw only the surface of things it is for the reason that most things have nothing but a surface. He did not pretend—perhaps because he did not know how—he did not pretend to see any depths in a life that is only a film of unsteady appearances stretched over regions deep indeed, but which have nothing to do with the half-truths, half-thoughts, and whole illusions of existence. The road to these distant regions does not lie through the domain of Art or the domain of Science where well-known voices quarrel noisily in a misty emptiness; it is a path of toilsome silence upon which travel men simple and unknown, with closed lips, or, may be, whispering their pain softly—only to themselves.

But Daudet did not whisper; he spoke loudly, with animation, with a clear felicity of tone—as a bird sings. He saw life around him with extreme clearness, and he felt it as it is—thinner than air and more elusive than a flash of lightning. He hastened to offer it his compassion, his indignation, his wonder, his sympathy, without giving a moment of thought to the momentous issues that are supposed to lurk in the logic of such sentiments. He tolerated the little foibles, the small ruffianisms, the grave mistakes; the only thing he distinctly would not forgive was hardness of heart. This unpractical attitude would have been fatal to a better man, but his readers have forgiven him. Withal he is chivalrous to exiled queens and deformed sempstresses, he is pityingly tender to broken-down actors, to

ruined gentlemen, to stupid Academicians; he is
glad of the joys of the commonplace people in a
commonplace way—and he never makes a secret
of all this. No, the man was not an artist. What
if his creations are illumined by the sunshine
of his temperament so vividly that they stand
before us infinitely more real than the dingy
illusions surrounding our everyday existence?
The misguided man is for ever pottering amongst
them, lifting up his voice, dotting his i's in
the wrong places. He takes Tartarin by the
arm, he does not conceal his interest in the
Nabob's cheques, his sympathy for an honest
Academician *plus bête que nature*, his hate for an
architect *plus mauvais que la gale;* he is in the thick
of it all. He feels with the Duc de Mora and
with Felicia Ruys—and he lets you see it. He
does not sit on a pedestal in the hieratic and
imbecile pose of some cheap god whose greatness
consists in being too stupid to care. He cares
immensely for his Nabobs, his kings, his book-
keepers, his Colettes, and his Saphos. He
vibrates together with his universe, and with
lamentable simplicity follows M. de Montpavon
on that last walk along the Boulevards.

'*Monsieur de Montpavon marche à la mort,*' and
the creator of that unlucky *gentilhomme* follows
with stealthy footsteps, with wide eyes, with an
impressively pointing finger. And who wouldn't
look? But it is hard; it is sometimes very hard
to forgive him the dotted i's, the pointing finger,
this making plain of obvious mysteries. '*Monsieur
de Montpavon marche à la mort,*' and presently on
the crowded pavement, takes off his hat with

punctilious courtesy to the doctor's wife, who, elegant and unhappy, is bound on the same pilgrimage. This is too much! We feel we cannot forgive him such meetings, the constant whisper of his presence. We feel we cannot, till suddenly the very *naïveté* of it all touches us with the revealed suggestion of a truth. Then we see that the man is not false; all this is done in transparent good faith. The man is not melodramatic; he is only picturesque. He may not be an artist, but he comes as near the truth as some of the greatest. His creations are *seen;* you can look into their very eyes, and these are as thoughtless as the eyes of any wise generation that has in its hands the fame of writers. Yes, they are seen, and the man who is not an artist is seen also, commiserating, indignant, joyous, human and alive in their very midst. Inevitably they *marchent à la mort*—and they are very near the truth of our common destiny: their fate is poignant, it is intensely interesting, and of not the slightest consequence.

Henry W. Nevinson

1856-1941

A FAREWELL TO FLEET STREET

IT is still early, but dinner is over—not the club dinner with its buzzing conversation, nor yet the restaurant dinner, hurried into the ten minutes between someone's momentous speech and the leader that has to be written on it. The suburban dinner is over, and there was no need to hurry. They tell me I shall be healthier now. What do I care about being healthier?

Shall I sit with a novel over the fire? Shall I take life at second-hand and work up an interest in imaginary loves and the exigencies of shadows? What are all the firesides and fictions of the world to me that I should loiter here and doze, doze, as good as die?

They tell me it is a fine thing to take a little walk before bed-time. I go out into the suburban street. A thin, wet mist hangs over the silent and monotonous houses, and blurs the electric lamps along our road. There will be a fog in Fleet Street to-night, but everyone is too busy to notice it. How friendly a fog made us all! How jolly it was that night when I ran straight into a *Chronicle* man, and got a lead of him by a short head over the same curse! There's no chance of running into anyone here, let alone cursing! A few figures slouch past and disappear; the last postman goes his round, knocking at one house in ten; up and down the asphalt path leading into the obscurity of the Common a wretched woman wanders in vain; the long, pointed windows of a chapel glimmer with yellowish light through the dingy air, and I hear the faint groans of a harmonium cheering the people dismally home. The groaning ceases, the lights go out, service is over; it will soon be time for decent people to be in bed.

In Fleet Street the telegrams will now be falling thick as—No, I won't say it! No Vallombrosa for me, nor any other journalistic tag! I remember once a young sub-editor had got as far as, 'The cry is still——' when I took him by the throat. I have done the State some service.

Our sub-editors' room is humming now: a low murmur of questions, rapid orders, the rustle of paper, the quick alarum of telephones. Boys keep bringing telegrams in orange envelopes. Each sub-editor is bent over his little lot of news. One sorts out the speeches from bundles of flimsy. The middle of Lloyd George's speech has got mixed up with Balfour's peroration. If he left them mixed, would anyone be the less wise? Perhaps the speakers might notice it, and that man from Wiltshire would be sure to write saying he had always supported Mr. Balfour, and heartily welcomed this fresh evidence of his consistency.

'Six columns speeches in already; how much?' asks the sub-editor. 'Column and quarter,' comes answer from the head of the table, and the cutting begins. Another sub-editor pieces together an interview about the approaching comet. 'Keep comet to three sticks,' comes the order, and the comet's perihelion is abbreviated. Another guts a blue-book on prison statistics as savagely as though he were disembowelling the whole criminal population.

There's the telephone ringing. 'Hullo, hullo!' calls a sub-editor quietly. 'Who are you? Margate mystery? Go ahead. They've found the corpse? All right. Keep it to a column, but send good story. Horrible mutilations? Good. Glimpse the corpse yourself if you can. Yes. Send full mutilations. Will call for them at eleven. Good-bye.' 'You doing the Archbishop, Mr. Jones?' asks the head of the table. 'Cup-tie at Sunderland,' answers Mr. Jones, and all the time the boys go in and out with those orange-coloured bulletins of the world's health.

What's a man to do at night out here? Let's have a look at all these posters displayed in front of the Free Library, where a few poor creatures are still reading last night's news for the warmth. Next week there's a concert of chamber-music in the Town Hall. I suppose I might go to that, just to 'kill time,' as they say. Think of a journalist wanting to kill time! Or to kill anything but another fellow's 'stuff,' and sometimes an editor! Then there's a boxing competition at the St. John's Arms, and a subscription dance in the Nelson Rooms, and a lecture on Dante, with illustrations from contemporary art, for working men and women, at the Institute. Also there's something called the Why-Be-Lonesome Club

for promoting friendly social intercourse among
the young and old of all classes. I suppose I
might go to that too. It sounds comprehensive.

There seems no need to be dull in the suburbs.
A man in a cart is still crying coke down the
street. Another desires to sell clothes-props. A
brace of lovers come stealing out of the Common
through the mist, careless of mud and soaking
grass. I suppose people would say I'm too old to
make love on a County Council bench. In love's
cash-books the balance-sheet of years is kept
with remorseless accuracy.

The foreign editors are waiting now in their
silent room, and the telegrams come to them
from the ends of the world. They fold them in
packets together by countries or continents—the
Indian stuff, the Russian stuff, the Egyptian,
Balkan, Austrian, South African, Persian,
Japanese, American, Spanish, and all the rest.
They'll have pretty nearly seven columns by
this time, and the order will come 'Two-and-a-
half foreign.' Then the piecing and cutting will
begin. One of them sits in a telephone box with
bands across his head, and repeats a message
from our Paris correspondent. Through our
Paris man we can talk with Berlin and Rome.

From this rising ground I can see the light of
the city reflected on the misty air, and somewhere mingled in that light are the big lamps
down in Fleet Street. The City's voice comes to
me like a confused murmur through a telephone
when the words are unintelligible. The only
distinct sounds are the dripping of the moisture
from the trees in suburban gardens, and the

voice of an old lady imploring her pet dog to return from his evening walk.

The voice of all the world is now heard in that silent room. From moment to moment news is coming of treaties and revolutions, of sultans deposed and kings enthroned, of commerce and failures, of shipwrecks, earthquakes, and explorations, of wars and flooded camps and sieges, of intrigue, diplomacy, and assassination, of love, murder, revenge, and all the public joy and sorrow and business of mankind. All the voices of fear, hope, and lamentation echo in that silent little room; and maps hang on the walls, and guide-books are always ready, for who knows where the next event may come to pass upon this energetic little earth, already twisting for a hundred million years around the sun?

The editor must be back by now. Calm and decisive, he takes his seat in his own room, like the conductor of an orchestra preparing to raise his baton now that the tuning-up is finished. The leader-writers are coming in for their instructions. No need for much consultation to-night—not for the first leader anyhow. For the second—well, there are a good many things one could suggest: Turkey or Persia or the eternal German Dreadnought for a foreign subject; the stage censorship or the price of cotton; and the cup-ties, or the extinction of hats for both sexes as a light note to finish with. He's always labouring to invent 'something light,' is the editor. He says we must sometimes consider the public; just as though we wrote the rest of the paper for our own private fun.

But there's no doubt about the first leader to-night. There's only one subject on which it would be a shock to every reader in the morning not to find it written. And, my word! what a subject it is! What seriousness and indignation and conviction one could get into it! I should begin by restating the situation. You must always assume that the reader's ignorance is new every morning, as love should be; and anyone who happens to know something about it likes to see he was right. I should work in adroit references to this evening's speeches, and that would fill the first paragraph—say, three sides of my copy, or something over. In the second paragraph I'd show the immense issues involved in the present contest, and expose the fallacies of our opponents who attempt to belittle the matter as temporary and unlikely to recur—say, three sides of my copy again, but not a word more. And, then, in the third paragraph, I'd adjure the Government, in the name of all their party hold sacred, to stand firm, and I'd appeal to the people of this great Empire never to allow their ancient liberties to be encroached upon or overridden by a set of irresponsible—well, in short, I should be like General Sherman when at the crisis of a battle he used to say, 'Now, let everything go in'—four sides of my copy, or even five if the stuff is running well.

Somebody must be writing that leader now. Possibly he is doing it better than I should, but I hope not. When Hannibal wandered all those years in Asia at the Court of silly Antiochus this or stupid Prusias the other, and knew that

Carthage was falling to ruin while he alone might have saved her if only she had allowed him, would he have rejoiced to hear that some-one else was succeeding better than himself—had traversed the Alps with a bigger army, had won a second Cannæ, and even at Zama snatched a decisive victory? Hannibal might have re-joiced. He was a very exceptional man.

But here's a poor creature still playing the clarionet down the street, on the pretence of giving pleasure worth a penny. Yes, my boy, I know you're out of work, and that is why you play the 'Last Rose of Summer' and 'When other Lips.' I am out of work, too, and I can't play anything. You say you learnt when a boy, and once played in the orchestra at Drury Lane; but now you've come to wandering about sub-urban streets, and having finished 'When other Lips,' you will quite naturally play 'My Lodg-ing's on the Cold Ground.' Only last night I was playing in an orchestra myself, not a hundred miles (obsolete journalistic tag!)—not a hundred miles from Drury Lane. It was a grand orchestra, that of ours. Night by night it played the symphony of the world, and each night a new symphony was performed, without rehearsal. The drums of our orchestra were the echoes of thundering wars; the flutes and soft recorders were the eloquence of an Empire's statesmen; and our 'cellos and violins wailed with the pity of all mankind. In that vast orchestra I played the horn that sounds the charge, or with its sharp réveillé vexes the ear of night before the sun is up. Here is your penny, my brother in affliction. I, too, have once joined in the music of a star, and now wander the suburban streets.

That leader-writer has not finished yet, but the proofs of the beginning of his article will be coming down. In an hour or so his work will be over, and he will pass out into the street exhausted, but happy with the sense of function fulfilled. Fleet Street is quieter now. The lamps gleam through the fog, a motor-'bus thunders by, a few late messengers flit along with the latest telegrams, and some stragglers from the restaurants come singing past the Temple. For a few moments there is silence but for the leader-writer's quick footsteps on the pavement. He is some hours in front of the morning's news, and in a few hours more half a million people will be reading what he has just written, and will quote it to each other as their own. How often I have had whole sentences of my stuff thrown at me as conclusive arguments almost before the printing ink was dry!

Here I stand, beside a solitary lamp-post upon a suburban acclivity. The light of the city's existence—I think my successor would say, of her pulsating and palpitating or ebullient existence —is pale upon the sky, and the murmur of her voice sounds like large but distant waves. I stand alone, and near me there is no sound but the complaint of a homeless tramp swearing at the cold as he settles down upon a bench for the night.

How I used to swear at that boy for not coming quick enough to fetch my copy! I knew the young scoundrel's step—I knew the step of every man and boy in that office. I knew the way each of them went up and down the stairs, and coughed or whistled or spat. What knowledge dies with me now that I am gone! *Qualis artifex pereo!* But that boy—how I should love to be swearing at him now! I wonder whether he misses me? I hope he does. 'It would be an assurance most dear,' as an old song of exile used to say.

Sir Walter Raleigh

1861–1922

DON QUIXOTE[1]

A SPANISH knight, about fifty years of age,
who lived in great poverty in a village of La
Mancha, gave himself up so entirely to reading
the romances of chivalry, of which he had a
large collection, that in the end they turned his
brain, and nothing would satisfy him but that
he must ride abroad on his old horse, armed with
spear and helmet, a knight-errant, to encounter
all adventures, and to redress the innumerable
wrongs of the world. He induced a neighbour
of his, a poor and ignorant peasant called Sancho
Panza, mounted on a very good ass, to accom-
pany him as squire. The knight saw the world
only in the mirror of his beloved romances; he
mistook inns for enchanted castles, windmills
for giants, and country wenches for exiled prin-
cesses. His high spirit and his courage never
failed him, but his illusions led him into endless
trouble. In the name of justice and chivalry he
intruded himself on all whom he met, and
assaulted all whom he took to be making an
oppressive or discourteous use of power. He and
his poor squire were beaten, trounced, cheated,
and ridiculed on all hands, until in the end, by

[1] Miguel de Cervantes Saavedra, born at Alcalá de
Henares, 1547; died at Madrid, 23 April 1616.

the kindliness of his old friends in the village, and with the help of some new friends who had been touched by the amiable and generous character of his illusions, the knight was cured of his whimsies and was led back to his home in the village, there to die.

That is the story of Don Quixote: it seems a slight framework for what, without much extravagance, may be called the wisest and most splendid book in the world. It is an old man's book; there is in it all the wisdom of a fiery heart that has learned patience. Shakespeare and Cervantes died on the same day, but if Cervantes had died at the same age as Shakespeare we should have had no 'Don Quixote.' Shakespeare himself has written nothing so full of the diverse stuff of experience, so quietly and steadily illuminated by gentle wisdom, so open-eyed in discerning the strength of the world; and Shakespeare himself is not more courageous in championing the rights of the gallant heart. Suppose the Governor of Barataria had been called on to decide the cause between these two great authors. His judgments were often wonderfully simple and obvious. Perhaps he would have ruled that whereas Shakespeare died at the age of fifty-two and Cervantes lived seventeen years longer, a man shall give his days and nights to the study of Shakespeare until he is older than ever Shakespeare was, and then, for the solace of his later years, shall pass on to the graver school of Cervantes. Not every man lives longer than Shakespeare; and, of those who do, not every man masters the art and craft of growing

older with the passage of years, so that, by this
rule, the Spanish gentleman would have a
much smaller circle of intimates than the High
Bailiff's son of Stratford. And so he has; yet his
world-wide popularity is none the less assured.
He has always attracted, and will always attract,
a great company of readers who take a simple
and legitimate delight in the comic distresses of
the deluded Don, in the tricks put upon him,
in the woful absurdity of his appearance, in the
many love-stories and love-songs that he hears,
in the variety of the characters that he meets,
in the wealth of the incidents and events that
spring up, a joyous crop, wherever he sets his
foot, and not least, perhaps, in the beatings,
poundings, scratchings, and tumblings in the
mire that are his daily portion. That is to say,
those who care little or nothing for Don Quixote
may yet take pleasure in the life that is in his
book; and his book is full of life.

We have no very ample record of the life
experiences of Cervantes, which are distilled in
this, his greatest book.[1] We know that he was a

---

[1] The authentic facts concerning the life of Cervantes
have been collected and stated with admirable scholarly
precision by Professor Fitzmaurice Kelly, in his recent
'Miguel de Cervantes Saavedra, a Memoir' (Clarendon
Press, 1913). In this biography is embodied all that can
be learned from the large array of documents discovered
and published within the last twenty years by the late
Cristobal Pérez Pastor. The resulting addition to our
knowledge will disappoint those who are not accustomed
to the perspective of the law. A man's small debts and
worries are recorded on parchment; the crucial events of
his life find no historian but himself. To compile a life of
Cervantes from this wilderness of documents is as difficult

soldier, and fought against the Turks at Lepanto, where his left hand was maimed for life; that he was made prisoner some years later by the Moors, and suffered five years' captivity at Algiers; that he attempted with others to escape, and when discovered and cross-examined took the whole responsibility on himself; that at last he was ransomed by the efforts of his family and friends, and returned to Spain, there to live as best he could the life of a poor man of letters, with intermittent Government employ, for thirty-six more years. He wrote sonnets and plays, pawned his family's goods, and was well acquainted with the inside of prisons. He published the First Part of 'Don Quixote' in 1605—that is to say, in his fifty-eighth year—and thenceforward enjoyed a high reputation, though his poverty continued. In 1615 the Second Part of 'Don Quixote' appeared, wherein the author makes delightful play with the First Part by treating it as a book well known to all the characters of the story. In the following year he died, clothed in the Franciscan habit, and was buried in the convent of the Barefooted Trinitarian Nuns in Madrid. No stone marks his grave, but his spirit still wanders the world in the person of the finest gentleman of all the realms of fact and fable, who still maintains in discourse with all whom he meets that the thing of which the world has most need is knights-

as it must always be to write the life of a soldier and poet from the evidence supplied by his washing-bills and tax-papers. Mr. Fitzmaurice Kelly has performed his task modestly and judiciously.

errant, to do honour to women, to fight for the cause of the oppressed, and to right the wrong. 'This, then, gentlemen,' he may still be heard saying, 'it is to be a knight-errant, and what I have spoken of is the order of chivalry, in the which, as I have already said, I, though a sinner, have made profession; the same which these famous knights profess do I profess; and that is why I am travelling through these deserts and solitary places, in quest of adventures, with deliberate resolve to offer my arm and my person to the most dangerous adventure which fortune may present, in aid of the weak and needy.' And the world is still incredulous and dazed. 'By these words which he uttered,' says the author in brief comment on the foregoing speech, 'the travellers were quite convinced that Don Quixote was out of his wits.'

It has often been said, and is still sometimes repeated by good students of Cervantes, that his main object in writing 'Don Quixote' was to put an end to the influence of the romances of chivalry. It is true that these romances were the fashionable reading of his age, that many of them were trash, and that some of them were pernicious trash. It is true also that the very scheme of his book lends itself to a scathing exposure of their weaknesses, and that the moral is pointed in the scene of the Inquisition of the Books, where the priest, the barber, the housekeeper, and the niece destroy the greater part of his library by fire. But how came it that Cervantes knew the romances so well, and dwelt on some of their incidents in such loving detail?

Moreover, it is worth noting that not a few of them are excluded by name from the general condemnation. 'Amadis of Gaul' is spared, because it is 'the best of all books of the kind.' Equal praise is given to 'Palmerin of England'; while of 'Tirante the White' the priest himself declares that it is a treasure of delight and a mine of pastime.

> 'Truly, I declare to you, gossip, that in its style this is the best book in the world. Here the knights eat and sleep, and die in their beds, and make their wills before they die, with other things in which the rest of the books of this kind are wanting.'

But even stronger evidence of the esteem that Cervantes felt for the best of the romances is to be found in his habit of linking their names with the poems of Homer and Virgil. So, in the course of instruction given by Don Quixote to Sancho Panza, while they dwelt in the wilds of the Sierra Morena, Ulysses is cited as the model of prudence and patience, Aeneas as the greatest of pious sons and expert captains, and Amadis as the 'pole star, the morning star, the sun of valiant and enamoured knights, whom all we have to copy, who do battle under the banner of love and chivalry.' It would indeed be a strange thing if a book which is so brave an exercise of the creative imagination were mainly destructive in its aim, and deserved no higher honour than a scavenger. The truth is that the book is so many-sided that all kinds of tastes and beliefs can find their warrant in it. The soul

of it is an irony so profound that but few of its
readers have explored it to the depths. It is like
a mine, deep below deep; and much good
treasure is to be found at the more easily
accessible levels. All irony criticises the imperfect ideas and theories of mankind, not by
substituting for them other ideas and other
theories, less imperfect, but by placing the facts
of life, in mute comment, alongside of the
theories. The Ruler of the World is the great
master of irony; and man has been permitted
to share some part of his enjoyment in the
purifying power of fact. The weaker and more
querulous members of the race commonly try
to enlist the facts in the service of their pet ideas.
A grave and deep spirit like Cervantes knows
that the facts will endure no such servitude.
They will not take orders from those who call
for their verdict, nor will they be content to
speak only when they are asked to speak. They
intrude suddenly, in the most amazing and
irrelevant fashion, on the carefully ordered plans
of humanity. They cannot be explained away,
and many a man who thought to have guarded
himself against surprise has been surprised by
love and death.

Every one sees the irony of 'Don Quixote' in
its first degree, and enjoys it in its more obvious
forms. This absurd old gentleman, who tries to
put his antiquated ideas into action in a busy,
selfish, prosy world, is a figure of fun even to the
meanest intelligence. But, with more thought,
there comes a check to our frivolity. Is not all
virtue and all goodness in the same case as Don

Quixote? Does the author, after all, mean to say that the world is right, and that those who try to better it are wrong? If that is what he means, how is it that at every step of our journey we come to like the Don better, until in the end we can hardly put a limit to our love and reverence for him? Is it possible that the criticism is double-edged, and that what we are celebrating with our laughter is the failure of the world?

A wonderful thing in Cervantes' handling of his story is his absolute honesty and candour. He does not mince matters. His world behaves as the world may be expected to behave when its daily interests are violently disordered by a lunatic. Failure upon failure dogs the steps of poor Don Quixote, and he has no popularity to redeem his material disasters. 'He who writes of me,' says the Don pensively, in his discussion with the bachelor Sampson, 'will please very few'; and the only comfort the bachelor can find for him is that the number of fools is infinite, and that the First Part of his adventures has delighted them all. As an example of Cervantes' treatment take one of the earliest of these adventures, the rescue of the boy Andres from the hands of his oppressor. As he rode away from the inn, on the first day of his knighthood, while yet he was unfurnished with a squire, Don Quixote heard cries of complaint from a thicket near by. He thanked Heaven for giving him so early an opportunity of service, and turned his horse aside to where he found a farmer beating a boy. Don Quixote, with all knightly formality, called the farmer a coward, and challenged him to single combat. The farmer, terrified by the strange apparition, explained that the boy was his servant and by gross carelessness had lost sheep for him at the rate of one a day. The matter was at last settled by the farmer liberating the boy and promising to pay him in full his arrears of wages; whereupon the knight rode away, well pleased. Then the farmer tied up the boy again, and beat him more severely than ever, till at the last he loosed him, and told him to go and seek redress from his champion. 'So the boy departed sobbing, and his master stayed behind laughing, and after this manner did the valorous Don Quixote right that wrong.' Later on, when the knight and his squire are in the wilds, with the company whom chance has gathered around them, the boy appears again, and Don Quixote narrates the story of his deliverance as an illustration of the benefits conferred on the world by knight-errantry.

'All that your worship says is true,' replies the lad, 'but the end of the business was very much the contrary of what your worship imagines.' 'How contrary?' said Don Quixote. 'Did he not pay thee, then?' 'He not only did not pay me,' said the boy, 'but as soon as your worship had got outside the wood, and we were alone, he tied me again to the same tree, and gave me so many lashes that he left me flayed like St. Bartholomew; and at every lash he gave me, he uttered some jest or scoff, to make a mock of your worship; and if I had not felt so much pain, I would have laughed at what he said. . . . For all this your worship is to blame, because if you had held on your way, and had not meddled with other people's business, my master would have been content to give me a dozen or two lashes, and afterwards he would have released me and paid me what he owed. But as your worship insulted him and called him bad names, his anger was kindled, and as he could not avenge himself on you, he let fly the tempest on me.'

Don Quixote sadly admits his error, and confesses that he ought to have remembered that 'no churl keeps the word he gives if he finds that it does not suit him to keep it.' But he promises Andres that he will yet see him righted; and with that the boy's terror awakes. 'For the love of God, sir knight-errant,' he says, 'if you meet me again, and see me being cut to pieces, do not rescue me, nor help me, but leave me to my pain; for, however great it be, it cannot be greater than will come to me from the help of your worship—whom, with all the knights-errant ever born into the world, may God confound!' With that he ran away, and Don Quixote stood very much abashed by his story, so that the rest of the company had to take great care that they did not laugh outright and put him to confusion.

At no point in the story does Cervantes permit the reader to forget that the righter of wrongs must not look in this world for either success or praise. The indignities heaped upon that gentle

and heoric soul almost revolt the reader, as
Charles Lamb remarked. He is beaten and
kicked; he has his teeth knocked out, and con-
soles himself with the thought that these hard-
ships are incident to his profession; his face is
all bedaubed with mud, and he answers with
grave politeness to the mocks of those who
deride him. When he stands sentry on the back
of his horse at the inn, to guard the sleepers, the
stable wench, Maritornes, gets him to reach up
his hand to an upper window, or rather a round
hole in the wall of the hayloft, whereupon she
slips a running noose over his wrist and ties the
rope firmly to a bar within the loft. In this
posture, and in continual danger of being hung
by the arm if his horse should move away, he
stands till dawn, when four travellers knock at
the gate of the inn. He at once challenges them
for their discourtesy in disturbing the slumbers
of those whom he is guarding. Even the Duke
and the Duchess, who feel kindly to Don Quixote
and take him under their care, are quite ready
to play rough practical jokes on him. It is while
he is their guest that his face is all scratched and
clawed by frightened cats turned loose in his
bedroom at night. His friends in the village
were kinder than this, but they, to get him home,
carried him through the country in a latticed
cage on poles, like a wild beast, for the admiration of the populace; and he bethought himself,
'As I am a new knight in the world, and the first
that hath revived the forgotten exercise of
chivalry, these are newly invented forms of
enchantment.' His spirit rises superior to all

his misfortunes, and his mind remains as serene as a cloudless sky.

But Don Quixote, it may be objected, is mad. Here the irony of Cervantes finds a deeper level. Don Quixote is a high-minded idealist, who sees all things by the light of his own lofty preconceptions. To him every woman is beautiful and adorable; everything that is said to him is worthy to be heard with attention and respect; every community of men, even the casual assemblage of lodgers at an inn, is a society founded on strict rules of mutual consideration and esteem. He shapes his behaviour in accordance with these ideas, and is laughed at for his pains. But he has a squire, Sancho Panza, who is a realist and loves food and sleep, who sees the world as it is, by the light of common day. Sancho, it might be supposed, is sane, and supplies a sure standard whereby to measure his master's deviations from the normal. Not at all; Sancho, in his own way, is as mad as his master. If the one is betrayed by fantasy, the other is betrayed, with as ludicrous a result, by common sense. The thing is well seen in the question of the island, the government of which is to be entrusted to Sancho when Don Quixote comes into his kingdom. Sancho, though he would have seen through the pretences of any merely corrupt bargainer, recognises at once that his master is disinterested and truthful, and he believes all he hears about the island. He spends much thought on the scheme, and passes many criticisms on it. Sometimes he protests that he is quite unfit for the position of a governor, and that his wife would cut a poor figure as a governor's lady. At other times he vehemently asserts that many men of much less ability than himself are governors, and eat every day off silver plate. Then he hears that, if an island should not come to hand, he is to be rewarded with a slice of a continent, and at once he stipulates that his domain shall be situated on the coast, so that he may put his subjects to a profitable use by selling them into slavery. It is not a gloss upon Cervantes to say that Sancho is mad; the suggestion is made, with significant repetition, in the book itself. 'As the Lord liveth,' says the barber, addressing the squire, 'I begin to think that thou oughtest to keep him company in the cage, and that thou art as much enchanted as he. In an evil day wast thou impregnated with his promises, and it was a sorrowful hour when the island of thy longings entered thy skull.'

So these two, in the opinion of the neighbours, are both mad, yet most of the wisdom of the book is theirs, and when neither of them is talking, the book falls into mere commonplace. And this also is many times recognised and commented on in the book itself. Sometimes it is the knight, and sometimes the squire, whose conversation makes the hearers marvel that one who talks with so much wisdom, justice, and discernment should act so foolishly. Certainly the book is a paradise of delightful discourse wherein all topics are handled and are presented in a new guise. The dramatic setting, which is the meaning of the book, is never forgotten; yet the things said are so good that when they are taken out of their setting they shine still, though with diminished splendour. What could be better than Don Quixote's treatment of the question of lineage, when he is considering his future claim to marry the beautiful daughter of a Christian or paynim King? 'There are two kinds of lineage,' he remarks. 'The difference is this—that some were what they are not, and others are what they were not; and when the thing is looked into I might prove to be one of those who had a great and famous origin, with which the King, my father-in-law who is to be, must be content.' Or what could be wiser than Sancho's account of his resignation of the governorship? 'Yesterday morning I left the island as I found it, with the same streets, houses, and tiles which they had when I went there. I have borrowed nothing of nobody, nor mixed myself up with the making of profits, and though I thought to make some profitable laws, I did not make any of them, for I was afraid they would not be kept, which would be just the same as if they had never been made.' Many of those who come across the pair in the course of their wanderings fall under the fascination of their talk. Not only so, but the world of imagination in which the two wanderers live proves so attractive, the infection of their ideas is so strong, that, long before the end of the story is reached, a motley company of people, from the Duke and Duchess down to the villagers, have set their own business aside in order to take part in the make-believe, and to be the persons of Don

Quixote's dream. There was never any Kingdom of Barataria; but the hearts of all who knew
him were set on seeing how Sancho would com-
port himself in the office of Governor, so the
Duke lent a village for the purpose, and it was
put in order and furnished with officers of State
for the part that it had to play. In this way some
of the fancies of the talkers almost struggle into
existence, and the dream of Don Quixote makes
the happiness it does not find.

Nothing in the story is more touching than the
steadily growing attachment and mutual admiration of the knight and the squire. Each deeply
respects the wisdom of the other, though Don
Quixote, whose taste in speech is courtly, many
times complains of Sancho's swarm of proverbs.
Each is influenced by the other; the knight
insists on treating the squire with the courtesies
due to an equal, and poor Sancho, in the end,
declares that not all the governments of the
world shall tempt him away from the service of
his beloved master. What, then, are we to think,
and what does their creator think, of those two
madmen, whose lips drop wisdom? 'Mark you,
Sancho,' said Don Quixote, 'there are two kinds
of beauty—one of the soul, and another of the
body. That of the soul excelleth in knowledge,
in modesty, in fine conduct, in liberality and
good breeding; and all these virtues are found
in, and may belong to, an ugly man. . . . I see
full well, Sancho, that I am not beautiful, but
I know also that I am not deformed, and it is
enough for a man of honour to be no monster;
he may be well loved, if he possesses those gifts

of soul which I have mentioned.' Sometimes, at the height of his frenzy, the knight seems almost inspired. So, when the shepherds have entertained him, he offers, by way of thanks, to maintain against all comers the fame and beauty of the shepherdesses, and utters his wonderful little speech on gratitude:

'For the most part, he who receives is inferior to him who gives; and hence God is above all, because he is, above all, the great giver; and the gifts of man cannot be equal to those of God, for there is an infinite distance between them; and the narrowness and insufficiency of the gifts of man is eked out by gratitude.'

There cannot be too much of this kind of madness. Well may Don Antonio cry out on the bachelor Sampson, who dresses himself as the Knight of the Silver Moon and overthrows Don Quixote in fight:

'O sir, may God forgive you the wrong you have done to all the world in desiring to make a sane man of the most gracious madman that the world contains! Do you not perceive that the profit which shall come from the healing of Don Quixote can never be equal to the pleasure which is caused by his ecstasies?'

What if the world itself is mad, not with the ecstasy of Don Quixote, nor with the thrifty madness of Sancho, but with a flat kind of madness, a makeshift compromise between faith and doubt? All men have a vein of Quixotry somewhere in their nature. They can be counted on, in most things, to follow the beaten path of interest and custom, till suddenly there comes along some question on which they refuse to appeal to interest; they take their stand on principle, and are adamant. All men know in themselves the mood of Sancho, when he says:

> 'I have heard the preachers preach that we should love our Lord for himself alone, without being moved to it by the hope of glory or the fear of pain; but, for my own part, I would love him for what he is able to do for me.'

These two moods, the mood of Quixote and the mood of Sancho, seem to divide between them most of the splendours and most of the comforts of human life. It is rare to find either mood in its perfection. A man who should consistently indulge in himself the mood of the unregenerate Sancho would be a rogue, though, if he preserved good temper in his doings, he would be a pleasant rogue. The man who would maintain in himself the mood of Quixote would be something very like a saint. The saints of the Church Militant would find no puzzle and no obscurity in the character of the Knight of La Mancha. Some of them, perhaps, would understand, better than Don Quixote understood, that the full record of his doings, compiled by Cervantes, is both a tribute to the saintly character, and a criticism of it. They certainly could not fail to discover the religious kernel of the book, as the world, in the easy confidence of its own superiority, has failed to discover it. They would know that whoso loseth his life shall save it; they would not find it difficult to understand how Don Quixote, and, in his own degree, Sancho, was willing to be a fool, that he, and the world with him, might be made wise. Above all, they would appreciate the more squalid misadventures of Don Quixote, for, unlike the public, which recognises the saint by his aureole, they would know, none better, that the way they have chosen is the way of contempt, and that Christianity was nursed in a manger.

Maurice Henry Hewlett
1861–1923

MASCALLS

We cut out of the high road by a sunk lane between dogwood hedges and ragged elms, I and a young squire of my acquaintance who lives and reigns not far from here. Beyond the trees there showed up the gable-end and chimneys of a house, and anon we came to a flint-and-stone wall, a blank space of masonry, wherein one barred window. The place might have been a convent in some Tuscan *vicolo*, so blind a look it had; but in our country, when a little house faces the sun, it has no use for windows to the north. We reached a door in the wall, tumbled down a flight of steps, and stood, as it were, upon the shore of a lake of light, with nothing before us but sunshot air, and across that radiant emptiness the further hills rolling away towards Somerset. Two great ilexes guard the entry, and make so dry a shelter that the angle of the wall with their covering serves as a wood-shed. A terrace-walk runs along the rim of the vale, from which the garden, enclosed in its white wall and red-tile coping, falls sharply down to the river. The wall ends there in a freakish gazebo overhanging the water, which once might have covered a boat-house, but now has a homelier use. Upon the terrace is Mascalls, the old stone house.

Mascalls has a quiet and seemly, plain face, much like that of some old labourer which has been bleached and scorched by the suns of fifty summers. It would be bald-looking, almost too severely to the purpose, but for one ample bow-window, the after-thought of some Mascall of the Regency. That was about the date at which it took its present shape, for while the ashlar might be of any age, and no doubt had served a much older house, its windows were all sashed in the way of 1810 or so, and a line of billets had been set under the eaves when a tile roof took the place of thatch. But antiquity was below us and about us—a mullioned window to the cellar, a huge tithe barn close by, built in Pelasgian blocks. The front door, with a coquettish stuccoed pediment which reminded me somehow of Jane Austen, stood open; and there, bowing, appealing with her faded eyes, stood the wife of the last Mascall who could be suffered to hold Mascalls, a patient, sad-faced woman, rendered by cares rather than years to look any age. She made us free of the place with a courtesy which never fails her countrywomen, though one of us had decreed that morning that she must leave. We made our rueful survey. We saw the wreck of a sturdy old house. From attic to cellar the tale was the same. Parting walls, sagging ceilings, gaping floor-boards, dry-rotten joists, damp-eaten, rat-gnawed, it was falling about the family's heads. To put the place in order again would cost a small fortune in these days, which could only be recovered by rent. But rent was what the family could not find—so what were you to do? My friend was humane, but he had to pay his way. His land was not a luxury, it was his livelihood. He was in as mortgagee on a foreclosure. The word had been spoken. Mascall could no longer hold Mascalls.

Yet what a pleasant seat for an old house, on a ridge above the eddying chalk-stream, full in the sun, with a view over the valley into the heart of the West! What a shady orchard of cider-apples, what a sheltered, ripe old walled-garden, what a green water-meadow edging the brook! The place is so much 'seated in the mean,' as Shakespeare says; it has the homely comfort, the plainness, the gentle every-dayness which makes our country beloved of all who come to know it. A country of half-tones, of silver-greys and amber-yellows, of mild wet winds, misted mornings and temperate noons; a country of Quaker habit. To be driven from it, if you have lived there all your life, and laboured its earth, and gone out and in: brought your bride there, got your children there, seen your old father die and borne him thence to the churchyard, returning then to know that you are Mascall of Mascalls; as it was in the beginning, is now . . . and then—to slip back and back, to feel your hold loosening, to be shiftless to help, in your own holding on sufferance, by squatter's right . . . and then—bidden to go! How can a man bear that?

There is neither script nor memory in the parish which does not recall a Mascall at Mascalls. The name there goes back to the fifteenth century; and if the house was called so

then it can only have been because there was
then a Mascall in it. And so you go back by
allowable guesswork to the first Mascall of all.
They were yeomen, free-holders, **or as good**, of
belike a hundred acres; and if 1810 to 1820 saw
the house refaced, new-roofed and made trim,
you must reflect that those were great years for
farming, with corn at 160s. and other things
according. Then came lean years; then temperament crept in; the Mascall blood ran thin;
the present man's grandfather failed, perhaps
in the hungry Forties; he mortgaged, could not
pay his interest; the squire's father foreclosed,
and since then Mascall's father and Mascall
himself have been labourers for hire. Even so
they could not keep afloat. Mascall, an honest
man, a steady, well-spoken man, but, as I read
him, a man with a temperament, lost way, could
not pick it up again. The house began to fall.
And one can't go on so for ever.

I can only guess what they feel about it, for,
being what they are, both of them, they will not
contend with fate. It is to be, they say, and wait
for it to come. Unable either to do or to say
anything, it is almost impossible to conceive lives
so expressionless as theirs. Barely, you would
think, a human life—except that they have
loved, and had children, and worked. But something was wanting besides expression. They
never leave their work, they never cease to work,
and yet they can't get on. Year by year they
have worked the daylight through, debt mount-
ing, the old house falling flake by flake like a
November woodland. Dock and thistle choke

their tillage, mud and dill-cup and marsh-marigold choke their gutters. Not only have they never complained, they have done no hand's turn to stem the ruin. It would seem as if the round of every day absorbed all the vital force they have to spend, that any intervals from toil which they might win went in vacant reverie. Mascall, I was told, has been seen of a Sunday morning standing in the road, doing nothing. Simply standing there. Not leaning over a gate, not smoking a pipe; but standing, doing nothing. Whether any intervals come Mrs. Mascall's way I don't know, but I doubt it. I saw a photograph in the house of one of its daughters. A pretty girl in white muslin, a sash round her waist, a flapping straw hat in her hand. Fair, blue-eyed obviously, like her mother. A pretty girl, but—temperament was in that vacant smile.

And so—Mascall of Mascalls no more; and the old homestead must to it again.

WIND IN THE DOWNS

THE Avon Valley is handsomely a fortnight ahead of mine, as I have proved over and over again, but from what I saw to-day I should suppose that the Wylye ran through a warmer soil than any other of the Five Rivers. I saw a tree just outside Wilton covered with golden knops on the point of breaking—and that in a wind which made my heart feel like doing the same thing. I dare swear that in Lord Pem-

broke's park there will be several in full leaf.
Avon will not provide such a sight yet awhile;
and Ebble not for three weeks. You get in this
country of ridge and hollow something approaching the sharp contrasts the South of France will
give you—something approaching them, and
yet, of course, if I can be understood, nothing
like them. I remember driving from Le Puy
to Pont Saint-Esprit—May the season. Le Puy
had been hot enough for any one; May weather
intensified by the crater in which the town
cowers and the tufa on which it roasts. From
there, and from May, we climbed into March
and fields of daffodil; from March into as bleak
a February as you could dread in the Jura, and
snow over all the waste; from that, down a
mountain slide, into the valley of the Ardèche,
where the hedgerows were full of dusty roses,
and the peasants making hay. You won't do
that in South Wilts., but you may have the
Chalke valley with its trees naked and sere, and
the slopes of its hills white with winter bents,
and over the plain come down into Wilton to
find magnolias in flower, and house fronts
smothered in Forsythia. Ours is the snuggest
valley but poorest soil of any of the five, and
our river, being the smallest, has not thrown
up a broad bed of silt on either bank in which
trees can grow tall and feel running water about
their roots.

When our Mistral began to blow, which was
ten days ago, I went up the drove immediately
behind my house, and could hardly find a sign
of a cowslip. I did find the leaves of one, but

there were no more on a ledge which will be
thick with them by and by. No wheatears to
be seen, and no March hares in their amorous
transports. The grass was as harsh as wire, the
moss, disintegrated by the rain and dried by
the wind, stood away from the earth like the
ribs of a rotten ship. To come presently upon
a little cloud of dog-violets was to be moved, as
the Ancient Mariner was, by 'a spring of love.'
Having blessed them unaware, I did it again,
very conscious of the act of worship. Beyond
that, further up the hill, one might have been
in mid-winter. I struggled to the Race Plain
where the wind, straight from Nova Zembla,
cut through my clothes like a knife. As usual,
I encountered a little scattered fleet of gypsies,
tacking into the jaws of it; a sorry nag straining
at a cart full of poles and miscellaneous junk;
women and young girls encumbered with babies
in their shawls, barefoot children padding about
on their white heels, and one smooth secret-
faced man, lord of the tattered seraglio, himself
well-clothed and unhampered. The women
were too distressed even to look their usual
petitions. I think they felt the wind rattling
their bones together. But the sultan hailed me,
and we conversed for a few moments behind a
furze-bush. They were from Sherborne, going
to the Forest, into what he called 'summer
quarters.' 'They will be glad of them, some of
your ladies,' I said, and he gave me a sharp
look. 'They are all right,' he said. 'They'll have
to wait, like the best of us.' He accepted a fill
of his pipe, lit it, turned it downwards, nodded,

plunged his hands, and went leisurely after his belongings. Myself, I went huddling home to a wood fire, feeling that he had the better of me in a many ways. For one thing, he kept half a dozen women in order—which I could not do even if I would; for another, he did not allow the mere wind to interfere with his good pleasure, his lordly ease of mind. I admire, while I cannot esteem, gypsies. Their ways are not our ways.

The Race Plain is their highway from the West to their headquarters in the New Forest, as once it was ours to London. Nearly every furze-clump all its length has the lewside blackened by the ruins of a fire. Night or day you will meet them coming or going, or pass a group of them snuggling or sleeping by a drift-wood fire. Very rarely they come to beg or hawk clothes-pegs in the village; but mostly they keep to their green road. Great poachers, of course; but beyond a few stray fowls we don't hear of much thieving. It is strange how little they mix, even now, with our people, not strange, therefore, that we know so little of them. That mystery is occasionally the begetter of romance. I said somewhere, confirming Borrow, that their girls scorn our young men, and am sure it is true of the main of them. Yet there are half-breeds among them, plainly; and such generalisations cannot be quite true. I heard of a case only the other day, where some green-eyed waif of theirs cast her spells upon a farm-lad, bewitched and bemused him until, for love of her, he was led into bad courses. He used to meet her at night, and their shelter in bad

weather was a deserted barn in the hillside, a
place locally known as Rats' Castle. From such
association he was led on and on, left his home,
threw up his work, and hid with her in the
hollows of the hills. His people thought he had
gone for a soldier, and made no more than
perfunctory search. Then, by and by, things
began to be missed—hens and their eggs, bread
out of bakers' carts, milk out of dairies, even
clothing from the washing-lines. And then, one
fine night, Rats' Castle was discovered to be
ablaze. The lad was taken and confessed to
everything, but the girl was not found. I hope
he got over his heart-attack during his term at
Devizes, which he served alone. He exonerated
her from all blame, took everything on his
shoulders; and as he was found near the burning
barn, and she not seen there, there was no
evidence against her, though plenty of suspicion.
He would not, perhaps could not, name her, but
she was well known to the police, and has since
been seen at fairs, or in the market. She was
pointed out to me in Sarum one Tuesday—
quite young, with hair lighter than her tan, with
narrowed, sidelong eyes, in a faded red blouse
and black skirt. She stood motionless, biting a
corner of her apron between her very white
teeth—half vicious, half wild-cat. Then I was
told the story, and was much moved to think
of what never did, and in the nature of things,
or of boy, never could have come out at the
inquiry: any hint, namely, of the wild stress of
passion, the lure of the romantic, or of what
answers to it, which drew the devoted simpleton

to forsake father and mother, industry and honesty, and to cleave to this *belle dame sans merci*, to thieve for her, and to take all the penalty. That is what he did; and he was not the first.

THE CRYSTAL VASE

I HAVE often wished that I could write a novel in which, as mostly in life, thank goodness, nothing happens. Jane Austen, it has been objected, forestalled me there, and it is true that she very nearly did—but not quite. It was a point for her art to make that the novel should have form. Form involved plot, plot a logic of events; events—well, that means that there were collisions. They may have been mild shocks, but persons did knock their heads together, and there were stars to be seen by somebody. In life, in a majority of cases, there are no stars, yet life does not on that account cease to be interesting; and even if stars should happen to be struck out, it is not the collision, nor the stars either, which interest us most. No, it is our state of soul, our mental process under the stress which we care about, and as mental process is always going on, and the state of the soul is never the same for two moments together, there is ample material for a novel of extreme interest, which need never finish, which might indeed be as perennial as a daily newspaper or the *Annual Register*. Why is it, do you suppose, that anybody, if he can, will read anybody else's letter?

It is because every man-Jack of us lives in a cage, cut off from every other man-Jack; because we are incapable of knowing what is going on in the mind of our nearest and dearest, and because we burn for the assurance we may get by evidence of homogeneity procurable from any human source. Man is a creature of social instinct condemned by his nature to be solitary. Creatures in all outward respects similar to himself are awhirl about him. They cannot help him, nor he them; he cannot even be sure, for all he may assume it, that they share his hope and calling.

> Ensphered in flesh we live and die,
>   And see a myriad souls adrift,
> Our likes, and send our voiceless cry
>   Shuddering across the void: 'The truth!
> Succour! The truth!' None can reply.

That is the state of our case. We can cope with mere events, comedy, tragedy, farce. The things that happen to us are not our life. They are imposed upon life, they come and go. But life is a secret process. We only see the accretions.

The novel which I dreamed of writing has recently been done, or rather begun, by Miss Dorothy Richardson. She betters the example of Jane Austen by telling us much more about what seems to be infinitely less, but is not so in reality. She dips into the well whereof Miss Austen skims the surface. She has essayed to report the mental process of a young woman's lifetime from moment to moment. In the course of four, if not five, volumes nothing has happened yet but the death of a mother and the marriage of a sister or so. She may write forty, and I shall be ready for the forty-first. Mental process, the states of the soul, emotional reaction—these as they are moved in us by other people are Miss Richardson's subject-matter, and according as these are handled is the interest we can devote to her novels. These fleeting things are Miss Richardson's game, and they are the things which interest us most in ourselves, and the things which we desire to know most about in our neighbours.

But, of course, it won't do. Miss Richardson does not, and cannot, tell us all. A novel is a piece of art which does not so much report life as transmute it. She takes up what she needs for her purpose, and that may not be our purpose. And so it is with poetry—we don't go to that for the facts, but for the essence of fact. The poet who told us all about himself at some particular pass would write a bad poem, for it is his affair to transfigure rather than transmute, to move us by beauty at least as much as by truth. What we look for so wistfully in each other is the raw material of poetry. We can make the finished article for ourselves, given enough matter; and indeed the poetry which is imagined in contemplation is apt to be much finer than that which has passed through the claws of prosody and syntax. The fact, to be short with it, is that literature has an eye upon the consumer. Whether it is marketable or not, it is intended for the public. Now no man will undress in public with design. It may be a pity, but so it is. Undesignedly, I don't say. It would be possible,

I think, by analysis, to track the successive waves of mental process in *In Memoriam*. Again, *The Angel in the House* brought Patmore as near to self-explication as a poet can go. Shakespeare's Sonnets offer a more doubtful field of experiment.

What then? Shall we go to the letter-writers —to Madame de Sévigné, to Gray, to Walpole and Cowper, Byron and Lamb? A letter-writer implies a letter-reader, and just that inadequacy of spoken communication will smother up our written words. Madame de Sévigné must placate her high-sniffing daughter; Gray must please himself; Walpole must at any cost be lively; Cowper must be urbane to Lady Hesketh or deprecate the judgment of the Reverend Mr. Newton. Byron was always before the looking-glass as he wrote; and as for Charles Lamb, do not suppose that he did anything but hide in his clouds of ink. Sir Sidney Colvin thinks that Keats revealed himself in his letters, but I cannot agree with him. Keats is one of the best letter-writers we have; he can be merry, fanciful, witty, thoughtful, even profound. He has a sardonic turn of language hardly to be equalled outside Shakespeare. 'Were it in my choice, I would reject a Petrarchal coronation— on account of my dying day, and because women have cancers.' Where will you match that but from Hamlet? But Keats knew himself. 'It is a wretched thing to confess, but it is a very fact, that not one word I can utter can be taken for granted as an opinion growing out of my identical Nature.' So I find him in his letters, swayed rather by his fancies than his states of soul, until indeed that soul of his was wrung by agony of mind and disease of body. Revelation, then, like gouts of blood, did issue, but of that I do not now write. No man is sane at such a crisis.

Parva componere magnis, there is a letter contained in 'The Early Diary of Frances Burney' (ed. Mrs. A. R. Ellis, 1899), more completely apocalyptic than anything else of the kind accessible to me. Its writer was Maria Allen, daughter of Dr. Burney's second wife, therefore half-sister to the charming Burney girls. She was a young lady who could let herself go, in act as well as on paper, and withal, as Fanny judged her, 'flighty, ridiculous, uncommon, lively, comical, entertaining, frank, and undisguised'—or because of it—she did contrive to unfold her panting and abounding young self more thoroughly than the many times more expert. You have her here in the pangs of a love-affair, of how long standing I don't know, but now evidently in a bad state of miss-fire. It was to end in elopement, post-chaise, clandestine marriage, in right eighteenth-century. Here it is in an earlier state, all mortification, pouting and hunching of the shoulder. I reproduce it with Maria's punctuation, which shows it to have proceeded, as no doubt she did herself, in gasps:

'I was at the Assembly, forced to go entirely against my own Inclination. But I always have sacrificed my own Inclinations to the will of other people—could not resist the pressing Importunity of—Bet Dickens—to go—tho' it proved Horribly stupid. I drank tea at the— told old Turner—I was determined not to dance—he would not believe me—a wager ensued—half a crown provided I followed my own Inclinations—agreed—Mr. Audley asked me. I refused—sat still—yet followed my own Inclinations. But four couple began—Martin (c'était Lui) was there—yet stupid—n'importe —quite Indifferent—on both sides—Who had I—to converse with the whole Evening—not a female friend—none there—not an acquaintance—All Dancing—who then—I've forgot— n'importe—I broke my earring—how—heaven knows—foolishly enough—one can't always keep on the Mask of Wisdom—well n'importe I danced a Minuet à quatre the latter end of the Eve—with a stupid Wretch—need I name him —They danced cotillions almost the whole Night—two sets—yet I did not join them—Miss Jenny Hawkins danced—with who—can't you guess—well—n'importe—'

There is more, but my pen is out of breath. Nobody but Mr. Jingle ever wrote like that; and in so far as Maria Allen may be said to have had a soul, there in its little spasms is the soul of Maria Allen, with all the *malentendus* of the ballroom and all the surgings of a love-affair at cross-purposes thrown in.

As for Fanny Burney's early diary, its careful and admirable editor claims that you have in it 'the only published, perhaps the only existing record of the life of an English girl, written of herself in the eighteenth century.' I believe that to be true. It is a record, and a faithful and very charming record of the externals of such a life. As such it is, to me, at least, a valuable thing. If

it does not unfold the amiable, brisk, and happy
Fanny herself, there are two simple reasons why
it could not. First, she was writing her journal
for the entertainment of old Mr. Crisp of Chess-
ington, the 'Daddy Crisp' of her best pages;
secondly, it is not at all likely that she knew of
anything to unfold. Nor, for that matter, was
Fanny herself of the kind that can unfold to
another person. Yet there is a charm all over
the book, which some may place here, some
there, but which all will confess. For me it is
not so much that Fanny herself is a charming
girl, and a girl of shrewd observation, of a
pointed pen, and an admirable gift of mimicry.
She has all that, and more—she has a good heart.
Her sister Susan is as good as she, and there are
many of Susan's letters. But the real charm of
the book, I think, is in the series of faithful
pictures it contains of the everyday round of an
everyday family. Dutch pictures all—passers-by,
a knock at the front door, callers—Mr. Young,
'in light blue embroidered with silver, a bag
and sword, and walking in the rain'; a jaunt
to Greenwich, a concert at home—the Agujari
in one of her humours; a masquerade—'a very
private one, at the house of Mr. Laluze. . . .
Hetty had for three months thought of nothing
else . . . she went as a Savoyard with a hurdy-
gurdy fastened round her waist. Nothing could
look more simple, innocent and pretty. My
dress was a close pink Persian vest covered with
a gauze in loose pleats. . . .' What else? Oh,
a visit to Teignmouth—Maria Allen now Mrs.
Ruston; another to Worcester; quiet days at

King's Lynn, where 'I have just finished *Henry
and Frances* . . . the greatest part of the last
volume is wrote by Henry, and on the gravest of
grave subjects, and that which is most dreadful
to our thoughts, Eternal Misery. . . .' Terrific
novel: but need I go on? There may be some to
whom a description of the nothings of our life
will be as flat as the nothings themselves—but I
am not of that party. The things themselves
interest me, and I confess the charm. It is the
charm of innocence and freshness, a morning
dew upon the words.

The Burneys, however, can do no more for us
than shed that auroral dew. They cannot re-
assure us of our normal humanity, since they
needed reassurance themselves.

Where, then, shall we turn? So far as I am
aware, to two only, except for two others whom
I leave out of account. Rousseau is one, for it is
long since I read him, but my recollection is that
the *Confessions* is a kind of novel, pre-meditated,
selective, done with great art. Marie Bashkirt-
seff is another. I have not read her at all. Of
the two who remain I leave Pepys also out of
account, because, though it may be good for us
to read Pepys, it is better to have read him and
be through with it. There, under the grace of
God, go a many besides Pepys, and among them
every boy who has ever befouled a wall with a
stump of pencil. We are left then with one whom
it is ill to name in the same fill of the inkpot,
'Wordsworth's exquisite sister,' as Keats, who
saw her once, at once knew her to be.

In Dorothy Wordsworth's journals, you may

have the delight of daily intercourse—*famigliar-
mente discorrendo*—with one of the purest and
noblest souls ever housed in flesh; to that you
may add the reassurance to be got from word
and implication beyond doubt. She tells us
much, but implies more. We may see deeply
into ourselves, but she sees deeply into a deeper
self than most of us can discern. It is not only
that, knowing her, we are grounded in the rudi-
ments of honour and lovely living; it is to learn
that human life can be so lived, and to conclude
that of that at least is the Kingdom of Heaven.

These journals are for fragments only of the
years which they cover, and as such exist for
Jan.–May, 1798 (Alfoxden); May–Dec., 1800,
Oct.–Dec., 1801, Jan.–July, 1802: all these at
Grasmere. They have been printed by Professor
Knight, and I have the assurance of Mr. Gordon
Wordsworth that what little has been omitted is
unimportant. Nothing is unimportant to me,
and I wish the whole had been given us; but
what we have is enough whereby to trace the
development of her extraordinary mind and of
her power of self-expression. The latter, undoubtedly, grew out of emotion, which gradually
culminated until the day of William Wordsworth's marriage. There it broke, and with it,
as if by a determination of the will, there the
revelation ceased. A new life began with the
coming of Mary Wordsworth to Dove Cottage,
a life of which Dorothy records the surface only.

The Alfoxden fragment (20 Jan.–22 May,
1798), written when she was twenty-seven, is
chiefly notable for its power of interpreting

landscape. That was a power which Wordsworth himself possessed in a high degree. There
can be no doubt, I think, that they egged each
other on, but I myself should find it hard to say
which was egger-on and which the egged. This
is the first sentence of it:

'20 Jan.—The green paths down the hill-
sides are channels for streams. The young
wheat is streaked by silver lines of water
running between the ridges, the sheep are
gathered together on the slopes. After the
wet dark days, the country seems more
populous. It peoples itself in the sunbeams.'

Here is one of a few days later:

'23rd.—Bright sunshine; went out at 3 o'cl.
The sea perfectly calm blue, streaked with
deeper colour by the clouds, and tongues or
points of sand; on our return of a gloomy red.
The sun gone down. The crescent moon,
Jupiter and Venus. The sound of the sea
distinctly heard on the tops of the hills, which
we could never hear in summer. We attribute
this partly to the bareness of the trees, but
chiefly to the absence of the singing birds,
the hum of insects, that noiseless noise which
lives in the summer air. The villages marked
out by beautiful beds of smoke. The turf
fading into the mountain road.'

She handles words, phrases, like notes or
chords of music, and never gets her landscape by
direct description. One more picture and I must
leave it:

'26.— . . . Walked to the top of a high hill to see a fortification. Again sat down to feed upon the prospect; a magnificent scene, *curiously* spread out for even minute inspection though so extensive that the mind is afraid to calculate its bounds. . . .'

Coleridge was with them most days, or they with him. Here is a curious point to note. Dorothy records:

'March 7th.—William and I drank tea at Coleridge's. Observed nothing particularly interesting. . . . One only leaf upon the top of a tree—the sole remaining leaf—danced round and round like a rag blown by the wind.'

And Coleridge has in *Christabel:*

The one red leaf, the last of its clan,
That dances as often as dance it can,
Hanging so light, and hanging so high,
On the topmost twig that looks up at the sky.

William, Dorothy, and Coleridge went to Hamburg at the end of that year, but in 1800 the brother and sister were in Grasmere; and the journal which opens with May 14, at once betrays the great passion of Dorothy's life:

'William and John set off into Yorkshire after dinner at half-past two o'clock, cold pork in their pockets. I left them at the turning of the Low-Wood bay under the trees. My heart was so full I could hardly speak to W., when I gave him a farewell kiss. I sate a long time upon a stone at the margin of the lake,

H*

and after a flood of tears my heart was easier. The lake looked to me, I know not why, dull and melancholy, and the weltering on the shore seemed a heavy sound. . . . I resolved to write a journal of the time till W. and J. return, and I set about keeping my resolve, because I will not quarrel with myself, and because I shall give William pleasure by it when he comes again. . . .'

'Because I will not quarrel with myself!' She is full of such illuminations. Here is another:

'Sunday, June 1st.—After tea went to Ambleside round the lakes. A very fine warm evening. Upon the side of Loughrigg *my heart dissolved in what I saw.*'

Now here is her account of a country funeral which she reads into, or out of, the countryside:

'Wednesday, 3rd Sept.— . . . a funeral at John Dawson's. . . . I was affected to tears while we stood in the house, the coffin lying before me. There were no near kindred, no children. When we got out of the dark house the sun was shining, and the prospect looked as divinely beautiful as I ever saw it. It seemed more sacred than I had ever seen it, *and yet more allied to human life.* I thought she was going to a quiet spot, and I could not help weeping very much. . . .'

The italics are mine. William was pleased to call her weeping 'nervous blubbering.'

And then we come to 1802, the great last year of a twin life; the last year of the five in which those two had lived as one soul and one heart. They were at Dove cottage, on something under £150 a year. Poems were thronging thick about them; they were living intensely. John was alive. Mary Hutchinson was at Sockburn. Coleridge was still Coleridge, not the bemused and futile mystic he was to become. As for Dorothy, she lives a thing enskied, floating from ecstasy to ecstasy. It is the third of March, and William is to go to London. 'Before we had quite finished breakfast Calvert's man brought the horses for Wm. We had a deal to do, pens to make, poems to be put in order for writing, to settle for the press, pack up. . . . Since he left me at half-past eleven (it is now two) I have been putting the drawers in order, laid by his clothes, which he had thrown here and there and everywhere, filed two months' newspapers, and got my dinner, two boiled eggs and two apple tarts. . . . The robins are singing sweetly. Now for my walk. I *will* be busy. I *will* look well, and be well when he comes back to me. O the Darling! Here is one of his bitter apples. I can hardly find it in my heart to throw it into the fire. . . . I walked round the two lakes, crossed the stepping-stones at Rydalefoot. Sate down where we always sit. I was full of thought of my darling. Blessings on him.' Where else in our literature will you find mood so tender, so intimately, so delicately related?

A week later, and William returned. With him, it seems, her descriptive powers. 'Monday morning—a soft rain and mist. We walked to Rydale for letters. The Vale looked very beautiful in excessive simplicity, yet at the same time, uncommon obscurity. The church stood alone, mountains behind. The meadows looked calm and rich, bordering on the still lake. Nothing else to be seen but lake and island.' Exquisite landscape. For its like we must go to Japan. Here is another. An interior. It is the 23rd of March, 'about ten o'clock, a quiet night. The fire flickers, and the watch ticks. I hear nothing save the breathing of my beloved as he now and then pushes his book forward, and turns over a leaf. . . .' No more, but the peace of it is profound, the art incomparable.

In April, between the 5th and 12th, William went into Yorkshire upon an errand which she knew and dreaded. Her trouble makes the words throb.

'Monday, 12th. . . . The ground covered with snow. Walked to T. Wilkinson's and sent for letters. The woman brought me one from William and Mary. It was a sharp windy night. Thomas Wilkinson came with me to Barton and questioned me like a catechiser all the way. Every question was like the snapping of a little thread about my heart. I was so full of thought of my half-read letter and other things. I was glad when he left me. Then I had time to look at the moon while I was thinking of my own thoughts. The moon travelled through the clouds, tinging them yellow as she passed along, with two stars near her, one larger than the other. . . . At this time William, as

I found the next day, was riding by himself between Middleham and Barnard Castle.'

I don't know where else to find the vague torment of thought, its way of enhancing colour and form in nature, more intensely observed. Next day: 'When I returned *William* was come. *The surprise shot through me.*' This woman was not so much poet as crystal vase. You can see the thought cloud and take shape.

The twin life was resumed for yet a little while. In the same month came her descriptions of the daffodils in Gowbarrow Park, and of the scene by Brothers Water, which prove to anybody in need of proof that she was William's well-spring of poesy. Not that the journal is necessarily involved. No need to suppose that he even read it. But that she could make him see, and be moved by, what she had seen is proved by this: '17th.— . . . I saw a robin chasing a scarlet butterfly this morning'; and 'Sunday, 18th.— . . . William wrote the poem on *The Robin and the Butterfly.*' No, beautiful beyond praise as the journals are, it is certain that she was more beautiful than they. And what a discerning, illuminative eye she had! 'As I lay down on the grass, I observed the glittering silver line on the ridge of the backs of the sheep, owing to their situation respecting the sun, which made them look beautiful, but with something of strangeness, like animals of another kind, as if belonging to a more splendid world. . . .' What a woman to go a-gypsying through the world with!

Then comes the end. . . . 'Thursday, 8th

July.— . . . In the afternoon, after we had talked a little, William fell asleep. I read *The Winter's Tale;* then I went to bed but did not sleep. The swallows stole in and out of their nest, and sat there, *whiles* quite still, *whiles* they sung low for two minutes or more at a time, just like a muffled robin. William was looking at *The Pedlar* when I got up. He arranged it, and after tea I wrote it out—280 lines. . . . The moon was behind. . . . We walked first to the top of the hill to see Rydale. It was dark and dull, but our own vale was very solemn—the shape of Helm Crag was quite distinct though black. We walked backwards and forwards on the White Moss path; there was a sky like white brightness on the lake. . . . O beautiful place! Dear Mary, William. The hour is come. . . . I must prepare to go. The swallows, I must leave them, the wall, the garden, the roses, all. Dear creatures, they sang last night after I was in bed; seemed to be singing to one another, just before they settled to rest for the night. Well, I must go. Farewell.'

Next day she set out with William to meet her secret dread, knowing that life in Rydale could never be the same again. Wordsworth married Mary Hutchinson on the 4th October, 1802. The secret is no secret now, for Dorothy was a crystal vase.

Logan Pearsall Smith
1865–1946

THE ROSE

THE old lady had always been proud of the great rose-tree in her garden, and was fond of telling how it had grown from a cutting she had brought years before from Italy, when she was first married. She and her husband had been travelling back in their carriage from Rome (it was before the time of railways), and on a bad piece of road south of Siena they had broken down, and had been forced to pass the night in a little house by the roadside. The accommodation was wretched of course; she had spent a sleepless night, and rising early had stood, wrapped up, at her window, with the cool air blowing on her face, to watch the dawn. She could still, after all these years, remember the blue mountains with the bright moon above them, and how a far-off town on one of the peaks had gradually grown whiter and whiter, till the moon faded, the mountains were touched with the pink of the rising sun, and suddenly the town was lit as by an illumination, one window after another catching and reflecting the sun's beams, till at last the whole little city twinkled and sparkled up in the sky like a nest of stars.

That morning, finding they would have to

wait while their carriage was being repaired, they had driven in a local conveyance up to the city on the mountain, where they had been told they would find better quarters; and there they had stayed two or three days. It was one of the miniature Italian cities with a high church, a pretentious piazza, a few narrow streets and little palaces, perched, all compact and complete, on the top of a mountain, within an enclosure of walls hardly larger than an English kitchen garden. But it was full of life and noise, echoing all day and all night with the sounds of feet and voices.

The Café of the simple inn where they stayed was the meeting-place of the notabilities of the little city; the *Sindaco*, the *avvocato*, the doctor, and a few others; and among them they noticed a beautiful, slim, talkative old man, with bright black eyes and snow-white hair—tall and straight and still with the figure of a youth, although the waiter told them with pride that the *Conte* was *molto vecchio*—would in fact be eighty in the following year. He was the last of his family, the waiter added—they had once been great and rich people—but he had no descendants; in fact the waiter mentioned with complacency, as if it were a story on which the locality prided itself, that the *Conte* had been unfortunate in love, and had never married.

The old gentleman, however, seemed cheerful enough; and it was plain that he took an interest in the strangers, and wished to make their acquaintance. This was soon effected by the friendly waiter; and after a little talk the

old man invited them to visit his villa and
garden which were just outside the walls of the
town. So the next afternoon, when the sun
began to descend, and they saw in glimpses
through doorways and windows, blue shadows
beginning to spread over the brown mountains,
they went to pay their visit. It was not much of
a place, a small, modernised, stucco villa, with
a hot pebbly garden, and in it a stone basin
with torpid gold fish, and a statue of Diana and
her hounds against the wall. But what gave a
glory to it was a gigantic rose-tree which clam-
bered over the house, almost smothering the
windows, and filling the air with the perfume of
its sweetness. Yes, it was a fine rose, the *Conte*
said proudly when they praised it, and he would
tell the Signora about it. And as they sat there,
drinking the wine he offered them, he alluded
with the cheerful indifference of old age to his
love affair, as though he took for granted that
they had heard of it already.

'The lady lived across the valley there beyond
that hill. I was a young man then, for it was
many years ago. I used to ride over to see her;
it was a long way, but I rode fast, for young men,
as no doubt the Signora knows, are impatient.
But the lady was not kind, she would keep me
waiting, oh, for hours; and one day when I had
waited very long I grew very angry, and as
I walked up and down in the garden where she
had told me she would see me, I broke one of
her roses, broke a branch from it; and when
I saw what I had done, I hid it inside my coat—
so—; and when I came home I planted it, and

the Signora sees how it has grown. If the Signora admires it, I must give her a cutting to plant also in her garden; I am told the English have beautiful gardens that are green, and not burnt with the sun like ours.'

The next day, when their mended carriage had come up to fetch them, and they were just starting to drive away from the inn, the *Conte's* old servant appeared with the rose-cutting neatly wrapped up, and the compliments and wishes for a *buon viaggio* from her master. The town collected to see them depart, and the children ran after their carriage through the gate of the little city. They heard a rush of feet behind them for a few moments, but soon they were far down toward the valley; the little town with all its noise and life was high above them on its mountain peak.

She had planted the rose at home, where it had grown and flourished in a wonderful manner; and every June the great mass of leaves and shoots still broke out into a passionate splendour of scent and crimson colour, as if in its root and fibres there still burnt the anger and thwarted desire of that Italian lover. Of course the old *Conte* must have died many years ago; she had forgotten his name, and had even forgotten the name of the mountain city that she had stayed in, after first seeing it twinkling at dawn in the sky, like a nest of stars.

John Galsworthy

1867–1933

A PORTRAIT

Iᴛ is at the age of eighty that I picture him without the vestige of a stoop, rather above middle height, of very well-proportioned figure, whose flatness of back and easy movements were the admiration of all who saw them. His iron-grey eyes had lost none of their colour, they were set in deep, so that their upper lids were invisible, and had a peculiar questioning directness, apt to change suddenly into twinkles. His head was of fine shape—one did not suspect that it required a specially made hat, being a size larger than almost any other head; it was framed in very silky silvery hair, brushed in an arch across his forehead, and falling in becoming curves over the tips of his ears; and he wore always a full white beard and moustaches, which concealed a jaw and chin of great determination cleft by a dimple. His nose had been broken in his early boyhood; it was the nose of a thinker, broad and of noticeable shape. The colour of his cheeks was a fine dry brown; his brow very capacious, both wide and high, and endowed with a singular serenity. But it was the balance and poise of his head which commanded so much attention. In a theatre, church, concert-hall, there was never any head so fine as his, for the silvery hair and beard lent to its massiveness a curious grace and delicacy.

The owner of that head could not but be endowed with force, sagacity, humour, and the sense of justice. It expressed, indeed, his essential quality—equanimity; for there were two men in him—he of the chin and jaw, a man of action and tenacity, and he of the nose and brow, the man of speculation and impersonality; yet these two were so curiously balanced and blended that there was no harsh ungraceful conflict. And what made this equanimity so memorable was the fact that both his power of action and his power of speculation were of high quality. He was not a commonplace person content with a little of both. He wanted and had wanted throughout life, if one may judge by records, a good deal of both, ever demanding with one half of him strong and continuous action, and with the other half, high and clean thought and behaviour. The desire for the best both in material and spiritual things remained with him through life. He felt things deeply; and but for his strange balance, and a yearning for inward peace which never seems to have deserted him, his ship might well have gone down in tragedy.

To those who had watched that journey, his voyage through life seemed favourable, always on the top of the weather. He had worked hard, and he had played hard, but never too hard. And though one might often see him irritated, I think no one ever saw him bored. He perceived **a** joke quicker than most of us; he was **never** eccentric, yet fundamentally independent of other people's opinions, and perhaps a little unconscious that there were better men than he. Not that he was conceited, for of this quality, so closely allied to stupidity and humbug, he had about as much as the babe unborn. He was, indeed, a natural foe to anæmia in any of its forms, just as he was instinctively hostile to gross bull-beef men and women. The words, 'a bullying chap,' were used by him as crushing dispraise. I can recall him now in his chair after dinner, listening to one, who, puffing his cigarette, is letting himself go on a stream of robustious, rather swaggering complacencies; with what a comprehending straight look he regards the speaker, not scornful, not sarcastic, but simply, as it were, saying: 'No, my young buck, for all your fine full-blooded talk, and all your red face, you are what I see you to be, and you will do what I tell you to do!' Such men had no chance with him when it came to the tug of war; he laid his will on them as if they had been children.

He was that rather rare thing, a pure-blooded Englishman; having no strain of Scotch, Welsh, Irish, or foreign blood in his pedigree for four hundred years at least. He sprang from a long line of farmers intermarrying with their kind in the most southern corner of Devonshire, and it is probable that Norse and British blood were combined in him in a high state of equality. Even in the actual situation of his place of origin, the principle of balance had been maintained, for the old farmhouse from which his grandfather had emerged had been perched close to the cliff. Thus, to the making of him had gone land and sea, the Norseman and the Celt.

Articled to the Law at the age of sixteen by his father, a Plymouth merchant, whose small ancient ships traded to the Mediterranean in fruits, leather, and wines, he had come to London, and at the earliest possible date (as was the habit with men in those times) had been entered on the rolls as a solicitor. Often has he told me of the dinner he gave in honour of that event. 'I was a thread-paper, then,' he would say (indeed, he never became fat).—'We began with a barrel of oysters.' About that and other festivities of his youth, there was all the rich and rollicking flavour of the days of Pickwick. He was practically dependent on his own exertions from the time he began to practise his profession, and it was characteristic of him that he never seems to have been hard pressed for money. The inherent sanity and moderation of his instincts preserved him, one imagines, from the financial ups and downs of most young men, for there was no niggardliness in him, and a certain breadth of conception characterised his money affairs throughout life. It was rather by the laws of gravity, therefore, whereby money judiciously employed attracts money, and the fact that he lived in that money-maker's Golden Age, the nineteenth century, that he had long been (at the age of eighty) a wealthy man. Money was to him the symbol of a well-spent, well-ordered life, provocative of warmth in his heart because he loved his children, and was careful of them to a fault. He did not marry till he was forty-five, but his feeling for the future of his family manifested itself with the birth of his first child. Selecting a fair and high locality, not too far away from London, he set himself at once to make a country place, where the little things should have fresh air, new milk, and all the fruits of the earth, home-grown round them. Quite wonderful was the forethought he lavished on that house and little estate stretching down the side of a hill, with its walled gardens, pasture, corn-land and coppice. All was solid, and of the best, from the low four-square red brick house with its concrete terrace and French windows, to the cow-houses down by the coppice. From the oak trees, hundreds of years old, on the lawns, to the peach trees just planted along the south sunny walls. But here too, there was no display for the sake of it, and no extravagance. Everything was at hand, from home-baked bread, to mushrooms wild and tame; from the stables with their squat clock-tower, to pigsties; from roses that won all the local prizes, to blue-bells; but nothing redundant or pretentious.

The place was an endless pleasure to him, who to the last preserved his power of taking interest, not only in great, but in little things. Each small triumph over difficulty—the securing of hot water in such a quarter, the better lighting of another, the rescue of the nectarines from wasps, the quality of his Alderney cows, the encouragement of rooks—afforded him as much simple and sincere satisfaction as every little victory he achieved in his profession, or in the life of the Companies which he directed. But with all his shrewd practical sense, and almost naïve pleasure in material advantage, he combined a very real spiritual life of his own. Nor was there anything ascetic in that inner life. It was mellow as the music of Mozart, his most beloved composer; Art and Nature both had their part in it. He was, for instance, very fond of opera, but only when it could be called 'grand'; and it grieved him that opera was no longer what it had been, yet was it secretly a grave satisfaction that he had known those classical glories denied to the present generation. He loved indeed almost all classical music, but (besides Mozart) especially Beethoven, Gluck, and Meyerbeer, whom he insisted (no less than Herbert Spencer) on considering a great composer. Wagner he tried very hard to appreciate and, after visiting Bayreuth, even persuaded himself that he had succeeded, though he never ceased to point out the great difference that existed between this person and Mozart. He loved the Old Masters of painting, having for favourites amongst the Italians: Rafael, Correggio, Titian, Tintoretto; and amongst Englishmen Reynolds and Romney. On the other hand, he regarded Hogarth and Rubens as coarse, but Vandyke he very much admired, because of his beautiful painting of hands, the hall-mark, he would maintain, of an artist's quality. I cannot remember his feeling about Rembrandt, but Turner he certainly distrusted as extravagant. Botticelli and the earlier masters he had not as yet quite learned to relish; and Impressionism, including Whistler, never really made conquest of his taste, though he always resolutely kept his mind open to what was modern—feeling himself young at heart.

Once on a spring day, getting over a stile, I remember him saying:

'Eighty! I can't believe it. Seems very queer. I don't feel it. Eighty!' And, pointing to a blackbird that was singing, he added: 'That takes the years off you!' His love of Nature was very intimate, simple, and unconscious. I can see him standing by the pond of a summer evening watching the great flocks of starlings that visited those fields; or, with his head a little to one side, listening rapturously to a skylark. He would contemplate, too, with a sort of serene passion, sunset effects, and every kind of view.

But his greatest joy in life had been his long summer holidays, in Italy or among the Alps, and his memory was a perfect storehouse of peaks, passes, and arrivals at Italian inns. He had been a great walker, and, as an old man, was still very active. I can remember him on horseback at the age of sixty, though he had never been a sportsman—not being in the way of hunting, having insufficient patience for fishing, and preferring to spend such time as he might have had for shooting, in communing with his beloved mountains. His love for all kinds of beauty, indeed, was strangely potent; and perhaps the more natural and deep for its innocence of all tradition and formal culture. He got it, I think, from his mother, of whom he always spoke with reverence as 'the most beautiful woman in the Three Towns.' Yes, his love of beauty was a sensuous, warm glow pervading the whole of him, secretly separating him from the majority of his associates. A pretty face, a beautiful figure, a mellow tune, the sight of dancing, a blackbird's song, the moon behind a poplar tree, starry nights, sweet scents, and the language of Shakespeare—all these moved him deeply, the more perhaps because he had never learned to express his feelings. His attempts at literature indeed were strangely naïve and stilted; his verse, in the comic vein, rather good; but all, as it were, like his period, ashamed to express any intimate feeling except in classical language. Yet his literary tastes were catholic; Milton was his favourite poet, Byron he also admired; Browning he did not care for; his favourite novelist was George Eliot, and, curiously enough—in later life—Turgenev. I well remember when the translated volumes of that author were coming out, how he would ask for another of those yellow books. He did not know why he liked them, with all those 'crack-jaw' Russian names; but assuredly it was because they were written by one who worshipped beauty.

The works of Dickens and Thackeray he read with appreciation, on the whole, finding the first perhaps a little too grotesque, and the second a little too satiric. Scott, Trollope, Marryat, Blackmore, Hardy, and Mark Twain also pleased him; but Meredith he thought too 'misty.'

A great theatre-goer all his life, he was very lukewarm towards modern actors, comparing them adversely with those constellations of the past, Edmund and Charles Kean, Charlie Mathews, Farren, Power, 'little Robson,' and Helen Faucit. He was, however, a great lover of Kate Vaughan's dancing; an illustration of the equanimity of one who had formed his taste on Taglioni.

Irving he would only accept in *Louis XI.*, *The Bells*, and, I think, *Charles I.*, and for his mannerisms he had a great aversion. There was something of the old grand manner about his theatre habits. He attended with the very best and thinnest lavender kid gloves on his hands, which he would hold up rather high and clap together at the end of an act which pleased him; even, on memorable occasions, adding the word 'Bravo.' He never went out before the end of a play, however vehemently he might call it 'poor stuff,' which, to be quite honest, he did about nine times out of ten. And he was ever ready to try again, having a sort of touching confidence in an art which had betrayed him so often. His opera hats were notable, usually of such age as to have lost shape, and surely the largest in London. Indeed, his dress was less varied than that of any man I have ever seen; but always neat and well-cut, for he went habitually to the best shops, and without eccentricity of any kind. He carried a repeating gold watch and thin round gold chain which passed, smooth and sinuous as a little snake, through a small black seal with a bird on it; and he never abandoned very well made side-spring boots with cork soles, greatly resenting the way other boots dirtied his hands, which were thin and brown with long polished nails, and blue veins outstanding. For reading only, he wore tortoise-shell eyeglasses, which he would perch low down on the bridge of his nose, so that he could look over them, for his eyes were very long-sighted. He was extremely fastidious in his linen, and all personal matters, yet impatient of being mollycoddled, or in any way over-valeted. Even on the finest days, he carried an umbrella, the ferrule of which, from his habit of stumping it on the pavement, had a worn and harassed look, and was rarely more than half present.

Having been a Conservative Liberal in politics till well past sixty, it was not until Disraeli's time that he became a Liberal Conservative. This was curious, for he always spoke doubtfully of 'Dizzy,' and even breathed the word 'humbug' in connection with him. Probably he was offended by what he termed 'the extravagance' in Dizzy's rival. For the Duke of Devonshire and Lord Salisbury he had respect without enthusiasm; and conceived for John Bright a great admiration as soon as he was dead. But on the whole the politician who had most attracted him had been Palmerston, because—if memory serves—he had in such admirable degree the faculty of 'astonishing their weak nerves.' For, though never a Jingo, and in later days both cautious and sane in his Imperialism, he had all a Briton's essential deep-rooted distrust of the foreigner. He felt that they were not quite safe, not quite sound, and must from time to time be made to feel this. Born two years after the Battle of Waterloo, he had inherited a certain high pride of island birth. And yet in one case, where he was for years in close contact with a foreigner he conceived for him so grave a respect, that it was quite amusing to watch the discomfiture of his traditional distrust. It was often a matter of wonder amongst those who knew him that a man of his ability and judgment had never even sought to make his mark in public affairs. Of the several reasons for this, the chief was, undoubtedly, the extraordinary balance of his temperament. To attain pre-eminence in any definite department of life would have warped and stunted too many of his instincts, removed too many of his interests; and so he never specialised in anything. He was quite unambitious, always taking the lead in whatever field he happened to be, by virtue of his great capacity and will-power, but never pushing himself, and apparently without any life-aim, but that of leading a sane, moderate, and harmonious existence.

And it is for this that he remains written on the national page, as the type of a lost and golden time, when life to each man seemed worth living for its own sake, without thought of its meaning as a whole, or much speculation as to its end. There was something classical, measured, and mellow in his march adown the years, as if he had been god-mothered by Harmony. And yet, though he said his prayers and went to church, he could not fairly have

been called a religious man; for at the time when
he formed his religious habits, 'religion' had as
yet received no shocks, and reigned triumphant
over an unconscious nation whose spirit was
sleeping; and when 'religion,' disturbed to its
foundations, began to die, and people all round
him were just becoming religious enough to
renounce the beliefs they no longer held, he was
too old to change, and continued to employ the
mechanism of a creed which had never really
been vital to him. He was in essence pagan: All
was right with his world! His love was absorbed
by Nature, and his wonder by the Great Starry
Scheme he felt all around. This was God to
him; for it was ever in the presence of the stars
that he was most moved to a sense of divine
order. Looking up at those tremulous cold companions he seemed more reverent, and awed,
than ever he was in the face of creeds or his
fellow man. Whether stirred by the sheer beauty
of Night, or by its dark immensity swarming
with those glittering worlds, he would stand
silent, and then, perhaps, say wistfully: 'What
little bits of things we are! Poor little wretches!'
Yes, it was then that he really worshipped,
adoring the great wonders of Eternity. No one
ever heard him talk with conviction of a future
life. He was far too self-reliant to accept what he
was told, save by his own inner voice; and that
did not speak to him with certainty. In fact,
as he grew old, to be uncertain of all such high
things was part of his real religion; it seemed to
him, I think, impertinent to pretend to intimate
knowledge of what was so much bigger than

himself. But neither his conventional creed, nor that awed uncertainty which was his real religion were ever out of hand; they jogged smoothly on in double harness, driven and guided by a supremer power—his reverence for Life. He abhorred fanaticism. In this he truly mirrored the spirit of that great peacefully expanding river, the Victorian Era, which began when he came of age. And yet, in speaking before him of deep or abstract things, it was not safe to reckon without his criticism, which would sometimes make powerfully shrewd deductions out of the sheer logical insight of a nature neither fundamentally concerned with other worlds, nor brought up to the ways of discussion. He was pre-eminently the son of a time between two ages—a past age of old, unquestioning faith in Authority; a future age of new faith, already born but not yet grown. Still sheltering in the shade of the old tree which was severed at the roots and toppling, he never, I think, clearly saw—though he may have had glimpses—that men, like children whose mother has departed from their home, were slowly being forced to trust in, and be good to, themselves and to one another, and so to form out of their necessity, desperately, unconsciously, their new great belief in Humanity. Yes, he was the son of *a time between two ages*—the product of an era without real faith—an individualist to the core.

His attitude towards the poor, for instance, was essentially that of man to man. Save that he could not tolerate impostors (one of his favourite words), and saw through them with almost startling rapidity, he was compassionate to any who had fallen on evil fortune, and especially to those who had been in any way connected with him. But in these almonary transactions he was always particularly secretive, as if rather doubting their sagacity, and the wisdom of allowing them to become known—himself making up and despatching the parcels of old clothes, and rather surreptitiously producing such coins and writing such cheques as were necessary. But 'the poor,' in bulk, were always to him the concern of the Poor Law pure and simple, and in no sense of the individual citizen. It was the same with malefactors, he might pity as well as condemn them, but the idea that the society to which he and they belonged was in any way responsible for them, would never have occurred to him. His sense of justice, like that of his period, was fundamentally based on the notion that every man had started with equal, or at all events, with quite sufficient opportunities, and must be judged as if he had. But, indeed, it was not the custom in his day to concern oneself with problems outside one's own class. Within that class, and in all matters domestic, no man was ever born with a nicer sense of justice. It was never overridden by his affections; very seldom, and that with a certain charming *naïveté*, by his interests. This sense of justice, however, in no way prevented him from being loved; for, in spite of a temper apt to take fire, flare up, and quickly die down again, he was one of the most loveable of men. There was not an ounce of dourness or asperity in his composition. His laughter was of a most infectious kind, singularly spontaneous and delightful, resembling the laughter of a child. The change which a joke wrought in the aspect of his large, dignified, and rather noble face, was disconcerting. It became wrinkled, or, as it were, crumpled; and such a twinkling overcame his eyes as was frequently only to be extinguished by moisture. 'That's rich!' was his favourite expression to describe what had tickled him; for he had preserved the use of Devonshire expressions, bringing them forth, from an intimate pet drawer of memory, and lingering over them with real gusto. He still loved, too, such Devonshire dishes of his boyhood, as 'junket' and 'toad in the hole'; and one of his favourite memories was that of the meals snatched at the old coaching Inn at Exeter, while they changed the horses of the Plymouth to the London coach. Twenty-four hours at ten miles an hour, without ever a break! Glorious drive! Glorious the joints of beef, the cherry brandy! Glorious the old stage coachman, a 'monstrous fat chap' who at that time ruled the road!

In the city, where his office was situate, he was wont, though at all times a very moderate eater, to frequent substantial, old-fashioned hostelries such as Roche's, Pim's, or Birch's, in preference to newer and more pretentious places of refreshment. He had a remarkable palate too, and though he drank very little, was, in his prime, considered as fine a judge of wine as any in London. Of tea he was particularly fond, and always consumed the very best Indian, made with extreme care, maintaining that the Chinese variety was only fit for persons of no taste.

He had little liking for his profession, believing it to be beneath him, and that Heaven had intended him for an advocate; in which he was probably right, for his masterful acumen could not have failed to assure him a foremost position at the Bar. And in him, I think, it is certain that a great Judge was lost to the State. Despite this contempt for what he called the 'pettifogging' character of his occupation, he always inspired profound respect in his clients; and among the shareholders of his Companies, of which he directed several, his integrity and judgment stood so high that he was enabled to pursue successfully a line of policy often too comprehensive, and far-seeing for the temper of the times. The reposeful dignity, and courage, of his head and figure when facing an awkward General Meeting could hardly have been exceeded. He sat, as it were, remote from its gusty temper, quietly determining its course.

Truly memorable were his conflicts with the only other man of his calibre on those Boards, and I cannot remember that he was ever beaten. He was at once the quicker tempered and more cautious. And if he had not the other's stoicism and iron nerve, he saw further into the matter in hand, was more unremitting in his effort, equally tenacious of purpose, and more magnetic. In fact, he had a way with him.

But, after all said, it was in his dealings with children that the best and sweetest side of his personality was manifested. With them he became completely tender, inexhaustibly interested in their interests, absurdly patient, and as careful as a mother. No child ever resisted him, or even dreamed of doing so. From the first moment they loved his white hair and beard, his 'feathers' as one little thing called them. They liked the touch of his thin hand, which was never wet or cold; and, holding to it, were always ready to walk with him—wandering with complete unanimity, not knowing quite where or for what reason. How often have I not watched him starting out on that high adventure with his grandson, his face turned gravely down towards a smaller face turned not quite so gravely up; and heard their voices tremendously concerned with all the things they might be going to do together! How often have I not seen them coming back, tired as cats, but still concerned about what was next going to happen! And children were always willing to play cricket with him because he bowled to them very slowly, pitching up what he called 'three-quarter' balls, and himself always getting 'out' almost before he went in. For, although he became in his later years a great connoisseur of cricket, spending many days at Lord's or the Oval, choosing out play of the very highest class, and quite impatient of the Eton and Harrow Match, he still performed in a somewhat rococo fashion, as of a man taught in the late twenties of the last century, and having occasion to revive that knowledge about 1895. He bent his back knee, and played with a perfectly crooked bat, to the end that when he did hit the ball, which was

not too often, it invariably climbed the air.
There was, too, about his batting, a certain
vein of recklessness or bravado, somewhat out of
keeping with his general character, so that, as
has been said, he was never in too long. And
when he got out he would pitch the bat down
as if he were annoyed, which would hugely
please his grandson, showing of course that he
had been trying his very best, as indeed, he
generally had. But his bowling was extremely
impressive, being effected with very bent knees,
and a general air of first putting the ball to the
eye, as if he were playing bowls; in this way he
would go on and on giving the boy 'an innings,'
and getting much too hot. In fielding he never
could remember on the spur of the moment
whether it was his knees or his feet that he ought
to close; and this, in combination with a habit
of bending rather cautiously, because he was
liable to lumbago, detracted somewhat from
his brilliance; but when the ball was once in
his hands, it was most exciting—impossible to
tell whether he would throw it at the running
batsman, the wicket, or the bowler, according as
the game appeared to him at the moment to be
double wicket, single wicket, or rounders. He
had lived in days when games were not the
be-all and end-all of existence, and had never
acquired a proper seriousness in such matters.
Those who passed from cricket with him to
cricket in the cold wide world found a change
for which at first they were unable to account.
But even more fascinating to children than his
way of playing cricket was his perfect identifica-

tion with whatever might be the matter in hand. The examination of a shell, the listening to the voice of the sea imprisoned in it, the making of a cocked hat out of the *Times* newspaper, the doing up of little buttons, the feeding of pigeons with crumbs, the holding fast of a tiny leg while walking beside a pony, all these things absorbed him completely, so that no visible trace was left of the man whose judgment on affairs was admirable and profound. Nor, whatever the provocation, could he ever bring himself to point the moral of anything to a child, having that utter toleration of their foibles which only comes from a natural and perfectly unconscious love of being with them. His face, habitually tranquil, wore in their presence a mellow look of almost devil-may-care serenity.

Their sayings, too, he treasured, as though they were pearls. First poems, such as:

> I sorr a worm,
> It was half-ly dead;
> I took a great spud,
> And speared through his head

were to him of singular fair promise. Their diagnoses of character, moreover, especially after visiting a circus, filled him with pure rapture, and he would frequently repeat this one:

'Father, is Uncle a clever man?'

'H'm! well—yes, certainly.'

'I never seen no specimens. He can't balance a pole on his nose, for instance.'

To the declining benison of their prayers, from their 'darling father and mother,' to 'all poor people who are in distress,' he loved to listen, not so much for the sentiments expressed, as because, in their little nightgowns, they looked so sweet, and were so roundabout in their way of getting to work.

Yes, children were of all living things his chosen friends, and they knew it.

But in his long life he made singularly few fast friendships with grown-up people, and, as far as I know, no enemies. For there was in him, despite his geniality, a very strong vein of fastidiousness, and such essential deep love of domination, that he found, perhaps, few men of his own age and standing to whom he did not feel natively superior. His most real and lifelong friendship was for a certain very big man with a profound hatred of humbug and a streak of 'the desperate character' in him. They held each other in the highest esteem, or, as they would probably have put it, swore by one another; the one grumbling at, but reverencing, the other's high and resolute equanimity; the other deploring and admiring the one's deep and generous recklessness. The expressions: 'Just like John, the careful fellow!' 'Just like Sil, reckless beggar!' were always on their lips; for like all their generation they were sparing of encomium; and great, indeed, must have been their emotion before they would show their feelings. Dear as they were to each other's hearts, they never talked together of spiritual things, they never spoke in generalities, but gravely smoking their cigars, discussed their acquaintances, investments, wine, their nephews and grandchildren, and the affairs of the State—

condemning the advertising fashion in which everything was now done. Once in a way they would tell a story—but they knew each other's stories too well; once in a way quote a line of Byron, Shakespeare, or Milton; or whistle to each other, inharmoniously, a bar or two from some song that Grisi, Mario, or Jenny Lind had sung. Once in a way memories of the heyday of their youth, those far-off golden hours, stealing over them, they would sit silent, with their grave steady eyes following the little rings of bluish smoke. . . . Yes, for all their lack of demonstration, they loved each other well.

I seem still to see the subject of this portrait standing at his friend's funeral one bleak November day, the pale autumn sunlight falling on the silver of his uncovered head a little bowed, and on his grave face, for once so sad. I hear the tones of his voice, still full and steady; and from the soul of his eyes, looking, as it were, through and through those forms of death to some deep conclusion of his own, I know how big and sane and sweet he was.

His breed is dying now, it has nearly gone. But as I remember him with that great quiet forehead, with his tenderness, and his glance which travelled to the heart of what it rested on, I despair of seeing his like again. For, with him there seems to me to have passed away a principle, a golden rule of life, nay, more, a spirit—the soul of Balance. It has stolen away, as in the early morning the stars steal out of the sky. *He* knew its tranquil secret, and where he is, there must it still be hovering.

G. S. Street

1867–1936

FOG

An acquaintance has kindly informed me that there is in these scribblings of mine too much introspection, meditation, reflection. 'Go out,' quoth he, 'into the beautiful world, and write down what you see there.' I think he is wrong. There is far too much description done as it is. It is easy to go to a place and easy to write a sort of cataloguing description when one goes. Fitly to describe any visible thing whatever is the work of an artist, I question not. But artists are few and easy work is tempting: it seems well to me that some of us scribblers should sit at home and think. The result may not be magnificent, but there is sufficient rarity in the exercise to give it a sort of an odd flavour which may not be so dull to everybody as to my acquaintance. I always follow advice, however, and so, having received this, I took my hat and went out into the beautiful world, with the intention—but it really is a base intention—of writing down what I saw there.

Unfortunately there was a thick fog. Now the cultivated reader is assured, of course, that a London fog is a beautiful thing. But the only writing Londoner who has never described one may as well cling to this negative distinction.

Besides, I doubt my æsthetic quality is old-fashioned. Curious, weird, interesting, I perceive a London fog to be: its beauty something eludes my gross vision. A mist, or a light fog, when one can see forty yards about one, has a fugitive fantastic charm, but so has not a dense and isolating vapour. I could write, with feeling and gratitude at least, of the beauty I saw at dusk, all last week, in the trees and distances of Hyde Park and Kensington Gardens. The lonely grace of the winter trees, their bare tracery, unspeakably delicate, clear against a purple or violet haze in the sky, and the pretty fairyland where the yellow lamps made spots of colour—all this was beauty wonderful and magical, and I blessed my lot for once that I could go and gaze on it day by day. Immediately thereafter to perceive that masses of dirty vapour had their beauty also was too swift a turn for my senses. So I will let the description alone. After all, it has been claimed for a fog that it is a blessing to men of letters, because it forces them in upon themselves, and this fog drove me once more to reflection, since it is fated I should disappoint my acquaintance.

Beauty or none, there is much to be said for a London fog. It gives us all that 'change' which we are always needing. When our world is all but invisible, and growing visible bit by bit looks utterly different from its accustomed self, the stupidest of us all can hardly fail to observe a change for our eyes at least as great as there would have been in going to Glasgow. When, arriving at one's house or one's club, that

monotonous diurnal incident seems an almost
incredible feat, accomplished with profound relief
and gratitude for a safe deliverance, one has at
least an unaccustomed sensation. One is not a
man going into his club, but a mariner saved from
shipwreck at the last gasp, to be greeted with
emotion by erst indifferent waiters. Yes, a fog
gives Londoners a more thorough change than
going to the Riviera to avoid it. Then it brings
out the kindness and cheerfulness, which are
their prime claim to honour, into strong relief.
True, it also throws into relief the incomparable
egoism of the prosperous among them. People
with no serious cares or worries in the world of
course bemoan and upbraid this trifling inconvenience. But the working, struggling Londoners, cabmen and 'busmen, you and I, display
our indomitable good-humour to advantage.
I stayed on top of a 'bus for half an hour in the
block on Monday at Hyde Park Corner and
talked with the driver. People are often disappointed in a 'bus-driver because they expect
a wit and a pretty swearer. They find neither,
but they find an overworked man of extraordinary cheerfulness, responsive, ready to
laugh. He is master of his business—a fact
emphasised by the fog—to a degree refreshing
to one whose experience of men professing some
practical calling is that the great majority, some
from mere stupidity, some from over-hasty
enthusiasm, are quite incompetent. When
finally I left him, his mate piloted me through
wheels and horses to the pavement, and I felt
I had been among folk who deserve to live. On

Sunday night I walked a mile to my abode, and made a point of asking my whereabouts of every one I met. Not one churlish or even hurried answer: politeness, jokes, reminiscences, laughter. We are a kindly people, and it is worth a fog to know it. Another pleasure of a fog is a mild but extended form of the pleasure we feel when we hear that a millionaire has broken his leg. The too fortunate are suffering a discontent health cannot remove. There was in that block a fat brougham containing an important-looking old man who foamed at the mouth, and one reflected that there was a temporary equality of fortunes.

Such are the pleasures we may take in a London fog. It has also a chastening lesson for us, being a regularly recurring proof that we are not yet civilised enough in the main to make any sacrifice for the public good uncompelled. We shall not provide the right kind of grate until there is a penalty for not doing so. Each citizen will argue that the cost is certain and the benefit, unless the others do the same, as he is sure they will not, insignificant. It is an allegory of more vital matters. The cave-man is strong in us yet. Let us humble ourselves. But if we are not intelligent enough to abolish fogs, let us be at least sophisticated enough to enjoy them.

PICCADILLY

Though I be fair as a powdered peruke,
    And once was a gaping silly,
Your Whitechapel Countess will prove, Lord Duke,
    She's a regular tiger lily:
She'll fight you with cold steel and she'll run you off
    your legs
    Down the length of Piccadilly.

Yes, there was a time when exciting things happened in Piccadilly, but one has to go for them, as Mr. Meredith has gone,[1] at least to the first quarter of the century. Nowadays the eyes of the nation are not fixed on a handful of social heroes and heroines, so that even were a discarded wife to chase her false fleeting lord along the edge of the Green Park few people would hear of the event, in spite of our wonderful Press. But I doubt if anything of interest, reported or not, ever happens now in Piccadilly. If our manners are less elaborate than our ancestors' were, we are certainly more self-contained. Few people 'let themselves go' anywhere, least of all in a public thoroughfare: the exceptions are controlled by the police. And I fancy the habit of interested sauntering has declined; we hurry from one stupid occasion to another in cabs and omnibuses, and we lose our acquaintances in the crowd. Our reminiscences will contain but few remarkable encounters in the street.

All the same, there is still a significance in Piccadilly. That is to say, from Bond Street to Hyde Park Corner: from Bond Street eastwards

[1] [In *The Amazing Marriage*.]

to the Circus there is no significance at all, merely shops and an obstructive flow of vacuous humanity. But walk from Bond Street westwards on a fine day about half-past twelve in the morning, and as you go down the slope you feel that you are in the spacious middle of social London, in the part of it that means Town—as Mr. Kipling sings to his banjo—to men who have known Town, when they hear the word in Australia or on the Niger. And that is the part that attracts them when they return. Some house in the country is dearer, perhaps, but they feel that they are back in Town when they walk down the slope of Piccadilly. Their minds may contain little of the social memories of the place: they may not think of the Duke in his duck trousers or of 'old Q' in his unrepentant age, but there, if anywhere, Town stirs in their blood.

I do not think it can be a merely personal and individual pleasure that comes to me when on a fine morning I look down Piccadilly from the top of the slope. I have observed it often in others, and I always fancy that people look brighter, with a blander eye on the world, here than elsewhere in London. For myself, I am conscious of a sort of ludicrous increase of importance, as though here one were less of an ant on an anthill and more of a necessary screw in the machine. I feel almost as one having a definite and not despicable place in the community, who can hold up his head and meet the world with a smile, not dodge it round a corner. Perhaps it is that one's mind unconsciously surveys its

memories of those who have strolled down
Piccadilly,—not only those whose achievements
or fortune have been infinitely greater, but those
who have come to infinitely worse grief; and it
unconsciously reminds itself that the descent is
not altogether completed. Some have so walked
down Piccadilly and continued their walking
till they did it on tottering but honoured feet:
others have walked down Piccadilly and walked
away into some unknown Inferno. I will not
trouble you with the associations of this or that
house: perhaps they too add to one's importance,
as one feels solemn in a graveyard.

There are folk who have no right in Piccadilly
of a morning. Those whose interests are com-
prised in their money gains and losses; those
whose clothes, whether old or new, are worn
uneasily; those who stare and scowl at their
neighbours, and those who cannot dissimulate
their success in life,—all these profane ones are
requested to absent themselves. In the afternoon let them return: regretfully then I abandon
Piccadilly to the plutocrat; by all means let him
arrive there from the City and stare at his kith
and kin in the crawling carriages. In the morning it is for amiable people, who saunter idly or
march with a brisk swing, people affable with
their eyes, who assume that those they meet are
their brothers and enjoy, they also, a pleasant
outlook on life, free from fret and snobbery and
every baseness. Let them sniff the morning air
and take the town as a natural place, and forget
its gorging gold and suffocated millions.

All this of fine mornings in general, and

especially of the early spring, before London is used up and all men's faces are grown pale with too effectual pleasures. In the afternoon, as I said, the place is different. Something fœtid has descended in the air, the red sheen is gone from the omnibuses, the idle saunter is exchanged for the painful crawl, and the brisk swing for the blatant swagger; the baser racial instincts have come atop.

In the evenings there is a new enchantment. But unless you be a triple-brass philosopher, to enjoy it you must drive; walking you find the national superiority in morals a little too disagreeable. But drive, drive up Piccadilly this time, not down, and observe the lines of lamps in the darkness, the one line by the seemly houses, the other by the black trees. Do they not suggest to you something vaguely, but pervadingly romantic?

In the morning there was the feeling of what social charm and interest there may be in a town; at night there is the feeling of its possibilities of adventure. It is, of course, quite a different romance from that of grey moors and distant lights in old windows: this romance is gay in its quality, even feverish. You may be driving home from a quiet dinner-party, to go quietly to bed; but do you not find a romance in this line of lamps leading into the heart of the town, where life, you imagine for a moment, is at some heat of interest? There it lies before you, multitudes of human things with hearts and fancies, countless abodes of mystery. You lean back and continue your course, without a regret, to your peaceful and respectable dwelling-place, but for a moment there was the sense of romance, a faint wave against your brain of the blood that craves adventure. A fleeting fancy: as I write it is gone: words do but riddle it. As you draw into the closer traffic, romance has flown, the closer sight of your fellow-creatures, unless you be very young, has killed it. Perhaps it was not a very edifying thing while it was with you. But nowhere else in London, as in Piccadilly by night, shall you feel it. And for it, as for my morning's stroll down the slope, do I count Piccadilly precious beyond words.

COCKNEY HUMOUR

So far I have dealt with places.[1] I must allow myself one less concrete subject, and end my unworthy appreciation of the town I live in by doing it, if I may, one slight service.

A gross injustice is done to London in the conceptions which most people hold of Cockney humour. Any vulgar joke you please is referred to this source, any writer of professedly funny books who happens to be without taste and education is called a Cockney humorist. This is very stupid, for Cockney humour, whether excellent in its average or not, is certainly distinctive, and it has nothing to do with vulgarity as such, nothing with the feebly forced jocosity of the writers to whom I have referred.

This jocosity, indeed, falsely and inconveniently called Cockney, may be usefully observed for a moment by way of contrast to the true

[1] [In a series of essays on London.]

Cockney humour. I trust that you will understand the sort of jocosity in books and journals to which I refer: I am too cowardly to name the books or the writers. It can lay no claim to being Cockney; it is not local in its nature, its producers are not necessarily Londoners; and its appreciators are the possessors of slow wits and vulgar tastes all over the country. Its local adjective is therefore misleading and unjust, and is to be from this moment abandoned. Conventional jocosity, like conventional sentimentalism, comes of fatness and idleness. It is essentially a quality of the comfortable classes, an excrescence of excessive materialism and want of mental exercise. It supplies the occasions of those whose minds move slowly and will not be stirred, but whose idle sides crave to be shaken. It is conventional therefore, and deals in stock and largely labelled figures, such as mothers-in-law and 'swells' with eye-glasses. It is always behind the times in the manners it depicts, for its patrons have been fed on a long tradition of it and must not be expected to use their eyes. It tends to an unthinking and unmanly brutality, gibing at old maids and women who have lost their looks—a brutality to which one notes with sorrow that one of the few real humorists of our times has committed himself. Its assumptions are all the old middle class ideas, the unquestioning acceptance of wealth as superiority, the contempt of art, and so forth. I do not wish to indict everybody who is amused by it, for we all must laugh, and good causes of laughter are not always known and accessible.

But it is essentially the amusement of stupid, clumsy, and unexercised minds. I protest with all the little vigour I have that its confusion with Cockney humour is abominable.

By Cockney humour I mean roughly the humour of London streets and public-houses. This I take to be distinctive: it is not understood in its fulness outside London, even by those of the same class and habits as the Londoners who produce and relish it. By 'produce' I mean invent and shout from the box-seat of an omnibus or from the press round the bar, for it seldom if ever finds its way into print. These Londoners live lives that are tolerably strenuous, always precarious, and often necessitous. Their minds do not run to fatness. Sentimentalism appeals to them only as following on beer or gin in a playhouse gallery, and is not then of a pernicious type; their sorrows are mostly connected with police-courts. They are the lower classes of London, and if they are not, as it has been somewhat dubiously said of the middle classes, the back-bone of the country, I claim for them at least that their wits, such as they may be, are in tolerably active exercise. Their humour is not conventional; it is fresh, and it lives. I do not mean that it is always first-rate—it is generally, no doubt, pretty poor in quality; but it is humour, and suits the moment: it is not a stereotyped and conventional pretence of it. It is coarse, to be sure, if you object to that. A vice of false refinement is to mistake coarseness for vulgarity, and to be offended by certain substantives and adjectives. If that is your unfortunate case, you cannot enjoy real Cockney humour. In fact, I am afraid that to savour it rightly you must be not only not prudish, but familiar enough with certain words of coarseness not to be surprised or preoccupied by them; you must remember that these words are in constant use by the folk you are observing, and must not overrate their force or importance. To omit the words is to miss the atmosphere. In some of Mr. Kipling's soldier ballads it is necessary for a right effect, to replace certain words for which he gives you tokens. They are quite harmless to the intelligent and genuinely refined. So in a Cockney story one must keep to its natural diction.

The most remarkable characteristic of Cockney humour is that it is absolutely unscrupulous. It has no reservations. Everything which comes within its horizon is a subject, an occasion, for jest. Now that—like it or dislike it—is a distinction. You do not find it in modern literature. And I am reminded that Cockney humour hardly comes into literature at all. The spirit of good Dr. Bowdler has kept it out. Dickens, who might have used it, refrained, for if you mention Sam Weller I reply that he had next to no humour at all—adding breathlessly, to keep my head from Dickens' worshippers, that Sam Weller was a wit. He had wit, certainly, and gave us a store of witticisms, but he had not humour. Also, Sam was not distinctively Cockney: his pronunciation, of the Borough it may have been, and as it exists in parts of contemporary Essex, was hardly Cockney at all. I have sometimes

met with a fragment of Cockney humour in the
Sporting Times—a departed contributor of that
paper observed or invented it with genius. But
with that exception I have not seen it reported.
There follows in the distinguished absence of
scruple the quality of brutality. But it is a
different thing from the mean and conventional
brutality I was reviling lately. It does not laugh
at old women as a matter of course. It consists
merely in ignoring the horrible or tragic side of
a funny situation. Everybody knows the old
story of the Cockney laughing after a fire.
' "Jump, yer silly fool," I says, "me and my
mite 's got a blanket!" An 'e did jump, and there
warn't no blanket, and 'e broke 'is —— neck.
Laugh? I 'aven't laughed so much,' etc. A
thousand apologies if the old story jars on your
refinement. But I maintain that the contrast of
expectation and the event is really humorous,
and the brutality which can laugh is surely
innocent. One finds such a brutality in Ro-
chester, who was a sort of aristocratic blackguard Cockney of genius.

Cockney humour is always ready, and in a
generation which is said to lack amusing talkers
its repartee should be cherished. As a rule they
are not exactly witty, they are too bald in form
for that, but they embody roughly a humorous
grasp of situations. I will not give you instances,
disliking to shirk the faithful record of my
memory, and being afraid you may think me
very vulgar as it is. To find them you must go
your ways among cabmen in their shelters, and
omnibus men, and flower-girls, and other people.

Cockney humour seems to have almost disappeared from the music halls; the last inspired exponent of it I remember was Bessie Bellwood. One meets it, of course, among people who are not Cockney nor lower class. The thoroughly dissipated young rake who has a humorous turn is much akin in his freer talk to the true Cockney humorist. One wonders if the quality will ever make a masterpiece of a book. Serious, long-faced realism is allowed a fairly free hand: one wonders if realism will ever be allowed to laugh, and humours of unscrupulous thoughts and unshackled tongues to come to their own again in our literature, as they partly came two centuries ago. Probably not.

A. Clutton-Brock

1868–1924

SUNDAY BEFORE THE WAR

On Sunday, in a remote valley in the West of England, where the people are few and scattered and placid, there was no more sign among them than among the quiet hills of the anxiety that holds the world. They had no news and seemed to want none. The postmaster had been ordered to stay all day in his little post-office, and that was something unusual that interested them, but only because it affected the postmaster.

It rained in the morning, but the afternoon was clear and glorious and shining, with all the distances revealed far into the heart of Wales and to the high ridges of the Welsh mountains. The cottages of that valley are not gathered into villages, but two or three together or lonely among their fruit-trees on the hillside; and the cottagers, who are always courteous and friendly, said a word or two as one went by, but just what they would have said on any other day and without any question about the war. Indeed, they seemed to know, or to wish to know, as little about that as the earth itself, which, beautiful there at any time, seemed that afternoon to wear an extreme and pathetic beauty. The country, more than any other in England, has the secret of peace. It is not wild, though it looks into the wildness of Wales; but all its cultivation, its orchards and hopyards and fields of golden wheat, seem to have the beauty of time upon them, as if men there had long lived happily upon the earth with no desire for change nor fear of decay. It is not the sad beauty of a past cut off from the present, but a mellowness that the present inherits from the past; and in the mellowness all the hillside seems a garden to the spacious farmhouses and the little cottages; each led up to by its own narrow, flowery lane. There the meadows are all lawns with the lustrous green of spring even in August, and often over-shadowed by old fruit-trees—cherry, or apple, or pear; and on Sunday after the rain there was an April glory and freshness added to the quiet of the later summer.

Nowhere and never in the world can there have been a deeper peace; and the bells from the little red church down by the river seemed to be the music of it, as the song of birds is the music of spring. There one saw how beautiful the life of man can be, and how men by the innocent labours of many generations can give to the earth a beauty it has never known in its wildness. And all this peace, one knew, was threatened; and the threat came into one's mind as if it were a soundless message from over the great eastward plain; and with it the beauty seemed unsubstantial and strange, as if it were sinking away into the past, as if it were only a memory of childhood.

So it is always when the mind is troubled among happy things, and then one almost wishes they could share one's troubles and become more real with it. It seemed on that Sunday that a golden age had lasted till yesterday, and that the earth had still to learn the news of its ending. And this change had come, not by the will of God, not even by the will of man, but because some few men far away were afraid to be open and generous with each other. There was a power in their hands so great that it frightened them. There was a spring that they knew they must not touch, and, like mischievous and nervous children, they had touched it at last, and now all the world was to suffer for their mischief.

So the next morning one saw a reservist in his uniform saying goodbye to his wife and children at his cottage-gate and then walking up the hill that leads out of the valley with a cheerful smile still on his face. There was the first open sign of trouble, a very little one, and he made the least of it; and, after all, this valley is very far from any possible war, and its harvest and its vintage of perry and cider will surely be gathered in peace.

But what happiness can there be in that peace, or what security in the mind of man, when the madness of war is let loose in so many other valleys? Here there is a beauty inherited from the past, and added to the earth by man's will; but the men here are of the same nature and subject to the same madness as those who are gathering to fight on the frontiers. We are all men with the same power of making and destroying, with the same divine foresight mocked by the same animal blindness. We ourselves may not be in fault to-day, but it is human beings in no way different from us who are doing what we abhor and they abhor even while they do it. There is a fate, coming from the beast in our own past, that the present man in us has not yet mastered, and for the moment that fate seems a malignity in the nature of the universe that mocks us even in the beauty of these lonely hills. But it is not so, for we are not separate and indifferent like the beasts; and if one nation for the moment forgets our common humanity and its future, then another must take over that sacred charge and guard it without hatred or fear until the madness is passed. May that be our task now, so that we may wage war only for the future peace of the world and with the lasting courage that needs no stimulant of hate.

ON FRIENDSHIP

FRIENDSHIP is above reason, for, though you find virtues in a friend, he was your friend before you found them. It is a gift that we offer because we must; to give it as the reward of virtue would be to set a price upon it, and those who do that have no friendship to give. If you choose your friends on the ground that you are virtuous and want virtuous company, you are no nearer to true friendship than if you choose them for commercial reasons. Besides, who are you that you should be setting a price upon your friendship? It is enough for any man that he has the divine power of making friends, and he must leave it to that power to determine who his friends shall be. For, though you may choose the virtuous to be your friends, they may not choose you; indeed, friendship cannot grow where there is any calculated choice. It comes, like sleep, when you are not thinking about it; and you should be grateful, without any misgiving, when it comes.

So no man who knows what friendship is ever gave up a friend because he turns out to be disreputable. His only reason for giving up a friend is that he has ceased to care for him; and, when that happens, he should reproach himself for this mortal poverty of affection, not the friend for having proved unworthy. For it is inhuman presumption to say of any man that he is unworthy of your friendship, just as it is to say of any woman, when you have fallen out of love with her, that she is unworthy of your love. In friendship and in love we are always humble, because we see that a free gift has been given to us; and to lose that humility because we have lost friendship or love is to take a pride in what should shame us.

We have our judgments and our penalties as part of the political mechanism that is forced upon us so that we may continue to live; but friendship is not friendship at all unless it teaches us that these are not part of our real life. They have to be; and we pay men, and clothe them in wigs and scarlet, to sit in judgment on other men. So we are tempted to play this game of judgment ourselves, even though no one has paid us to do it. It is only in the warmth of friendship that we see how cold a thing it is to judge and how stupid to take a pleasure in judging; for we recognise this warmth as a positive good, a richness in our natures, while the coldness that sets us judging is a poverty. Just as our criticism of a work of art begins only when we have ceased to experience it, so our criticism of our friends begins only when we have ceased to experience them, when our minds can no longer remain at the height of intimacy. But this criticism is harmless if we know it for what it is, merely the natural reaction, the cold fit that comes after the warm, and if we do not suppose that our coldness is wiser than our warmth.

There are men who cannot be friends except when they are under an illusion that their friends are perfect, and when the illusion passes there is an end of their friendship. But true friendship has no illusions, for it reaches to that part of a man's nature that is beyond his imperfections, and in doing so it takes all of them for granted. It does not even assume that he is better than other men, for there is egotism in assuming that. A man is your friend, not because of his superiorities, but because there is something open from your nature to his, a way that is closed between you and most men. You and he understand each other, as the phrase is; your relation with him is a rare success among a multitude of failures, and if you are proud of the success you should be ashamed of the failure.

There is nothing so fatal to friendship as this egotism of accounting for it by some superiority in the friend. If you do that you will become a member of a set, all, in their assertion of each others' merits, implying their own, and all uneasy lest they are giving more than they get. For if you insist upon the virtues of your friend, you expect him to insist upon your virtues, and there is a competition between you which makes friendship a burden rather than a rest. Criticism then becomes a treachery, for it implies that you are beginning to doubt those superiorities upon which your friendship is supposed to be based. But when no superiorities are assumed, criticism is only the exercise of a natural curiosity. It is because a man is your friend, and you like him so much and know him so well, that you are curious about him. You are in fact an expert upon him, and like to show your expert knowledge. And you are an expert because in the warmth of friendship his disguises melt away from him, and he shows himself to you just as he is. Indeed, that is the test of friendship and the delight of it, that because we are no longer afraid of being thought worse than we are we do not try to seem better. We know that it is not our virtues that have won us friendship, and we do not fear to lose it through our vices. We have reached that blessed state of being nearer to heaven than anything else in this life, in which affection does not depend upon judgment; and we are like gods, who have no need even to forgive, because they know. It is a rare state, and never attained to in its perfection. We can approach it only if we know what friendship is and really desire it, and especially if we admire the man who is a friend without ever wondering at his choice of friends or blaming him for his faithfulness to them whatever evil they may do.

E. V. Lucas

1868–1938

VILLE D'AVRAY

'When next you are in Paris,' said a lady at dinner, 'be sure to go to Cabassud's. For lunch. It is a delicious place.'

'Cabassud's?'

'Yes. At Ville d'Avray. You sit and eat in little arbours.'

And at once there floated through my mind a single detached line from one of the *Proverbs in Porcelain*—

April, Ville d'Avray, Ma'amselle Rose,

—the only line I have retained.

That was months ago, but I remembered the name, and when I was next in Paris I went out to the little courtly village of white houses and chestnut trees, bent not only on finding Cabassud but also the Corot monument, for it was at Ville d'Avray that Corot lived.

As it happens, Corot and Cabassud are side by side, on the edge of a little *étang*: one of the two *étangs*—the other is across the road—which he painted so often, again and again, under different effects of light, all his life. His admirers may think of him as searching France for these placid meres in which the sky is reflected so tenderly and with such lustre; but they are wrong. The frugal old boy, frugal only to be kind, knew a trick worth two of that. All he did was to leave his house, a few steps away, and find his subjects here, within reach of lunch at home; and it is fitting that his fine great head, benign and simple, in stone, set up in homage by many friends, should be here, so near the water and the reeds that he loved; fitting also that in the decorative border above it should be a lark singing, for it was as a lark that, in a famous passage, Corot once symbolised himself: a lark singing his little songs in a quiet sky, in contra-distinction to some contemporary—I forget which one—who was an eagle. Delacroix probably.

Whether any other artists are painting at Ville d'Avray to-day I cannot say; but I can say that a certain craftsman in clay has made it his home, for, greatly daring, I pushed open the unlatched door of his studio, under the impression that it might be a house to let (looking over houses to let being an amusement that never palls), and there I found arrays of exquisitely shaped little vases and bowls in soft neutral hues, and two or three potter's wheels, and vessels containing liquid of every colour of the prism. The potter himself was absent, and it was perhaps just as well; for I have no French to explain trespass in.

I heard afterwards, from one of Cabassud's friendly waiters, that he was a Russian refugee. Should by any chance these words meet his eyes, I hope he will accept my apology. 'Gently, potter, gently, pray.'

A few minutes later I had another thrill—for this was a red-letter day indeed.

It is curious how seldom, even if one haunts rivers for the purpose, one sees a kingfisher: I mean those of us who want to see them, who think there is no bird more exciting. Others see them often. I have a friend who composes music in a little summer house beside the Thames, and one Sunday morning while he was at work a kingfisher flew into the room, and in attempting to fly out again crashed against the window, so that the musician had to nurse it back to consciousness. But I doubt if he really valued the privilege; I think he looked upon it as an interruption. Another friend of mine, a biologist, complained that a kingfisher had swooped on his little pool of goldfish and carried them off. Complained! And the rural postman once told me where young kingfishers could be seen every morning at play—half a dozen of them—but his voice had no emotion in it as he told me, his eyes were dry, and when I went to the place there were none. Nor were there any when, recently, I walked beside the Test at Stockbridge, or beside the Avon at Fordingbridge, or beside the Itchen at Winchester.

It began to seem, indeed, as if none but the unadventurous achieved the fair, until at Ville d'Avray, as I stood between the two lakes, a kingfisher flashed by, my first for years. Only for a moment. It flashed across my vision for only a moment—burning, beautiful—and was gone; but I had seen it.

And Cabassud's?

Why is it that in France eating in the open air is a refined art, while in England it is almost always repulsive? Think of the horrors of restaurants that cater for day trippers here, and then contrast them with the comfort and distinction of Cabassud's, where one sits and eats in arbours, just as my informant had said, and everything is clean and comely and efficient. Although it was as late as October, there was a huge dish of *fraises de bois*, and a huge dish of *framboises*, with concomitant cream, enough for every one. And the service was quick. And all the while I was eating I was peering through the trees for another glimpse of darting blue, but it never came. Next spring, if I get to Paris, I shall go to Cabassud's again, full of new hope, and I advise every sojourner in the French capital to do the same. Let our motto be—

April, Ville d'Avray....

Yes, and why not a Ma'amselle Rose?

Hilaire Belloc

1870–1953

ON AN UNKNOWN COUNTRY

TEN years ago, I think, or perhaps a little less or perhaps a little more, I came in the Euston Road—that thoroughfare of Empire—upon a young man a little younger than myself whom I knew, though I did not know him very well. It was drizzling and the second-hand booksellers (who are rare in this thoroughfare) were beginning to put out the waterproof covers over their wares. This disturbed my acquaintance, because he was engaged upon buying a cheap book that should really satisfy him.

Now this was difficult, for he had no hobby, and the book which should satisfy him must be one that should describe or summon up, or, it is better to say, hint at—or, the theologians would say, reveal, or the Platonists would say *recall*—the Unknown Country, which he thought was his very home.

I had known his habit of seeking such books for two years, and had half wondered at it and half sympathised. It was an appetite partly satisfied by almost any work that brought to him the vision of a place in the mind which he had always intensely desired, but to which, as he had then long guessed, and as he is now quite certain, no human paths directly lead. He would buy

K

with avidity travels to the moon and to the planets, from the most worthless to the best. He loved Utopias and did not disregard even so prosaic a category as books of real travel, so long as by exaggeration or by a glamour in the style they gave him a full draught of that drug which he desired. Whether this satisfaction the young man sought was a satisfaction in illusion (I have used the word 'drug' with hesitation), or whether it was, as he persistently maintained, the satisfaction of a memory, or whether it was, as I am often tempted to think, the satisfaction of a thirst which will ultimately be quenched in every human soul I cannot tell. Whatever it was, he sought it with more than the appetite with which a hungry man seeks food. He sought it with something that was not hunger but passion.

That evening he found a book.

It is well known that men purchase with difficulty second-hand books upon the stalls, and that in some mysterious way the sellers of these books are content to provide a kind of library for the poorer and more eager of the public, and a library admirable in this, that it is accessible upon every shelf and exposes a man to no control, except that he must not steal, and even in this it is nothing but the force of public law that interferes. My friend therefore would in the natural course of things have dipped into the book and left it there; but a better luck persuaded him. Whether it was the beginning of the rain or a sudden loneliness in such terrible weather and in such a terrible town, compelling him to seek a more permanent companionship

with another mind, or whether it was my
sudden arrival and shame lest his poverty
should appear in his refusing to buy the book—
whatever it was, he bought that same. And
since he bought the Book I also have known it
and have found in it, as he did, the most complete expression that I know of the Unknown
Country, of which he was a citizen—oddly a
citizen, as I then thought, wisely as I now
conceive.

All that can best be expressed in words should
be expressed in verse, but verse is a slow thing to
create; nay, it is not really created: it is a secre-
tion of the mind, it is a pearl that gathers round
some irritant and slowly expresses the very
essence of beauty and of desire that has lain long,
potential and unexpressed, in the mind of the
man who secretes it. God knows that this
Unknown Country has been hit off in verse a
hundred times. If I were perfectly sure of my
accents I would quote two lines from the
Odyssey in which the Unknown Country stands
out as clear as does a sudden vision from a
mountain ridge when the mist lifts after a long
climb and one sees beneath one an unexpected
and glorious land; such a vision as greets a man
when he comes over the Saldeu into the simple
and secluded Republic of the Andorrans. Then,
again, the Germans in their idioms have flashed
it out, I am assured, for I remember a woman
telling me that there was a song by Schiller
which exactly gave the revelation of which I
speak. In English, thank Heaven, emotion of
this kind, emotion necessary to the life of the

soul, is very abundantly furnished. As, who does not know the lines:

> Blessed with that which is not in the word
> Of man nor his conception: Blessed Land!

Then there is also the whole group of glimpses which Shakespeare amused himself by scattering as might a man who had a great oak chest full of jewels and who now and then, out of kindly fun, poured out a handful and gave them to his guests. I quote from memory, but I think certain of the lines run more or less like this:

> Look how the dawn in russet mantle clad,
> Stands on the steep of yon high eastern hill.

And again:

> Night's candles are burnt out, and jocund day
> Stands tiptoe on the misty mountain tops.

Which moves me to digress. . . . How on earth did any living man pull it off as well as that? I remember arguing with a man who very genuinely thought the talent of Shakespeare was exaggerated in public opinion, and discovering at the end of a long wrangle that he was not considering Shakespeare as a poet. But as a poet, then, how on earth did he manage it?

Keats did it continually, especially in the *Hyperion*. Milton does it so well in the Fourth Book of *Paradise Lost* that I defy any man of a sane understanding to read the whole of that book before going to bed and not to wake up next morning as though he had been on a journey. William Morris does it, especially in the verses about a prayer over the corn; and as for Virgil, the poet Virgil, he does it continually like a man whose very trade it is. Who does not remember the swimmer who saw Italy from the top of the wave?

Here also let me digress. How do the poets do it? (I do not mean where do they get their power, as I was asking just now of Shakespeare, but how do the words, simple or complex, produce that effect?) Very often there is not any adjective, sometimes not any qualification at all: often only one subject with its predicate and its statement and its object. There is never any detail of description, but the scene rises, more vivid in colour, more exact in outline, more wonderful in influence, than anything we can see with our eyes, except perhaps those things we see in the few moments of intense emotion which come to us, we know not whence, and expand out into completion and into manhood.

Catullus does it. He does it so powerfully in the opening lines of

> *Vesper adest . . .*

that a man reads the first couplet of that Hymeneal, and immediately perceives the Apennines.

The nameless translator of the Highland song does it, especially when he advances that battering line—

> And we in dreams behold the Hebrides.

They all do it, bless their hearts, the poets, which leads me back again to the mournful reflection that it cannot be done in prose. . . .

Little friends, my readers, I wish it could be

done in prose, for if it could, and if I knew how
to do it, I would here present to you that Unknown Country in such a fashion that every
landscape which you should see henceforth
would be transformed, by the appearing through
it, the shining and uplifting through it, of the
Unknown Country upon which reposes this
tedious and repetitive world.

Now you may say to me that prose can do it,
and you may quote to me the end of the *Pilgrim's
Progress*, a very remarkable piece of writing. Or,
better still, as we shall be more agreed upon it,
the general impression left upon the mind by
the book which set me writing—Mr. Hudson's
Crystal Age. I do not deny that prose can do it,
but when it does it, it is hardly to be called prose,
for it is inspired. Note carefully the passages in
which the trick is worked in prose (for instance,
in the story of Ruth in the Bible, where it is done
with complete success), you still perceive an in-
cantation and a spell. Indeed this same episode
of Ruth in exile has inspired two splendid
passages of European verse, of which it is difficult
to say which is the more national, and therefore
the greatest, Victor Hugo's in the *Légende des
Siècles* or Keats's astounding four lines.

．　　．　　．　　．　　．　　．

There was a shepherd the other day up at
Findon Fair who had come from the east by
Lewes with sheep, and who had in his eyes that
reminiscence of horizons which makes the eyes
of shepherds and of mountaineers different from
the eyes of other men. He was occupied when
I came upon him in pulling Mr. Fulton's sheep

by one hind leg so that they should go the way they were desired to go. It happened that day that Mr. Fulton's sheep were not sold, and the shepherd went driving them back through Findon Village, and up on to the high Downs. I went with him to hear what he had to say, for shepherds talk quite differently from other men. And when we came on to the shoulder of Chanctonbury and looked down upon the Weald, which stretched out like the Plains of Heaven, he said to me: 'I never come here but it seems like a different place down below, and as though it were not the place where I have gone afoot with sheep under the hills. It seems different when you are looking down at it.' He added that he had never known why. Then I knew that he, like myself, was perpetually in perception of the Unknown Country, and I was very pleased. But we did not say anything more to each other about it until we got down into Steyning. Then we drank together and we still said nothing more about it, so that to this day all we know of the matter is what we knew when we started, and what you knew when I began to write this, and what you are now no further informed upon, namely, that there is an Unknown Country lying beneath the places that we know, and appearing only in moments of revelation.

Whether we shall reach this country at last or whether we shall not, it is impossible to determine.

Max Beerbohm
1872–

'A CLERGYMAN'

Fʀᴀɢᴍᴇɴᴛᴀʀʏ, pale, momentary; almost
nothing; glimpsed and gone; as it were, a faint
human hand thrust up, never to reappear, from
beneath the rolling waters of Time, he forever
haunts my memory and solicits my weak imagination. Nothing is told of him but that once,
abruptly, he asked a question, and received an
answer.

This was on the afternoon of April 7th, 1778,
at Streatham, in the well-appointed house of
Mr. Thrale. Johnson, on the morning of that
day, had entertained Boswell at breakfast in
Bolt Court, and invited him to dine at Thrale
Hall. The two took coach and arrived early.
It seems that Sir John Pringle had asked Boswell
to ask Johnson 'what were the best English
sermons for style.' In the interval before dinner,
accordingly, Boswell reeled off the names of
several divines whose prose might or might not
win commendation. 'Atterbury?' he suggested.
'Jᴏʜɴsᴏɴ: Yes, Sir, one of the best. Bᴏsᴡᴇʟʟ:
Tillotson? Jᴏʜɴsᴏɴ: Why, not now. I should
not advise any one to imitate Tillotson's style;
though I don't know; I should be cautious of
censuring anything that has been applauded by
so many suffrages.—South is one of the best, if

you except his peculiarities, and his violence, and sometimes coarseness of language.——Seed has a very fine style; but he is not very theological. Jortin's sermons are very elegant. Sherlock's style, too, is very elegant, though he has not made it his principal study.——And you may add Smalridge. BOSWELL: I like Ogden's Sermons on Prayer very much, both for neatness of style and subtility of reasoning. JOHNSON: I should like to read all that Ogden has written. BOSWELL: What I want to know is, what sermons afford the best specimen of English pulpit eloquence. JOHNSON: We have no sermons addressed to the passions, that are good for anything; if you mean that kind of eloquence. A CLERGYMAN, whose name I do not recollect: Were not Dodd's sermons addressed to the passions? JOHNSON: They were nothing, Sir, be they addressed to what they may.'

The suddenness of it! Bang!——and the rabbit that had popped from its burrow was no more.

I know not which is the more startling—the début of the unfortunate clergyman, or the instantaneousness of his end. Why hadn't Boswell told us there was a clergyman present? Well, we may be sure that so careful and acute an artist had some good reason. And I suppose the clergyman was left to take us unawares because just so did he take the company. Had we been told he was there, we might have expected that sooner or later he would join in the conversation. He would have had a place in our minds. We may assume that in the minds of the company around Johnson he had no place.

K*

He sat forgotten, overlooked; so that his self-assertion startled every one just as on Boswell's page it startles us. In Johnson's massive and magnetic presence only some very remarkable man, such as Mr. Burke, was sharply distinguishable from the rest. Others might, if they had something in them, stand out slightly. This unfortunate clergyman may have had something in him, but I judge that he lacked the gift of seeming as if he had. That deficiency, however, does not account for the horrid fate that befell him. One of Johnson's strongest and most inveterate feelings was his veneration for the Cloth. To any one in Holy Orders he habitually listened with a grave and charming deference. To-day, moreover, he was in excellent good humour. He was at the Thrales', where he so loved to be; the day was fine; a fine dinner was in close prospect; and he had had what he always declared to be the sum of human felicity —a ride in a coach. Nor was there in the question put by the clergyman anything likely to enrage him. Dodd was one whom Johnson had befriended in adversity; and it had always been agreed that Dodd in his pulpit was very emotional. What drew the blasting flash must have been not the question itself, but the manner in which it was asked. And I think we can guess what that manner was.

Say the words aloud: 'Were not Dodd's sermons addressed to the passions?' They are words which, if you have any dramatic and histrionic sense, *cannot* be said except in a high, thin voice.

You may, from sheer perversity, utter them in

a rich and sonorous baritone or bass. But if you do so, they sound utterly unnatural. To make them carry the conviction of human utterance, you have no choice; you must pipe them.

Remember, now, Johnson was very deaf. Even the people whom he knew well, the people to whose voices he was accustomed, had to address him very loudly. It is probable that this unregarded, young, shy clergyman, when at length he suddenly mustered courage to 'cut in,' let his high, thin voice soar *too* high, insomuch that it was a kind of scream. On no other hypothesis can we account for the ferocity with which Johnson turned and rended him. Johnson didn't, we may be sure, mean to be cruel. The old lion, startled, just struck out blindly. But the force of paw and claws was not the less lethal. We have endless testimony to the strength of Johnson's voice; and the very cadence of those words, 'They were nothing, Sir, be they addressed to what they may,' convinces me that the old lion's jaws never gave forth a louder roar. Boswell does not record that there was any further conversation before the announcement of dinner. Perhaps the whole company had been temporarily deafened. But I am not bothering about *them*. My heart goes out to the poor dear clergyman exclusively.

I said a moment ago that he was young and shy; and I admit that I slipped those epithets in without having justified them to you by due process of induction. Your quick mind will have already supplied what I omitted. A man with a high, thin voice, and without power to impress

any one with a sense of his importance, a man so
null in effect that even the retentive mind of
Boswell did not retain his very name, would
assuredly not be a self-confident man. Even if
he were not naturally shy, social courage would
soon have been sapped in him, and would in
time have been destroyed, by experience. That
he had not yet given himself up as a bad job,
that he still had faint wild hopes, is proved by
the fact that he did snatch the opportunity for
asking that question. He must, accordingly,
have been young. Was he the curate of the
neighbouring church? I think so. It would
account for his having been invited. I see him
as he sits there listening to the great Doctor's
pronouncement on Atterbury and those others.
He sits on the edge of a chair in the background.
He has colourless eyes, fixed earnestly, and a
face almost as pale as the clerical bands beneath
his somewhat receding chin. His forehead is
high and narrow, his hair mouse-coloured. His
hands are clasped tight before him, the knuckles
standing out sharply. This constriction does not
mean that he is steeling himself to speak. He has
no positive intention of speaking. Very much,
nevertheless, is he wishing in the back of his
mind that he *could* say something—something
whereat the great Doctor would turn on him
and say, after a pause for thought, 'Why yes, Sir.
That is most justly observed' or 'Sir, this has
never occurred to me. I thank you'—thereby
fixing the observer for ever high in the esteem
of all. And now in a flash the chance presents
itself. 'We have,' shouts Johnson, 'no sermons

addressed to the passions, that are good for anything.' I see the curate's frame quiver with sudden impulse, and his mouth fly open, and—— no, I can't bear it, I shut my eyes and ears. But audible, even so, is something shrill, followed by something thunderous.

Presently I re-open my eyes. The crimson has not yet faded from that young face yonder, and slowly down either cheek falls a glistening tear. Shades of Atterbury and Tillotson! Such weakness shames the Established Church. What would Jortin and Smalridge have said?—what Seed and South? And, by the way, who *were* they, these worthies? It is a solemn thought that so little is conveyed to us by names which to the palæo-Georgians conveyed so much. We discern a dim, composite picture of a big man in a big wig and a billowing black gown, with a big congregation beneath him. But we are not anxious to hear what he is saying. We know it is all very elegant. We know it will be printed and be bound in finely-tooled full calf, and no palæo-Georgian gentleman's library will be complete without it. Literate people in those days were comparatively few; but, bating that, one may say that sermons were as much in request as novels are to-day. I wonder, will mankind continue to be capricious? It is a very solemn thought indeed that no more than a hundred-and-fifty years hence the novelists of our time, with all their moral and political and sociological outlook and influence, will perhaps shine as indistinctly as do those old preachers, with all their elegance, now. 'Yes, Sir,' some great

pundit may be telling a disciple at this moment,
'Wells is one of the best. Galsworthy is one of
the best, if you except his concern for delicacy
of style. Mrs. Ward has a very firm grasp of
problems, but is not very creational.—Caine's
books are very edifying. I should like to read all
that Caine has written. Miss Corelli, too, is very
edifying. And you may add Upton Sinclair.'
'What I want to know,' says the disciple, 'is what
English novels may be selected as specially en-
thralling.' The pundit answers: 'We have no
novels addressed to the passions that are good
for anything, if you mean that kind of enthral-
ment.' And here some poor wretch (whose name
the disciple will not remember) inquires: 'Are
not Mrs. Glyn's novels addressed to the passions?'
and is in due form annihilated. Can it be that a
time will come when readers of this passage in
our pundit's Life will take more interest in the
poor nameless wretch than in all the bearers of
those great names put together, being no more
able or anxious to discriminate between (say)
Mrs. Ward and Mr. Sinclair than we are to
set Ogden above Sherlock, or Sherlock above
Ogden? It seems impossible. But we must remember that things are not always what they
seem.

Every man illustrious in his day, however
much he may be gratified by his fame, looks with
an eager eye to posterity for a continuance of
past favours, and would even live the remainder
of his life in obscurity if by so doing he could
insure that future generations would preserve a
correct attitude towards him forever. This is

very natural and human, but, like so many very
natural and human things, very silly. Tillotson
and the rest need not, after all, be pitied for our
neglect of them. They either know nothing
about it, or are above such terrene trifles. Let
us keep our pity for the seething mass of divines
who were *not* elegantly verbose, and had no fun
or glory while they lasted. And let us keep a
specially large portion for one whose lot was so
much worse than merely undistinguished. If that
nameless curate had not been at the Thrales'
that day, or, being there, had kept the silence
that so well became him, his life would have
been drab enough, in all conscience. But at any
rate an unpromising career would not have been
nipped in the bud. And that is what in fact
happened, I'm sure of it. A robust man might
have rallied under the blow. Not so our friend.
Those who knew him in infancy had not
expected that he would be reared. Better for
him had they been right. It is well to grow up
and be ordained, but not if you are delicate and
very sensitive, and shall happen to annoy the
greatest, the most stentorian and roughest of
contemporary personages. 'A Clergyman' never
held up his head or smiled again after the brief
encounter recorded for us by Boswell. He sank
into a rapid decline. Before the next blossoming
of Thrale Hall's almond trees he was no more.
I like to think that he died forgiving Dr. Johnson.

H. M. Tomlinson

1873-

THE MASTER

THIS master of a ship I remember first as a slim lad, with a shy smile, and large hands that were lonely beyond his outgrown reefer jacket. His cap was always too small for him, and the soiled frontal badge of his line became a coloured button beyond his forelock. He used to come home occasionally—and it was always when we were on the point of forgetting him altogether. He came with a huge bolster in a cab, as though out of the past and nowhere. There is a tradition, a book tradition, that the boy apprenticed to the sea acquires saucy eyes, and a self-reliance always ready to dare to that bleak extreme the very thought of which horrifies those who are lawful and cautious. They know better who live where the ships are. He used to bring his young shipmates to see us, and they were like himself. Their eyes were downcast. They showed no self-reliance. Their shyness and politeness, when the occasion was quite simple, were absurdly incommensurate even with modesty. Their sisters, not nearly so polite, used to mock them.

As our own shy lad was never with us for long, his departure being as abrupt and unannounced as his appearance, we could willingly endure him. But he was extraneous to the household.

He had the impeding nature of a new and super-fluous piece of furniture which is in the way, yet never knows it, and placidly stays where it is, in its wooden manner, till it is placed elsewhere. There was a morning when, as he was leaving the house, during one of his brief visits to his home, I noticed to my astonishment that he had grown taller than myself. How had that happened? And where? I had followed him to the door that morning because, looking down at his cap which he was nervously handling, he had told me he was going then to an examination. About a week later he announced, in a casual way, that he had got his master's ticket. After the first shock of surprise, caused by the fact that this information was an unexpected warning of our advance in years, we were amused, and we congratulated him. Naturally he had got his certificate as master mariner. Why not? Nearly all the mates we knew got it, sooner or later. That was bound to come. But very soon after that he gave us a genuine surprise, and made us anxious. He informed us, as casually, that he had been appointed master to a ship; a very different matter from merely possessing the licence to command.

We were even alarmed. This was serious. He could not do it. He was not the man to make a command for anything. A fellow who, not so long ago, used to walk a mile with a telegram because he had not the strength of character to face the lady clerk in the post office round the corner, was hardly the man to overawe a crowd of hard characters gathered by chance from

Tower Hill, socialise them, and direct them successfully in subduing the conflicting elements of a difficult enterprise. Not he. But we said nothing to discourage him.

Of course, he was a delightful fellow. He often amused us, and he did not always know why. He was frank, he was gentle, but that large vacancy, the sea, where he had spent most of his young life, had made him—well, slow. You know what I mean. He was curiously innocent of those dangers of great cities which are nothing to us because we know they are there. Yet he was always on the alert for thieves and parasites. I think he enjoyed his belief in their crafty omnipresence ashore. Proud of his alert and knowing intelligence, he would relate a long story of the way he had not only frustrated an artful shark, but had enjoyed the process in perfect safety. That we, who rarely went out of London, never had such adventures, did not strike him as worth a thought or two. He never paused in his merriment to consider the strange fact that to him, alone of our household, such wayside adventures fell. With a shrewd air he would inform us that he was about to put the savings of a voyage into an advertised trap which a country parson would have stepped over without a second contemptuous glance.

He took his ship away. The affair was not discussed at home, though each of us gave it some private despondency. We followed him silently, apprehensively, through the reports in the *Shipping Gazette*. He made point after point safely—St. Vincent, Gilbraltar, Suez, Aden—

after him we went across to Colombo, Singapore, and at length we learned that he was safe at Batavia. He had got that steamer out all right. He got her home again, too. After his first adventure as master he made voyage after voyage with no more excitement in them than you would find in Sunday walks in a suburb. It was plain luck; or else navigation and seamanship were greatly overrated arts.

A day came when he invited me to go with him part of his voyage. I could leave the ship at Bordeaux. I went. You must remember that we had never seen his ship. And there he was, walking with me to the dock from a Welsh railway station, a man in a cheap mackintosh, with an umbrella I will not describe, and he was carrying a brown paper parcel. He was appropriately crowned with a bowler hat several sizes too small for him. Glancing up at his profile, I actually wondered whether the turmoil was now going on in his mind over that confession which now he was bound to make: that he was not the master of a ship, and never had been.

There she was, a bulky modern freighter, full of derricks and time-saving appliances, and her funnel lording it over the neighbourhood. The man with the parcel under his arm led me up the gangway. I was not yet convinced. I was, indeed, less sure than ever that he could be the master of this huge community of engines and men. He did not accord with it.

We were no sooner on deck than a man in uniform, grey-haired, with a seamed and resolute face, which anyone would have recognised at

once as a sailor's, approached us. He was introduced as the chief officer. He had a tale of woe:
trouble with the dock-master, with the steve-
dores, with the cargo, with many things. He
did not appear to know what to do with them.
He was asking this boy of ours.

The skipper began to speak. At that moment
I was gazing at the funnel, trying to decipher a
monogram upon it; but I heard a new voice,
rapid and incisive, sure of its subject, resolving
doubts, and making the crooked straight. It
was the man with the brown paper parcel. It
was still under his arm—in fact, the parcel contained pink pyjamas, and there was hardly
enough paper. The respect of the mate was not
lessened by this.

The skipper went to gaze down a hatchway.
He walked to the other side of the ship, and in-
spected something there. Conned her length,
called up in a friendly but authoritative way to
an engineer standing by an amidship rail above.
He came back to the mate, and with an easy
precision directed his will on others, through his
deputy, up to the time of sailing. He beckoned
to me, who also, apparently, was under his
august orders, and turned, as though perfectly
aware that in this place I should follow him
meekly, in full obedience.

Our steamer moved out at midnight, in a
drive of wind and rain. There were bewildering and unrelated lights about us. Peremptory
challenges were shouted to us from nowhere.
Sirens blared out of dark voids. And there was
the skipper on the bridge, the lad who caused

us amusement at home, with this confusion in
the dark about him, and an immense insentient
mass moving with him at his will; and he had
his hands in his pockets, and turned to tell me
what a cold night it was. The pier-head search-
light showed his face, alert, serene, with his
brows knitted in a little frown, and his underlip
projecting as the sign of the pride of those who
look direct into the eyes of an opponent, and
care not at all. In my berth that night I searched
for a moral for this narrative, but went to sleep
before I found it.

G. K. Chesterton

1874–1936

FRENCH AND ENGLISH

I⊤ is obvious that there is a great deal of difference between being international and being cosmopolitan. All good men are international. Nearly all bad men are cosmopolitan. If we are to be international we must be national. And it is largely because those who call themselves the friends of peace have not dwelt sufficiently on this distinction that they do not impress the bulk of any of the nations to which they belong. International peace means a peace between nations, not a peace after the destruction of nations, like the Buddhist peace after the destruction of personality. The golden age of the good European is like the heaven of the Christian: it is a place where people will love each other; not like the heaven of the Hindu, a place where they will be each other. And in the case of national character this can be seen in a curious way. It will generally be found, I think, that the more a man really appreciates and admires the soul of another people the less he will attempt to imitate it; he will be conscious that there is something in it too deep and too unmanageable to imitate. The Englishman who has a fancy for France will try to be French; the Englishman who admires France will remain obstinately

English. This is to be particularly noticed in the case of our relations with the French, because it is one of the outstanding peculiarities of the French that their vices are all on the surface, and their extraordinary virtues concealed. One might almost say that their vices are the flower of their virtues.

Thus their obscenity is the expression of their passionate love of dragging all things into the light. The avarice of their peasants means the independence of their peasants. What the English call their rudeness in the streets is a phase of their social equality. The worried look of their women is connected with the responsibility of their women; and a certain unconscious brutality of hurry and gesture in the men is related to their inexhaustible and extraordinary military courage. Of all countries, therefore, France is the worst country for a superficial fool to admire. Let a fool hate France: if the fool loves it he will soon be a knave. He will certainly admire it, not only for the things that are not creditable, but actually for the things that are not there. He will admire the grace and indolence of the most industrious people in the world. He will admire the romance and fantasy of the most determinedly respectable and commonplace people in the world. This mistake the Englishman will make if he admires France too hastily; but the mistake that he makes about France will be slight compared with the mistake that he makes about himself. An Englishman who professes really to like French realistic novels, really to be at home in a French modern

theatre, really to experience no shock on first
seeing the savage French caricatures, is making
a mistake very dangerous for his own sincerity.
He is admiring something he does not understand. He is reaping where he has not sown,
and taking up where he has not laid down; he
is trying to taste the fruit when he has never
toiled over the tree. He is trying to pluck the
exquisite fruit of French cynicism, when he has
never tilled the rude but rich soil of French
virtue.

The thing can only be made clear to Englishmen by turning it round. Suppose a Frenchman came out of democratic France to live in
England, where the shadow of the great houses
still falls everywhere, and where even freedom
was, in its origin, aristocratic. If the Frenchman
saw our aristocracy and liked it, if he saw our
snobbishness and liked it, if he set himself to
imitate it, we all know what we should feel.
We all know that we should feel that that particular Frenchman was a repulsive little gnat.
He would be imitating English aristocracy; he would
be imitating the English vice. But he would not
even understand the vice he plagiarised: especially he would not understand that the vice is
partly a virtue. He would not understand those
elements in the English which balance snobbishness and make it human: the great kindness of
the English, their hospitality, their unconscious
poetry, their sentimental conservatism, which
really admires the gentry. The French Royalist
sees that the English like their King. But he
does not grasp that while it is base to worship

a King, it is almost noble to worship a power-less King. The impotence of the Hanoverian Sovereigns has raised the English loyal subject almost to the chivalry and dignity of a Jacobite. The Frenchman sees that the English servant is respectful: he does not realise that he is also disrespectful; that there is an English legend of the humorous and faithful servant, who is as much a personality as his master; the Caleb Balderstone, the Sam Weller. He sees that the English do admire a nobleman; he does not allow for the fact that they admire a nobleman most when he does not behave like one. They like a noble to be unconscious and amiable: the slave may be humble, but the master must not be proud. The master is Life, as they would like to enjoy it; and among the joys they desire in him there is none which they desire more sin-cerely than that of generosity, of throwing money about among mankind, or, to use the noble mediæval word, largesse—the joy of large-ness. That is why a cabman tells you you are no gentleman if you give him his correct fare. Not only his pocket, but his soul is hurt. You have wounded his ideal. You have defaced his vision of the perfect aristocrat. All this is really very subtle and elusive; it is very difficult to separate what is mere slavishness from what is a sort of vicarious nobility in the English love of a lord. And no Frenchman could easily grasp it at all. He would think it was mere slavishness; and if he liked it, he would be a slave. So every Englishman must (at first) feel French candour to be mere brutality. And if he likes it, he is a brute. These national merits must not be understood so easily. It requires long years of plenitude and quiet, the slow growth of great parks, the seasoning of oaken beams, the dark enrichment of red wine in cellars and in inns, all the leisure and the life of England through many centuries, to produce at last the generous and genial fruit of English snobbishness. And it requires battery and barricade, songs in the streets, and ragged men dead for an idea, to produce and justify the terrible flower of French indecency.

When I was in Paris a short time ago, I went with an English friend of mine to an extremely brilliant and rapid succession of French plays, each occupying about twenty minutes. They were all astonishingly effective; but there was one of them which was so effective that my friend and I fought about it outside, and had almost to be separated by the police. It was intended to indicate how men really behaved in a wreck or naval disaster, how they break down, how they scream, how they fight each other without object and in a mere hatred of everything. And then there was added, with all that horrible irony which Voltaire began, a scene in which a great statesman made a speech over their bodies, saying that they were all heroes and had died in a fraternal embrace. My friend and I came out of this theatre, and as he had lived long in Paris, he said, like a Frenchman: 'What admirable artistic arrangement! Is it not exquisite?' 'No,' I replied, assuming as far as possible the traditional attitude of John Bull in the pictures in *Punch*—'No, it is not exquisite. Perhaps it is unmeaning; if it is unmeaning I do not mind. But if it has a meaning I know what the meaning is; it is that under all their pageant of chivalry men are not only beasts, but even hunted beasts. I do not know much of humanity, especially when humanity talks in French. But I know when a thing is meant to uplift the human soul, and when it is meant to depress it. I know that *Cyrano de Bergerac* (where the actors talked even quicker) was meant to encourage man. And I know that this was meant to discourage him.' 'These sentimental and moral views of art,' began my friend, but I broke into his words as a light broke into my mind. 'Let me say to you,' I said, 'what Jaurès said to Liebknecht at the Socialist Conference: "You have not died on the barricades." You are an Englishman, as I am, and you ought to be as amiable as I am. These people have some right to be terrible in art, for they have been terrible in politics. They may endure mock tortures on the stage; they have seen real tortures in the streets. They have been hurt for the idea of Democracy. They have been hurt for the idea of Catholicism. It is not so utterly unnatural to them that they should be hurt for the idea of literature. But, by blazes, it is altogether unnatural to me! And the worst thing of all is that I, who am an Englishman, loving comfort, should find comfort in such things as this. The French do not seek comfort here, but rather unrest. This restless people seeks to keep itself in a perpetual agony of the revolutionary mood. Frenchmen, seeking revolution, may find the humiliation of humanity inspiring. But God forbid that two pleasure-seeking Englishmen should ever find it pleasant!'

CARLYLE'S 'PAST AND PRESENT'—AN INTRODUCTION

'PAST AND PRESENT' was published in 1843 and was the fourth of the important works of Carlyle. Its humour, eloquence, and imaginative energy must remain a permanent possession, but its peculiar historical force and value can scarcely be appreciated except in connection with the date. At the time when almost every eminent historian described the past as a mere foil to the present, Carlyle actually uses the flimsy and degraded present as a foil to the past. The average history-book used in schoolrooms commonly began a chapter with some such words as these: 'How surprised those rude barbarians would have been had they known that their rough ox-wagons would some day be replaced by steam-engines at thirty miles an hour, that their superstitious ordeals would end in enlightened courts of justice and beneficent Acts of Parliament.' The point of Carlyle's book is rather to reverse the phrase and exclaim, 'How horrified the men of the Middle Ages would have been if they had known that their plain customs and kingships would ever degenerate into the dirt and slavery of Manchester and the tomfooleries of Chancery and St. Stephen's.'

The term 'reactionary' is generally used as a

term of offence, just as the term 'progressive' is used as a term of praise; but only once in a hundred times is either of them used so as to convey any meaning or truth. Yet though the words have become a mere hackneyed cant, they have their proper use. Progress means persistence in the direction of one object maintained for a considerable period; reaction means some upheaval of disgust or contradiction, which overthrows the recent persistence and appeals back, perhaps, to its opposite. Thus we might truly say that English poetry from Cowley to Akenside progressed towards clearness and metrical accuracy. And we might truly say that Coleridge's *Ancient Mariner* was a reaction against this progress, the writing of a mere mad ballad in order to show how much more life there was in the old barbaric mysticism than in the recent easy-going rationality. Progress happens, in short, whenever men can endure one tendency for a long time. And reaction happens whenever some particular man can endure it no longer. These definitions are simple but I believe them to be comprehensive. A progressive is always a conservative; he conserves the direction of progress. A reactionary is always a rebel.

In this sense strictly and in no other Carlyle can lawfully be called a reactionary. His revolt against the trend of his time was literally a reaction, just as being seasick is a reaction. And such revolt and rejection raise much the same problem as sickness; it is certainly better to reject that which one cannot assimilate; but it makes a man feel rather sad and empty afterwards.

All scepticism is like seasickness in this respect. If you cannot enjoy the universe it is better to throw it up; but it will leave you weak and sensitive and any spirit that you touch will infallibly fly to your head. So the sceptic is always unnaturally open to the raids of superstition and eccentricity. Carlyle was in the final sense a good man, he was in every conceivable sense a great man. But when all is allowed, he was essentially a sick man; if you like, a seasick man, in the sense that his malady had been created by facing primary and magnificent elements. A sort of divine disgust was the passion that he was sent on earth to preach; he preached it with wonderful humour, poetry, pungent inventiveness, and encyclopædic variety, but it was disgust that was his motive; it was the insurgent mood called reaction. And remember that if it be true that all reactionaries are rebels, it is even more certain that most rebels are reactionaries. Every sudden movement which has gone forward has looked back. The Renaissance looked back to pagan art; the French Revolution looked back to pagan politics. And it was in the same way that mediæval art was looked back to by Ruskin and mediæval politics by Carlyle.

Carlyle's great work 'Past and Present' is the most emphatic example of this return and appeal of his to the polity and ethics of the Middle Ages. And it is this part of the book that is by far the most certain and solid. It is much more broadly certain that he is right about 'Past' than about 'Present.' He sees much more vividly and humanly the things that he has not seen, the events of veiled centuries and obscure tribes than he sees the events that are really happening around him in the streets of London. And the cause of this lies in his character as a reactionary; a reactionary, as we have said, means a conservative in revolt. His startling grip and graphic power in the description of people like Rufus or Abbot Samson comes chiefly from this: that he was to a certain extent in the same position as they. We shall never even begin to understand the Middle Ages until we realise that nobody really believed that the Roman Empire was dead until close upon the Reformation. For nearly a thousand years men believed not that the Empire was dead, but that it was decidedly ill, and therefore they naturally looked back to the previous period when it had been quite well. In Carlyle's time an enlightened man, a civilised man, a speculative man, meant a man who was always looking to the future. But in Rufus's time an enlightened, civilised, and speculative man meant a man who looked almost entirely to the past, in the hope of renewing its lost wisdom and liberty. Carlyle is slightly confused by this contradiction; but on the whole he deals with it admirably. In so far as Rufus lived in to-morrow Rufus was only a self-willed savage. In so far as Anselm lived in yesterday, Anselm was what we now call a liberal and even a free-thinker.

In two respects, indeed, Carlyle's version of the Middle Ages is really incorrect; not incorrect in detail (for in defiance of those dons

who always wished to prove an imaginative man
inaccurate, Carlyle was a very accurate historian) but incorrect in spirit, and conception.
First of all he makes the Middle Ages much too
German—or what comes to the same thing,
much too barbarous. Nobody of course can tell
for certain how much Teutonic blood mixed
with the dying Empire or whether it did anything to revive it. The mixture, if it took place
at all, took place at the time of which we have
the worst records, the full midnight of the ninth
century. But that when Europe rose again in a
new civilisation it was not a specially German
civilisation is quite certain. Almost any object
the eye may chance to fall on may illustrate the
Southern origin everywhere. Why is the arms
of Scotland a lion? Nobody ever saw a lion in
Scotland nor in Germany from which the
northern energy is traced. It is quite obvious
that such symbols must have spread northward
from a base on the Mediterranean. If chivalry
was merely German, why was it called chivalry,
which comes from the French for a horse? In
short, the Teutons may very possibly have
quickened Europe unconsciously with a clean
and fresh physical stock, but they certainly did
not consciously give it its new system and order;
that came, as much as the old system and order,
from Rome.

But there is a second and more serious defect
in Carlyle's picture; and that is that while he
admired the Middle Ages and had great natural
sympathy with religion, he happened to dislike,
or rather not to understand, the religion of the

Middle Ages. He preferred a religion of prophets, of inspired but irresponsible people suddenly appearing in a Babylonian city or a Scotch town and telling people, with great poetic force, that they were damned. Now it was a mark and may have been a defect of mediæval religion that it distrusted prophets. It preferred priests, because priests are not so arrogant. It disliked the man whose only message was himself; it always dreaded him as an egoist and sometimes lynched him as a heretic. Thus Carlyle vividly describes the dignity and decision of Anselm; yet he has not got the right Anselm, and if he had he would not like him. How utterly un-Carlylian is the image of a man really weeping with a sense of unworthiness when called to a high post, actually having the crozier forced into his hand and the mitre thrust by violence on to his head. According to Carlyle's theory of morals, Anselm should have leaped forward crying, 'I am the Able Man; give me scope; the tools to him that can use them.' There are two words that sum up the whole mediæval paradox, and Carlyle could never have made head or tail of them; and the words are 'Nolo episcopari.'

It is true to say of Carlyle that his conception of the past was a vision, that is, a thing splendid and even inspired but still personal and liable to error. But it must be added that Carlyle's view of the present was a vision too. To him Chelsea was a vision and Houndsditch was a vision; they had all the unnatural clearness of visions, but they also had some of the distortion.

Certain things, indeed, he said with a startling thoroughness and exactitude for which we cannot too much thank him. For example, he perceived that poverty was very much more of a fact in the streets than it was a fact in the books of political science. Nothing is finer in the history of the fiercest satire than the passage in which Carlyle describes the typhus patient thrown out of the tenement, who was forced to prove her sisterhood with the other people by giving them all a fever. But he had also this quality of the highest visionary artist, that the things he had not seen at all he was quite wrong about; I mean the things he had not visualised either with the eye of the spirit or that of the body. He is always wrong, and even outrageously wrong, about anything in which he is not intensely interested. Thus he is splendidly picturesque and yet precise about the Normans and the great twelfth-century expansion of Catholicism. But he is dreary, disingenuous, and even demonstrably wrong about the Spaniards and the great sixteenth-century expansion of Catholicism. His good history of the first and his bad history of the second seem really to arise from nothing but the mere fact that he was glad of the first incident and rather sorry for the last. He could only be the fine historian of his best work when his best passions or prejudices were engaged. He could only be accurate when he was excited.

About one thing he was heroically excited, and over that his great spirit is likely to preside for many a year to come; for it is certainly the task of our time. He is already the first prophet of the Socialists and the great voice against the social wrong. He has, indeed, almost all the qualities of the Socialists, their strenuousness, their steady protest, their single eye, also something of their Puritanism and their unconscious but instinctive dislike of democracy. Carlyle was the first who called in political inequality to remedy economic inequality, but he will not be the last. But when many reformers have been inspired by his lurid irony and fierce chiaroscuro of contrasts to attempt some solution of our social evil by sheer mastery and stroke of State, he will at least remain the greatest of them. He is a power eternally opposing certain social facts to certain necessary political fictions, and as such he will have honour for ever. It is amusing to recall his contempt for mere 'votes' and to wonder how he would have got on with the Suffragettes.

W. Somerset Maugham

1874-

THE BEAST OF BURDEN

At first when you see the coolie on the road, bearing his load, it is as a pleasing object that he strikes the eye. In his blue rags, a blue of all colours from indigo to turquoise and then to the paleness of a milky sky, he fits the landscape. He seems exactly right as he trudges along the narrow causeway between the rice fields or climbs a green hill. His clothing consists of no more than a short coat and a pair of trousers; and if he had a suit which was at the beginning all of a piece, he never thinks when it comes to patching to choose a bit of stuff of the same colour. He takes anything that comes handy. From sun and rain he protects his head with a straw hat shaped like an extinguisher with a preposterously wide, flat brim.

You see a string of coolies come along, one after the other, each with a pole on his shoulders from the ends of which hang two great bales, and they make an agreeable pattern. It is amusing to watch their hurrying reflections in the padi water. You watch their faces as they pass you. They are good-natured faces and frank, you would have said, if it had not been drilled into you that the oriental is inscrutable; and when you see them lying down with their loads under a banyan tree by a wayside shrine, smoking and chatting gaily, if you have tried to lift the bales they carry for thirty miles or more a day, it seems natural to feel admiration for their endurance and their spirit. But you will be thought somewhat absurd if you mention your admiration to the old residents of China. You will be told with a tolerant shrug of the shoulders that the coolies are animals and for two thousand years from father to son have carried burdens, so it is no wonder if they do it cheerfully. And indeed you can see for yourself that they begin early, for you will encounter little children with a yoke on their shoulders staggering under the weight of vegetable baskets.

The day wears on and it grows warmer. The coolies take off their coats and walk stripped to the waist. Then sometimes in a man resting for an instant, his load on the ground but the pole still on his shoulders so that he has to rest slightly crouched, you see the poor tired heart beating against the ribs: you see it as plainly as in some cases of heart disease in the out-patients' room of a hospital. It is strangely distressing to watch. Then also you see the coolies' backs. The pressure of the pole for long years, day after day, has made hard red scars, and sometimes even there are open sores, great sores without bandages or dressing that rub against the wood; but the strangest thing of all is that sometimes, as though nature sought to adapt man for these cruel uses to which he **is** put, an odd malformation seems to have arisen so that there is a sort of hump, like a camel's, against which the pole rests. But beating heart or angry sore, bitter rain or burning sun notwithstanding, they go on eternally, from dawn till dusk, year in year out, from childhood to the extreme of age. You see old men without an ounce of fat on their bodies, their skin loose on their bones, wizened, their little faces wrinkled and apelike, with hair thin and grey; and they totter under their burdens to the edge of the grave in which at last they shall have rest. And still the coolies go, not exactly running, but not walking either, sidling quickly, with their eyes on the ground to choose the spot to place their feet, and on their faces a strained, anxious expression. You can make no longer a pattern of them as they wend their way. Their effort oppresses you. You are filled with a useless compassion.

In China it is man that is the beast of burden.

'*To be harassed by the wear and tear of life, and to pass rapidly through it without the possibility of arresting one's course,—is not this pitiful indeed? To labour without ceasing, and then, without living to enjoy the fruit, worn out, to depart, suddenly, one knows not whither,—is not that a just cause for grief?*'

So wrote the Chinese mystic.

Basil de Selincourt

1876–

THE ENGLISH SECRET

THE problem of education is in the forefront of public attention at the present time, and the Government, like the country, has been seriously preoccupied with it. Within the last few years four reports have been issued, devoted in turn to the teaching of the classics, of modern languages, of science, and of English. Each of these reports has been the work of a committee not of mere specialists, but of men who combine special knowledge with a wide outlook on affairs; and yet, broadly considered, the result of their deliberations has been in each case to claim more attention, both relatively and absolutely, for the particular branch of study which they had been asked to examine. The total effect of their labours, therefore, is to convince us, as we were otherwise only too willing to believe, that youth is shorter than it should be. We misquote La Fontaine, and say with a sigh:

> Il nous en faut au moins un siècle bien compté,
> Car vingt ans, ce n'est pas la peine!

The human mind matures too rapidly. We have taken our bias and fallen into a routine, before we have assimilated a hundredth part of the information which we need or learned the use of a quarter of those delicate tools which are the furniture of our intellectual workshop. As the experience of the race widens and the scope of the normal life is enlarged, our children seem doomed to a more and more unenviable lot. With three or four different teachers competing for every hour of their time, it is difficult to see how they are to secure the background of repose which seems to be a condition of all growth and of the mind's most of all. The watched pot never boils. Once we begin to pursue our ideals of education in an atmosphere charged, however little, with excitement and self-consciousness, we shall stifle the very faculties we wish to develop and defeat the ends we have in view, though they be in themselves the highest and the best.

Perhaps, then, it is not wholly a misfortune that, at a time when important developments in the organisation of our educational system are looked for, the Government should find itself temporarily deprived of the means of carrying them out. The war overwhelmed us financially; but it did more and worse: our faculty of experience itself was dislodged by it. All the reports on education were written under the impact of the shock. The nation, the Empire, had pulled through, but on a margin of strength with which no one could feel satisfied. The impulse was strong to profit at once from all our bitter lessons of insufficiency and to apply the necessary remedies. We did not know enough about our neighbours, we must all learn French and German; we were behindhand in invention and in the chemistry and mechanics of production, it was because science had been inadequately taught; compared with the Canadian or the New Zealander, we were mere sleep-walkers, we must above all find ourselves and discover what we stood for, we must learn English; and, of course, the disposition to pursue any of these accomplishments at the expense of the classics must be resisted to the last gasp. Such, expressed in the crudest possible terms, is the upshot of the different advices which have been tendered to a distracted Government. The whole of them are clearly of the nature of good resolutions.

The framers of the report on the teaching of English were deeply impressed by the prominence accorded in the systematised education of France to the national language and literature. They seem to have realised imperfectly how much our problem is complicated in this country by the fact that the people we have to educate is the English people. It is a comparatively easy matter to educate a Frenchman. Not only is he alive from the start, asking for it, tingling with susceptibilities and reverberations; he also finds ready to hand that incomparable instrument, French: a language which has set its house in order and, having understood itself, can make a confident appeal to the intelligence of which it is to be the pattern. How different the nature and the condition of our English children, who, every time we return from beyond the Channel, strike us, beside the shining porcelain of those clear French faces, as so much half-formed, unreflecting clay! They are not consumed with anxiety to learn anything; least of all has it ever crossed their minds that they must learn English. And how shall we teach it to them, when the few of us who have begun to know what it is know it to be a tissue of accommodations, a thing with which order, method, and all that the developing mind first apprehends and rests upon have nothing to do—in a word, a kind of miraculous flowering of man's still unconscious wisdom, preserved to us as a compensation for our many blunderings, as a reward for our patience in confusion and our fundamental faith in life?

It was natural that the war, with its vicissitudes and difficult victory, should be followed by an outbreak of patriotism. No people is, in the last resort, more patriotic than the English, or readier to make ultimate sacrifices for the safety and welfare of their country. Yet our patriotism is normally of the kind which is not exhibited. The tendency which many must have noticed among us in these last years to 'discover' and to 'push' English literature or English music, to say nothing of trade or the Empire, and to conjure up a sense of magical virtue which must attach to these things because they are English, is uncharacteristic of our race. England, as good judges know, was once the leading country of the world in music, and there is no reason why she should not regain that position; but she is likeliest to regain it if she is allowed to retain her natural unconcern about her own performances and to think the works of Smith, Brown, and Robinson as dull as, or even a little duller than, they are. The case of our literature is still more vital. What attitude are we to take towards the strong and growing movement of which Sir Henry Newbolt's report is but one sign—the movement which aims at raising English to a leading place in education and conceives of it as offering in itself all that is necessary to the development of the mind and the ripening of every faculty?

This movement is, of course, primarily a 'humanistic' movement: its ostensible aim is to make our education more living and more real; so far as this is its direction, our sympathy with it is unqualified. But it is tinged also with that narrower, that un-English patriotism; and so it comes about that the ardent claims it advances in support of an English culture suffer from a defect, the last, we may be sure, their advocates could suspect in them: they are inadequate. The English language, English literature, stand, in our view, for something even greater than the report allows. There was an old dilemma of the schools about the teaching of virtue, a dilemma which arose largely because virtue is unseizable, an influence permeating and proceeding from the whole man, an atmosphere. The quality of the English spirit is similar; we believe it to be a question of the subtlest and most serious import how far and by what processes it can be taught, if indeed it can be directly taught at all.

Here we must at once make a distinction. The spirit which we identify as essentially English appears in innumerable simplicities of form, which still fall naturally from the lips of any English child. Who does not know the lovely carol refrain?

> The rising of the sun
> And the running of the deer,
> The playing of the merry organ,
> Sweet singing in the choir.

There is not a village in the land to which its sweetness is not native and congenial. But the constituents of that sweetness, the rhymes that are no rhymes, the ebb and flow of rhythm, the incoherencies of thought, the incompleteness, the audacity, the impressionism, the post-impressionism—how many understand or could hope to understand these things? Just as the true appreciation of Milton has been said to be the last reward of the scholar, so a finished critical delight in these racial innocencies is given to those alone who have traced the interplay of thought and form in poetry through all its elaborations. We need to have seen where Euripides failed on one side, or Racine on another, before we are qualified to appreciate this anonymous English success.

In so far, then, as the teaching of English means the assurance to English children of an immediate experience of the English spirit as it lives in English letters, or English music, or English life, who can overestimate the importance of this? It could be done, if the teachers were unsophisticated like their pupils. But the teachers, alas! must be educated and cannot be more than partially educated men. They know that they must pronounce their *h*'s where others pronounce them and must mind their *p*'s and *q*'s.

The glimmerings of method and principle to which they have been introduced at Oxford or at Birmingham have amazed instead of enlightening them; their native sense of beauty has withered and the love of bathos flourishes in its place. They drape the windows of poetry with Nottingham lace curtains and keep an aspidistra in a pot behind; and the fault is with English, not with them. For it has none of the qualities that can recommend it to intermediate appreciation. Every Frenchman is a stylist; the veriest peasant discriminates between accuracy and inaccuracy in the use of words, taking as his model a luminous prose. The corresponding Englishman is unaware of the existence of any model. He reads the Bible, he reads *John Bull*, and believes that the prophet Isaiah and Mr. Bottomley teach the same righteousness in the same manner.

The point is vital, and needs our more scrupulous and wider consideration. The English spirit, we hold, is distinguished in all its manifestations, and not least in its language and literature, by its power to carry forward and preserve under stress qualities which, in one after another of the races that have contributed most to the civilisation of the world, we see sacrificed to the attainment of some special function. It is the normal tendency of the mind, as it confronts the impact of experience and steers its way through the adverse current, to submit its faculties to division, to distinguish the different methods which are applicable to different contingencies, and so to furnish itself with certain specific implements or limbs. Now our physical limbs themselves are subject to this grave disadvantage, that having them in one kind we cannot have them in another. The birds when they took to flying sacrificed the use of fingers and hands for ever, to become the beautiful and ineffectual angels we see to-day. The case is infinitely more serious where the development of the mind is at stake. The mind is a mirror, and its most precious attribute is responsiveness. But, as it forms itself to the mould of the world, it tends to warp to-morrow's experience by refractions from the experience of yesterday. The lesson which it has the greatest difficulty in learning is that all specialisation of its powers must be conducted under a reserve, and that its life is its faculty to remain, if we may express it so, whole before a world that is whole. The chief exponent of this truth in recent years has been a prominent French philosopher. But the broad tendencies of French civilisation are diametrically and dangerously opposed to it. Only the other day, one of the leaders of French criticism, M. René Doumic, summarising the merit and virtue of Louis XIV and his time, wrote:

'Il a humilié la nature devant la raison, en qui réside toute la noblesse de l'homme. Ainsi il a exalté nos énergies traditionnelles et amené à son plein épanouissement l'âme de la race.'

The weak spot in French intellectual armour could not be better indicated. No doubt, reason may more nearly claim to represent the wholeness of the mind than any other faculty, especially if we use the word in its most comprehensive significance. But it is not and never can be the whole; least of all when it looks for its triumphs in the humiliation of nature. The French, then, with all the high specialisation and pride of their intellectual consciousness, have divided the mind and, in dividing, limited it. The English, without knowing what they were about, have in a singular degree preserved it whole. Our usual name for this wholeness is simply common sense. Respecting Nature instead of 'humiliating' her, watching facts as they are instead of demonstrating what they must and shall be, we have built up our Constitution, our Empire, and all those astonishing combinations of the theoretically senseless and the practically sane and sound which everywhere go by the name of English. Our conclusion is that this quality of the English mind, which we call common, has nothing common about it at all; it is a rarity, and it is of priceless value. To it more than to any other power we know belongs the task of guiding the spirit of man through the new phases of his development. We are trustees of the future of the world. Is that future to be brighter or is it to be gloomier than the past? On us more than on any other nation the answer depends, not primarily because of our position or our wealth—in these we are easily outdone,—but because long-rooted experience in the past has matured, without specialising, our power of vision. It is time, then, that we should reflect seriously upon the nature and implications of this remarkable gift, so that we may do nothing to weaken or undermine it. In framing a policy of education, above all, we must go warily; for a chief part of the educational process is the replacement of unconscious by conscious action of the mind, and, broadly speaking, this great English virtue is a virtue of unconsciousness.

It must, so far as the bulk of the nation is concerned, remain a virtue of unconsciousness. The difficulty which we found in the qualification of primary school teachers for the communication of the English spirit through music or letters is, we greatly fear, insuperable. We are not of those who hold that great art explains itself or that its appeal has an emotional universality like that of religion. Least of all do we find such a quality of æsthetic translucence in English masterpieces. Most of those who love our country and our literature must continue to love them without knowing why, and will risk their love itself if they insist on inquiring into the reason of it. But in minds susceptible of the highest and largest development the unconsciousness we speak of has, of course, never been more than partial, and the conditions of the time are less favourable to it every day. As life goes on the world offers our race less scope for the more obvious expression of its abilities. We shall expand less in the future, if only because there is no room for quick expansion now; and, since our development is to be internal, we must learn to look within. Even if there were no practical motive, our national age, our five hundred years of literary history, compel us to such a course. We cannot any longer ignore what we signify. We have to establish a system of English culture which can maintain as conscious virtue that loyalty to known truth, that simple receptiveness when the new fact appears, that attitude of reserve, that modesty in face of the unknown, that submission of logic to experience, which are now instinctive in us.

To put it otherwise, we have to decide what *learning English* really means. It is a problem in two parts. What is it to learn language? what is it to learn the English language? We are far too apt to suppose that language is the whole of education. It is, of course, more potent in its appeal than any other branch of study, and the highest developments are unattainable except by means of it. But, as an educational instrument, it has the disadvantage of appealing entirely to secondary and transposed experiences. It presents no tangible picture, it evokes no immediate response. It is liable, therefore, either to lead nowhere, in the case of minds to which its mutations do not occur readily, or, in the case of minds peculiarly apt to them, to lead into a world little related to our common experience— into an unreal world, in short. We are often disappointed that so few of those who pass through the educational mill learn to appreciate literature, to understand the best uses to which language can be put; but have we good reason for surprise? The experience of literature is one in which easier and more elementary experiences are implied, and in these easier experiences we offer the developing mind no practice. So far as we are aware, it is not recognised in English secondary education that the portals of experience are the eye and the ear: and that for the development and refinement of these senses, the gateways through which all wisdom must pass, there is in each case an art, an art ancillary to literature, and at once easier and more obviously educational because of its more direct appeal to instinctive physical responses. Music and the plastic arts, the one more abstract, the other more concrete than literature, are admirably qualified to bring out its central and inclusive place and to exhibit by contrast its delicate equilibrium. Music, particularly, in some respects the most elusive of the arts, furnishes the quickest approach to the conscious appreciation of all artistic effect; for while its mechanics are of mathematical simplicity and beauty (and an ideal educational instrument on that account), their meaning and value appear only when they are practically applied: they require us to take our part in various easy activities in which an artistic quality makes itself felt from the first. It is almost ludicrous to reflect that among the picked thousand English men and women who year by year base their culture upon an Hellenic inspiration not a tithe are acquainted with the relations of the musical scale which, in its still imperfect form, had already been seen by the Greeks to be the meeting ground of the arts and the sciences, more essential than the alphabet, and not less elementary. We cannot pursue this topic; if we have insisted on the value of the elements of music in education, what might we not also say of the urgent demand in England for the better training of the eye, when already our whole civilisation is menaced by the unheeded degradation of its visible expression? Here is a subject which would take us much too far. Our suggestion that music and the plastic arts are ancillary to literature has been made less in any hope of an early modification of our higher education to include them—though indeed there are already some signs of coming change—than as a means to the clearer presentment of the position of English literature as we conceive it.

For English, in our view, stands to other literatures in a relation analogous to that which we have given to literature itself among the arts. The stuff of music is the directly audible sound, of painting the visible forms of the world, and the scope of each of these arts is limited and clarified by its immediate appeal to sense. The stuff of literature involves a transcending of sense experience; for the shape and sound of words do not explain their meaning. To read is to be lifted by the power of a symbolic code into an ideal region; and in no art is the transition so difficult as in literature between the means and the end. The effects of poetry are not modelled upon primary appearances, or confined to any single attribute of things; its inspiration comes from a vision of concealed significances, its theme is the developing life of man. Now the English mind, as we have seen, has a native affinity for unanalysed adjustments and reactions. Here lies the secret of the greatness of our literature, here also the secret of its elusiveness. It comprehends better than any other the conditions and the opportunities of literary expression. To understand it is about as easy and about as difficult as to understand life itself. Possessed of the ultimate and essential gift, clinging in defiance of ridicule and the demands of consistency to their intuition of the relevant fact, the English, in their literature as elsewhere, disregard the appearances and superficialities of reason and method and retain, as by a miracle, just those elements which are vital to the work in hand. There is only one way of learning the secret of this extraordinary process: it is to learn everything else. The study of English literature is a study in compromise, in intuition; and the method of it is the study of the influences between which compromise has been made. The civilisation our literature reflects is a complex of many civilisations that have preceded it, the Greek and Roman above all; to know the world we live in presupposes knowledge of those precedent worlds. This, to our minds, is the unanswerable case for classical studies. English is unknowable without them. They are the road, and the only road, to conscious appreciation of our own thought and our own times.

A last word touching the relation of French and English culture. After the classics, no study is of greater importance for us than that of the language and literature of France. The breadth of purpose which distinguishes our literature has involved it in only too many technical uncertainties; one of the chief dangers attaching to the direct study of English, to English conceived as an instrument rather than as the end of education, is that it provides no safeguard against confusion between the virtue of breadth and the vice of uncertainty or bungling. French writers exhibit to us in an eminent degree the beauties of precision. Exquisite marksmen, they give us as we read them the delight of clearly distinguishing the rings of the target and of registering the impeccable shots. It is an experience of the greatest value for us. But again it is an experience fraught with dangers, and to these dangers only too many Englishmen succumb. France claims to be the Attica of modern Europe, and those to whom the literature of Athens is unfamiliar accede to the claim and suppose that the functions of literature, the life from which it receives and to which it gives inspiration, are better understood by our neighbours than by ourselves. If our conception is the true one, that idea is wholly illusory. English poetry, with all its failings, represents the Greek spirit expanded and, if partly clouded in the process, reinforced. French poetry is quintessential, a refinement of the refined; a model of method, it is comparatively insignificant in substance, because it has sacrificed truth to perfection and to reason life.

But the message of English literature, of the English spirit, is the culmination of all that the world has yet to offer to the inquiring mind. We cannot effectively receive it unless we are familiar with the elements it holds in solution, the pitfalls it has avoided, the experiences it has incorporated, and unless, when all these things are analysed and appreciated, we still hold fast to the organic principle of the whole, to its prevailing creative integrity. Moreover, the sense of our primary position can only be a misfortune to us unless it goes with a clear recognition of every inadequacy and error. Too much of our English criticism is insular, consisting in the admiration of incidental faults in what is great or of the meanderings of authors who have lost their way. Our poetry, still more our prose, has grown in a soil where weed and seed sprout with equal vigour, and it will be lamentable, it will be fatal, if the love of what is English should mean that we love both alike. English, let us remember it, offers us no standards of discrimination; that is the price it has to pay for its subtlety and comprehensiveness. The Englishman who is to enter perfectly into his inheritance must be a citizen of the world.

Edward Thomas

1878–1917

AUNT ANN'S COTTAGE

Two of us were walking together and talking nearly all the time, just as things occurred to our minds which were at rest in beautiful weather.

'Since we passed that white house behind the cedars,' I laughed, 'we have wandered from Gwithavon, the pure British name of a river in Essex, to a fishmonger's advertisement in the Battersea Park Road. Such are the operations of the majestic intellect. What do you think? Do you suppose the cavemen were very different, except that they can seldom have troubled about philology and would probably have eaten their philologers, and they did without fishmongers because fish were caught to eat and not to sell?'

'Well?' said Jones. 'I daresay what we have in common with the cavemen is what most helps us to go on living except in so far as we are fishmongers and philologers. Scratch a philologer and you will find a sort of caveman.'

'Yes: but isn't it a little disconcerting to think that two men who have been to one of our ancient universities should zigzag in this fashion? I think that to prove our self-respect we ought to go soberly back on our footsteps and see what sort of a pattern we made while we were in charge of the cavemen's god.'

'All right; but let it be simply for fun. It is a game I am very well used to. When we were children, my brother and I used to be sent to chapel to represent our parents who got up too late. After dinner we were put into a room to write down the main points of the sermon. My young brother, who was destined, as you now know, to be an atheist and a statistician, could do this perfectly well, and I could copy from him by right of primogeniture. For I, on the other hand, never heard more than a sentence at a time, and for that matter if I go to a public meeting nowadays to please a lady I never hear more than that. The difference is that now I am bored and impatient with myself and the lady for putting me into a foolish position, whereas nothing was more delightful than the half hour during which my brother listened to the sermon and I went wool-gathering. . . . I don't know who the original wool-gatherers were, but I always think they must have been uncommercial men whose task it was to wander over the mountains and be beforehand with the nesting birds, gathering from rock and thorn the locks of wool left by the sheep, a task that must take them into many a wild new place without overburdening them with wool or profit or applause at the end of the day. . . . While my brother was writing out the skeleton sermon, I used to wander backward over the windings of my chapel wool-gathering and of course strike out again here and there to right or left after more wool and more thorn and rock.

'The preacher was a mild, tall man, with a

mane of curling black hair, clean shaven, long white face, thin exquisitely formed lips, and a rich voice that murmured in a quiet musing manner that enchanted me so much that I was soon in a state of half dream. The light was dim as with gold dust. It was warm. The people around were soporific, too: I imagined them to be asleep and I alone awake, and my first steps had something of the thrill one feels in stealing out of a silent house at dawn. I listened to the preacher's voice and fixed my half-closed eyes on the ash-tree just outside one of the windows on the south side. As a rule the text alone was a sufficient portal to my wanderings. Alas! of all of them I can recall only one, and that because at the end of the sermon the preacher was seized with a fit of sneezing and I felt a slight pang because I finished my ramble at this painful moment. It was not at all an extraordinary wool-gathering, though.

'The text was the three verses in the first chapter of Genesis that describe the work of creation on the fifth day. In that musing way, as if he were oblivious of all but his ideas, which made me really fond of him, the preacher murmured: "Let the waters bring forth abundantly the moving creature that hath life, and fowl that may fly above the earth in the open firmament of heaven."

'That was enough. For me it was all the sermon. I saw at once a coast of red crags and a black sea that was white far below me where the waves got lost in the long corridors between the crags. The moon, newly formed to rule the night, stood full and large and white at the top of the arch of the sky that was black as the sea and without a cloud. And out of the waters were rising by twos and threes, but sometimes in multitudes like a cloud, the birds who were to fly in the open firmament of heaven. Sea birds with long white wings spread wide emerged singly out of the black, and paused on the surface and let their wings rise up like the sides of a lyre and then skimming low this way and that rose up in circles at last and screamed around the moon. Several had only risen a little way when they fell back into the sea and vanished, and these I supposed were destined to be deprived by the divine purpose of their wings and to become fish. Eagles as red as the encircling crags came up also, but they were always solitary and they ascended as upon a whirlwind in one or two long spirals, and blackening the moon for a moment they disappeared. The little birds that sing were usually born in cloudlets, white and yellow and dappled and blue, and, after hovering uncertainly at no great height, made for the crags, where they perched above the white foam and twittered in concert or, straying apart, sang shrill or soft and low or in stormy luxuriance after their own kind. And ever and anon the flocks of those who had soared now floated downwards across the moon and went over my head with necks outstretched and crying towards the mountains and moors and pools or sloped still lower and alighted and sailed on the waters, where they screamed each time the black surface yawned at a new birth

of white or many-coloured wings. Very soon
the sea was chequered from shore to horizon
with birds, and the sky was heaving continually
with others, so that the moon could be seen
either not at all or in slits and wedges, and the
crags were covered, as if with moss and leaves,
with birds, chiefly those that sing, and they
mingled their voices as if in a dawn of May.

'At a word from the preacher creeping in
upon me, I forgot about the fifth day of the
Creation, but not about the birds, and as it
was then February, I thought chiefly about
their nests and eggs. I went over in my mind
the different kinds I had taken the year before.
They were all in one long box procured from
the village shop where it used to hold bottles of
cheapest scent. I had not troubled to arrange
them, and in the chapel I saw the confusion of
the moorhen's and coot's big freckled eggs, and
between these, often in double layers, the blue
and the white and the olive, the spotted, the
blotched and the scrawled eggs. For a minute,
I forgot the eggs by thinking of a poem I had
begun to copy out and had laid away with the
eggs. It was the first poem I had ever read for
my own pleasure several times, and I had begun
to copy it in my best handwriting, the capitals
in red ink. I had got as far as "Some mute in-
glorious Milton here may. . . ." I tried to repeat
the verses but could not, and so I returned to
the eggs. I thought of the April past and the
April to come, when I should once more butt my
way through thickets of perpendicular and stiff
and bristling stems, through brier and thorn and

bramble in the double hedges; I would find the thrushes' nests in a certain oak and blackthorn copse where the birds used hardly anything but moss, and you could see them far away among the dark branches which seldom had many leaves but were furred over with lichens. I would go to all those little ponds shadowed by hazels close to the farms, where there was likely to be a solitary moorhen's home, and up into the pollard willow which used to have four starling's eggs at the bottom of a long narrow pocket. In all those spring days I had no aim but finding nests, and if I was not scrambling in a wood I walked with my head lifted up to the trees or turned aside to the hedges or bent down to the grass and undergrowth. I was not in the least curious about the eggs, or any question of numbers or variation in size, shape, or colour. Sun, rain, wind, deep mud, water over the boots and knees, scratches to arms and legs and face, dust in the eyes, fear of gamekeepers and farmers, excitement, dizziness, weariness, all were expressed by the plain or marked eggs in the scent box; they were all I had and I valued them in the same way and for the same reason as the athlete valued the parsley crown. I recalled the winning of this one and that, repenting sometimes that I had taken more than I should have done from the same nest, sometimes that I had not taken as many as would have been excusable: also, I blushed with annoyance because I had never revisited certain nests which were unfinished or empty when I discovered them—what a pity, perhaps the ploughboy robbed them completely. How careless the country boys were, putting them in their hats and forgetting all about them, often breaking them wantonly. I envied them their opportunities and despised them for taking them as a matter of course.

'I thought of the flowers I trampled over and the smell and the taste of the cowslips and primroses and various leaves and the young brier stems chewed and spat out again as I walked. I began to count up the Sundays that must go before there would be any chance of finding rooks' eggs. And that reminded me of the rookery in the half-dozen elms of a farmhouse home-field close by the best fishing place of all. The arrow-headed reeds grew in thick beds here and there and the water looked extraordinarily mysterious just this side of them, as if it might contain fabulous fish. Only last season I had left my line out there while I slipped through the neighbouring hedge to look for a reed-bunting's nest, and when I returned I had to pull in an empty line which the monster had gnawed through and escaped with hooks and bait. It was just there between the beds of arrow-head and that immense water-dock on the brink: I vowed to try again. Everybody had seen the monster or at least the swirl he made as he struck out into the deeps at a passing tread. "As long as my arm, I daresay," said the carter, and cracked his whip emphatically, with a suggestion that the fish was not to be caught by me. Well, we shall see.

'As usual, the idea of fishing was connected

with my Aunt Ann. There was none worth speaking of unless we stayed with her in our holidays. I often saw persons fishing, who certainly did not stay with her and probably would not have known of her if she was mentioned, but they never caught anything. The way their floats swam had not the right look. Now, I could have enjoyed fishing by those arrow-heads without a bait, so fishy did it look, especially on Sundays when no fishing was allowed: it was unbearable to see that look and have no rod or line.'

'Yes,' I interrupted, 'that fascinating look is quite indescribable, and I can quite understand how

> Simple Simon went a-fishing
> For to catch a whale,
> But all the water he had got
> Was in his mother's pail.

I have seen that look in tiny ponds and fished in one simply on the strength of it and against popular advice, but gave it up because I caught newts continually and nothing else. Do you know, when I lifted them up out of that strange water I shuddered and felt as if I were being punished by a spirit of the pond?'

'I have the same feeling about eels and never fish a second time where I have caught one: their twisting is utterly abandoned and unmingled protest and agony, and I feel that if men did not think even so would they writhe in pain or grief.

'To my wool-gathering. In the chapel I could see that shadowed water by the reeds and the float in the midst. In fact, I always could see that picture in my mind. I liked the water best when it was quite smooth; the mystery was greater, and I used to think I caught more fish out of it in that state. I hoped it would be a still summer and very warm. It was nearly three-quarters of a year since I was there by the rookery meadow last—eight months since I last tasted my aunt's doughy cake! I could see her making it, first stoning the raisins, while the dough was rising in a pan by the fire; when she thought I was not looking she stoned them with her teeth, but I did not mind, and now I come to think of it they were very white teeth, so that I can't think why no man ever married her for them alone. I suppose she was too busy, making cakes and wiping the dough off her fingers, and wondering if we had got drowned in the river, to think about lovers. I am glad no man did marry her; I mean, I was glad then. For she would probably have given up making doughy cakes full of raisins and spice if she had married. She existed for that and for supplying us with lamb and mint sauce and rhubarb tart with cream when we came in from bird's-nesting. How dull it must be for her, thought I in the chapel, all alone there and the fishing over and no birds laying yet, no nephews and, therefore, I supposed, no doughy cakes, for she could not be so greedy as to make them only for herself. She lived all alone in a little cottage in a row at the edge of a village. Hers was an end house. The rest were very neat, but hers was hidden by ivy which grew through the walls, up between the flagstones of the floor, and flapped in at the windows; it grew also over the panes, and was so dense that the mice ran up and down it, and you could see their pale silky bellies as they crossed the glass, if they did not look in over the sill and enter. The ivy was full of sparrows' nests, and it made the neighbours angry that she would not have them pulled out. We never thought of touching these nests, not if the neighbours' sons, who were acquaintances, suggested it. I wished I lived there always, always in a house covered with ivy, and kept by an aunt who baked and fried for you and tied up your cuts, and would clean half-a-hundred perchlings without a murmur, though at the end she had half covered her face and the windows with the flying scales. "Why don't you catch two or three really big ones?" she said, sighing for weariness, but still smiling at us, and putting on her crafty-looking spectacles. "Whew! if we could!" we said to one another: it seemed possible as we stood there, for she was a wonderful woman, and the house wonderful too—no anger, no sorrow, no fret, such a large fireplace, everything different from London and altogether better. The ticking of her three clocks was delicious, especially early in the morning as you lay awake, or when you got home tired, and it was twilight and no lamps. Everything had been like that in the house "ever so long," you could not tell how long; it was natural, like the trees; it was never stale; you never came down in the morning and felt you had done the same yesterday and would do the same to-morrow, as if each day was like a new badly-written line in a copy-book, with the same senseless, dismal words at the head of the page. Why couldn't we always live there? There was no chapel for us. Sunday was not the day of grim dulness when everybody was set free from work, only to show that he or she did not know what to do or not to do; if they had been chained slaves, they could not have been stiffer or more grim.

'In my fancy these adult people were a different race: I had no thought that I should become like that, and I laughed without a pang. How different my aunt with her face serene, kind, notwithstanding that she was bustling about all day and had trodden down her heels and let her hair break out into horns and wisps. I thought of the race of women and girls. I thought (with a little pity) they were very much nicer than men, thought more of you and were kinder. I would rather be a man, I mused, and yet I was sure women were better. I would not give up my right to be a man some day, but for the present there was no comparison between the two in my affections; there was not a man I should have missed. Odd things the women did, though. They always wore gloves when they went out, for example. Now, if I put on gloves, it was almost as bad as putting a handkerchief over my eyes, or cotton-wool in my ears. They picked flowers with gloved hands. Certainly they had their weaknesses. But think of the different ways of giving an apple. A man caused it to pass into your hands in a way that made it annoying to give thanks. A woman

M

gave herself with it, and it was as if the apple was part of her, and you took it away and ate it, sitting alone very peacefully and thinking of nothing. A boy threw it at you as if he wanted to knock your teeth out, and, of course, you threw it back at him again with the same intent. A girl gave it so that you wanted to give it back, if you were not somehow afraid. I thought of three girls who lived near my aunt, and would do anything I wanted, as if it was not I but they who wanted it. Perhaps it was. Perhaps they wanted nothing except to give. Well, and that was rather stupid, too.

'There the preacher's voice must have half released me from the spell, and I turned to a dozen things, as what o'clock it was, whether one of my pigeons would have laid its second egg when I got home, and how many I should have altogether in a year's time, whether Monday's post would bring a letter from a friend who was in Kent, going about the woods with a game-keeper who gave him squirrels, stoats, jays, mag-pies, an owl, and once a woodcock to skin. I recalled the sweet smell of the squirrels; it was abominable to kill them, but I liked skinning them. I went over the increasing row of books on my shelf. First came "The Compleat Angler," the thought of which gave me a brief entry into an indefinite alluring world of men rising early in the mornings and catching many fish, and talking to milkmaids who had sung songs with beautiful voices, and using strange baits. I wish I could say now how that book (a very poor edition) shut up between its gilded covers a different, embalmed, enchanted life without any care, from which life I emerged with the words "as wholesome as a pearch of Rhine," which recalled actual perch swimming in clear water in the green streets of the ponds on sunny days. Then there were Scott's poems, a book which then only meant a vision of armed men rising suddenly out of heather and rocks on a mountain side, and a fierce, plaided chief exclaiming:

And, Saxon, I am Rhoderick Dhu.

Next "Robinson Crusoe," "Grimm's Fairy Tales," "The Iliad," and a mass of almost babyish books, tattered and now untouched, but strictly preserved; and lastly, "The Adventures of King Arthur and the Round Table." As I reached this book, "Inexorable man," I heard the lady of the lake say to Merlin, "thy powers are resistless"; moonlit waters overhung by mountains and castles on their crags, boats with a dark, mysterious freight; knights trampling and glittering; sorceries, battles, dragons, kings and maidens, stormed or flitted through my mind, some only as words and phrases learnt by heart, some as pictures. It was a delicious but shadowy entertainment with an indefinable quality of remoteness tinged by the pale moonshine and the cold lake that finally suggested the reward and solid comfort of tea at my aunt's house, and thick slices, "cut ugly," of her doughy cake.

'Processions of living people, these also partly in words and partly in pictures, passed through my mind. They were faces peering above bundles of clothes, but some crying out for clearer recognition by means of tones of voice, decided and often repeated expressions of all the features acting together, and producing the effect which was their soul. They came up to me for judgment. Most I sent quickly away; others I stopped and, like a schoolmaster, compelled them to recite some chance word or deed of theirs tarrying in my memory. On they came, and I became conscious of the numbers at that moment surrounding me in the chapel seat. I looked at them and grew afraid of their silent solitude, and tried to keep myself distinct yet felt myself melting into the mass when the preacher quoted the words:

> He liveth best who loveth best
> All creatures great and small.

What he went on to say was lost. I looked at the people to see what they would do. The preacher said the words majestically, and I supposed them to be true. I was sorry for those squirrels which the gamekeeper shot, but I wanted to have their skins: with all these others I thought it must be different. They had listened to the sermon, they came to listen, and probably to learn and follow the true. I was expecting them to get up and go out, and show that they loved something very small, like an ant or fly. At that moment a small moth alighted on my knee, and I watched it creep and flutter up my leg to my shoulder. I did not feel that I loved it. The moth flew on to the upper part of a man's sleeve in front of me. He scarcely moved his head, but I knew he had seen the flight; he lifted his hand slowly, dropped it swiftly on the moth, whose scales powdered his coat, and then became rigid again. Evidently the words were not believed to be true. Why did poets say so many things that people seemed to like and did not believe, I wondered? But what if they were true, after all? I resolved to go on with my copying of Gray's *Elegy* that very afternoon, also not to collect moths. It entered my head that my aunt was merciless to mice; it was a grave objection, for she was to me the corner-stone of the universe. Here the sermon ended with a sneeze. I was very sorry for the preacher, but I fear I did not love him. As to moths, I never became a collector.'

'What a very consistent wool-gathering,' said I; 'I don't suppose the sermon was more so. And did you notice it was all pictorial? I'll be bound you don't go wool-gathering in that fashion now, and if the child is so much superior to us, how much more the caveman may have been!'

'Except that I don't believe any caveman ever had such an aunt as mine. There can have been no superfluous good women in those days, born simply to delight their sisters' and brothers' boys.'

'And now let us set out for Gwithavon!'

E. M. Forster

1879—

PHILO'S LITTLE TRIP

It was nearly a serious tumble—more serious than he anticipated. There were six in his party, all Hebrew gentlemen of position and intelligence, such as may be seen in these days filling a first-class carriage in the Cairo express on their way up to interview the Government. In those days the Government was not at Cairo but at Rome, and the six gentlemen were on their way to interview the Emperor Caligula. Observe them in their well-appointed little yacht, slipping out of the Mohammed Ali Square, which was then under water and part of the Eastern Harbour. Their faces are pale, partly from fasting, partly from anticipation, for the passage can be rough in February. And their mission was even more poignant than cotton. It concerned their faith. Jews at Alexandria had been killed and teased, and some Gentiles had, with the connivance of the Governor, erected a bronze chariot in their principal synagogue—not even a new chariot, for the horses had no tails or feet. It was a chariot once dedicated to—O Pollution! —Cleopatra. There it stood, and the Jews did not like to throw it down. And into their smaller synagogues, smaller objects, such as portraits of the Emperor, had been thrust. It is a delicate matter to complain to an Emperor about his own portrait, but Caligula was known to be a charming and reasonable young man, and the deputation had been selected for its tact.

As they crossed the harbour, the Temple of Cæsar stood out on the right, so impressive, so brilliant, that Philo could not repress his enthusiasm and recalled the view in after years.

> 'It is a piece incomparably above all others (he writes). It stands by a most commodious harbour, wonderfully high and large in proportion; an eminent sea mark: full of choice paintings and statues with donatives and oblatives in abundance; and then it is beautiful all over with gold and silver: the model curious and regular in the disposition of the parts, as galleries, libraries, porches, courts, halls, walks, and consecrated groves, as glorious as expense and art could make them, and everything in its proper place; besides that, the hope and comfort of seafaring men, either coming in or going out.'

When would he see his temple as he came in? Although Cleopatra had begun it for Antony, and Augustus finished it for himself, it filled him with love, as he turned from it with reluctance to the coast on the left, really more important, because Jehovah had translated the entire Bible into Greek there. There stood those seventy huts! O wonder! It was one of the anecdotes with which he hoped to rivet the attention of Caligula, when they arrived at Rome.

That charming and reasonable young man had

lately recovered from a severe illness, at which the whole civilised world rejoiced, and the Eternal City was full of embassies waiting to congratulate him. Among these, ominously enough, was a counter-deputation from Alexandria, strongly anti-Semite in tone. Philo watched it narrowly. The imperial invalid did not arrive till August, and at first things went pleasantly enough. He caught sight of the Jews one day as he was calling on his mother, seemed transported with delight and waved his hand to them, also sent a message that he would see them at once, but immediately left for Naples, and they had to follow him thither.

It was somewhere between Naples and Baiæ that the little trip came to its end. We cannot say where exactly, for the reason that the Emperor received the deputation over a considerable space of ground. He was continually on the trot throughout the audience, and they had to trot after him. He passed from room to room and from villa to villa, all of which, he told them, he had thrown open for their pleasure. They thanked him and tried to say more. He trotted on. With him ran the counter-deputation, and also a mob of concierges, housekeepers, glaziers, plumbers, upholsterers and decorators, to whom he kept flinging orders. At last he stopped. The Jews of Alexandria approached. And with a voice of thunder he cried, 'So you are the criminals who say I am not a god.' It was shattering, it was appalling, it was the very point they had hoped would not be raised. For they worshipped Jehovah only.

The counter-deputation shouted with delight, and the six Hebrew gentlemen cried in unison, 'Caligula! Caligula! do not be angry with us. We have sacrificed for you not once but three times—first at your accession, secondly when you were ill, thirdly when——' But the Emperor interrupted them with merciless logic. 'Exactly. For me and not to me,' and dashed off to inspect the ladies' apartments. After him they ran, hopeless of removing Cleopatra's chariot or of interesting him in the Septuagint. They would be lucky if they secured their lives. He climbed up to look at a ceiling. They climbed too. He ran along a plank; so did the Jews. They did not speak, partly from lack of breath, partly because they were afraid of his reply. At last, turning in their faces, he asked, 'Why don't you eat pork?' The counter-deputation shouted again. The Jews replied that different races ate different things, and one of them, to carry off the situation, said some people didn't eat lamb. 'Of course they don't,' said the Emperor, 'lamb is beastly.' The situation grew worse. A fit of fury had seized Caligula at the thought of lamb and he yelled, 'What are your laws? I wish to know what your laws are!' They began to tell him and he cried out, 'Shut those windows,' and ran away down a corridor. Then he turned with extraordinary gentleness and said, 'I beg your pardon, what were you saying?' They began to tell him of their laws, and he said, 'We'll have all the old pictures hung together here, I think.' Stopping anew, he looked round at his shattered train of ambassadors and artisans,

M*

and smiling, remarked, 'And these are the people who think I am not a god. I don't blame them. I merely pity them. They can go.' Philo led his party back to Alexandria, there to meditate on the accident that had so spoilt their little trip: Caligula was mad.

Yet did it signify—signify in the long run? The history of the Chosen People is full of such contretemps, but they survive and thrive. Six hundred years later, when Amr took the city, he found 40,000 Jews there. And look at them in the railway carriage now. Their faces are anxious and eloquent of past rebuffs. But they are travelling First.

Robert Lynd

1879–1949

THE HUMOUR OF HOAXES

IT was only the other day that Mr. G. A. Birmingham gave us a play about a hoax at the expense of an Irish village, in the course of which a statue was erected to an imaginary Irish-American General, the aide-de-camp of the Lord-Lieutenant coming down from Dublin to perform the unveiling ceremony. Lady Gregory, it may be remembered, had previously used a similar theme in *The Image*. And now comes the story of yet another statue hoax from Paris. On the whole the Paris joke is the best of the three. It was a stroke of genius to invent a great educationist called Hégésippe Simon. One can hardly blame the members of the Chamber of Deputies for falling to the lure of a name like that. Perhaps they should have been warned by the motto which M. Paul Bérault, of *L'Eclair*, the perpetrator of the hoax, quoted from among the sayings of the 'precursor' to whom he wished to erect a centenary statue. 'The darkness vanishes when the sun rises' is an aphorism which is almost too good to be true. M. Bérault, however, relying upon the innocence of human nature, sent a circular to a number of senators and deputies opposed to him in politics, announcing that, 'thanks to the

liberality of a generous donor, the disciples of
Hégésippe Simon have at length been able to
collect the funds necessary for the erection of a
monument which will rescue the precursor's
memory from oblivion,' and invited them to
become honorary members of a committee to
celebrate the event. Despite the fact that he
quoted the sentence about the darkness and the
sunrise, thirty of the politicians replied that they
would be delighted to help in the centenary rejoicings. M. Bérault thereupon published the
names with the story of the hoax he had practised
on them, and as a result, according to the newspaper correspondents, all Paris has been laughing at the joke, 'the good taste of which', adds
one of them, 'would hardly be relished in
England, where other political manners obtain.'

With all respect to this patriotic journalist,
I am afraid the love of hoaxing and practical
joking cannot be limited to the Latin, or even to
the Continental, races. It is a passion that is as
universal as lying, and a good deal older than
drinking. It is merely the instinct for lying,
indeed, turned to comic account. Christianity,
unable to suppress it entirely, had to come to
terms with it, and as a result we have one day of
the year, the First of April, devoted to the
humour of this particular sin. There are many
explanations of the origin of All Fools' Day, one
of which is that it is a fragmentary memorial of
the mock trial of Jesus, and another of which
refers it to the belief that it was on the first day
of April that Noah sent out the dove from the
Ark. But the Christian or Hebrew origin of the

festival appears to be unlikely in view of the fact that the Hindus have an All Fools' Day of their own, the Huli Festival, on almost exactly the same date. One may take it that it was in origin simply a great natural holiday, on which men enjoyed the licence of lying as they enjoy the licence of drinking on a Bank Holiday. There is no other sport for which humanity would be more likely to desire the occasional sanction of Church and State than the sport of making fools of our neighbours. We must have fools if we cannot have heroes. Some people, who are enthusiasts for destruction, indeed, would give us fools and knaves in the place of our heroes, and have even an idea that they would be serving some moral end in doing so. It is on an iconoclastic eagerness of one kind or another that nearly all hoaxing and practical joking is based. It consists chiefly in taking somebody down a peg. The boy who used to shout 'Wolf!', however, may have been merely an excessively artistic youth who enjoyed watching the varied expression on the faces of the sweating and disillusioned passers-by who ran to his assistance. Obviously, a man's face is a dozen times more interesting to look at when it is crimson with frustrated virtue than when it is placid with thought of the price of pigs.

This is not to justify the morality of hoaxing. It is to explain it as an art for art's sake. Murder can be, and has been, defended on the same grounds. It is to be feared, however, that few hoaxers or murderers can be named who pursued the hobby in the disinterested spirit of artists.

In most cases there is some motive of cruelty or dislike. One would not go to the trouble of murdering and hoaxing people if it did not hurt or vex somebody or other. Those who invent hoaxes are first cousins of the boy who ties kettles or lighted torches to cats' tails. It is the terror of the cat that amuses him. If the cat purred as the instruments of torture were fitted on to it the boy would feel that he had serious cause for complaint. There is no doubt a great deal of the cruelty of boys which is experimental rather than malicious—the practice of blowing up frogs, for instance. But, for the most part, it must be admitted, a spice of cruelty is counted a gain in human amusements. This is callous thoughtlessness in boys, but it is a deliberate enthusiasm in primitive man, out of which we have to be slowly civilised. There is probably no more popular game with the infancy of the streets than covering a brick with an old hat in the hope that some glorious fool will come along who will kick hat and brick together, and go limping and swearing on his way. One might easily produce a host of similar instances of the humour of the small boy who looks so like an angel and behaves so like a devil. There are, it may be, thousands of small boys who never perpetrated an act of such cheerful malice in their lives. But even they have usually some other outlet for their comic cruelty. The half of comic literature depends upon someone getting cudgelled or ducked in a well, or subjected to some pain. It is one of the paradoxes of comedy, indeed, that, even when we like the hero of it, we also like to see him hurt and humiliated. We are glad when Don Quixote is beaten to a jelly, and when his teeth are knocked down his throat. We rejoice at every discomfort that befalls poor Parson Adams. Humour, even when it reaches the pitch of genius, has still about it much of the elemental cruelty of the boy who arranges a pin upon the point of which his friend may sit down, or who pulls away a chair and sends someone sprawling.

Hoaxes, at the best, spring from a desire to harry our neighbours. As a rule, refined men and women have by this time given up the ambition to cause others physical pain, but one still hears of milder annoyances being practised with considerable spirit. It was Theodore Hook, I believe, who originated the practice of hoaxing tradesmen into delivering long caravans of goods at some house or other, to the fury of the householder and the disturbance of traffic. Every now and then the jest is still revived, whereupon everybody condemns it and—laughs at it. That is one of the oddest facts about the hoax as a form of humour. No one has a good word to say for it, and yet everyone who tells you the story of a hoax tells it with a chuckle. Some years ago a young gentleman from one of the Universities palmed himself off on an admiral— was it not?—as the Sultan of Zanzibar, and was entertained as such by the officers on board one of King George's ships. Everybody frowned at the young gentleman's taste, but nobody outside the Navy failed to enjoy the hoax as the best item of the day's news. Similarly, the Köpenick affair set not only all Germany but all Europe laughing. Skill and audacity always delight us for their own sakes; when it is rogueries that are skilful and audacious, they shock us into malicious appreciation. They are adventures standing on their heads. It is difficult not to forgive a clever impostor so long as it is not we on whom he has imposed.

As for the Hégésippe hoax, it may be that there is even an ethical element in our pleasure. Such a hoax as this is a pin stuck in pretentiousness. If it is an imposture, it is an imposture on impostors. One feels that it is good that members of Parliament should be exposed from time to time. Otherwise they might become puffed up. Still, there remains a very good reason why we should oppose a disapproving front to hoaxes of all sorts. We ourselves may be the next victim. Most of us have a Hégésippe Simon in our cupboard. Whether in literature, history, or politics, the human animal is much given to pretending to knowledge that he does not possess. There are some men whom one could inveigle quite easily into a discussion on plays of Shakespeare and Euripides which were never written. I remember how one evening two students concocted a poem beginning with the drivelling line, 'I stood upon the rolling of the years,' and foisted it on a noisy admirer of Keats as a work of the master. Similarly, in political arguments, one has known a man to invent sayings of Gladstone or Chamberlain without being challenged. This is, of course, not amusing in itself. It becomes amusing only when the other disputants, instead of confessing their ignorance, make a pretence of being acquainted with the invented quotation. It is our dread of appearing ignorant that leads us into the enactment of this kind of lying. We will go to any extreme rather than confess that we have never even heard of Hégésippe Simon. Luckily, Hégésippe Simon happens to be a person who can trip our pretentiousness up. But the senators and deputies who were willing to celebrate the precursor's centenary were probably not humbugs to any greater degree than if they had consented to celebrate the anniversary of Diderot or Rousseau or Alfred de Musset. It is utter imposture, this practice of doing honour to great names which mean less to one than a lump of sugar; and if an end could be put to centenary celebrations in all countries, no great harm would be done to public honesty. On the other hand, most public rejoicings over men of genius would be exceedingly small if all the speeches and applause had to come from the heart without any addition from those who merely like to be in the latest movement. Perhaps the adherents of Hégésippe Simon are necessary in order to make it profitable to be a man of genius at all. They are not only a useful claque, but they pay. That is why, even if William Shakespeare, Anatole France, and Bergson are only other and better names for Hégésippe, it would be madness to destroy such enthusiasm as has gathered round them. M. Bérault, by his light-hearted hoax on his political opponents, has struck at the very roots of popular homage to men of genius.

THIS BODY

THERE are occasional items of news in the papers that pull us up and tempt us to examine our attitude in regard to some question as if for the first time. One item of the kind was the announcement of the will of Edward Martyn, Irish revivalist and cousin of Mr. George Moore, in accordance with which his dead body was to be given to a medical school for dissection and the remains were afterwards to be buried, like other dissecting-room corpses, in a pauper's grave. Who, on reading this, could fail to turn round and ask himself whether he could endure the prospect of his body's being subjected, though past sense, to the knives of medical students? There are few people, indeed, who could be entirely indifferent on such a matter. If a man is careless of the fate of his body after death, as Socrates was, it is thought a sufficiently remarkable fact to be preserved in his biography. Christians ought, perhaps, of all people to have been most able to achieve this happy carelessness. But even the belief in the immortality of the soul has seldom persuaded human beings that a dead body is as worthless as the husk of a seed that has burst out of darkness into a flower. In the result, Christians have for centuries paid honour to dead bodies as though they were more noble than the living, and many a poor man has never had the hats of passers-by raised to him till he has driven through the streets as a corpse. I do not know how far modern Christians believe that after long ages at the sound of a trumpet the body that has been the prey of worms and of dusty time will actually rise out of the earth, recomposed into the likeness of a living man. Probably there are few who would now confess to any certainty about the matter. But many good men in the past believed that the dead body, far from being a worthless garment that the soul had cast off for ever, was the very garment that the soul would resume on its exaltation into Paradise. Even those Christians who despised the body alive glorified it in death, and a saint's body that he had kept starved and unclean as beneath contempt was revered after death as something with a divine power to perform miracles. This may seem, and is, paradoxical, but the awe of the living in presence of a dead body is natural to reflecting men. Certain savages, we are told, pay honour to the bodies of the dead only because they fear that, if they do not, the spirits of the dead will haunt them. But the civilised man, who has no such terrors, is as reverent because, perhaps, he sees in the dead body a sign and wonder that changes the aspect of the world for him and brings him to the very door of the mystery of his own life.

Whatever be the reason, the world has not yet outgrown the feeling that the dead must be honoured and not treated as refuse. The outcry during the War against the supposed German 'corpse-factory,' in which dead soldiers were turned into useful oils or chemicals for the munition factories, was something more than an expression of propagandist hypocrisy. It was absurd to believe that the Germans, being human beings, would sanction such a thing; but it was natural to believe that, if they did, they would themselves be so much the less human beings. And yet, if it is right to use a dead man's body for purposes of medicine, there is no logical reason why it should be a crime to use a dead man's body for purposes of war. It is arguable, indeed, that the needs of war are the more urgent, and that therefore the 'corpse-factory' should be less horrifying to us than the dissecting-room. As a matter of fact, the dissecting-room would horrify us a great deal more if it were not that we have nationalised (or municipalised) the bodies of friendless paupers. When anatomists sent their scouts into the graveyards to dig up the dead who had died solvent, the friends of the dead leagued themselves together and guarded the body by night till it had rotted in the earth. How many of us in our childhood grew up amid a thousand-and-one tales of body-snatchers! What devils they and the kidnappers seemed! How thrilling to hear of their adventures! We might laugh at them, as at the crimes of Bluebeard, but we laughed uneasily. Yet in another thousand years men may be looking back on the body-snatchers and kidnappers as among the saints of science, and Burke and Hare may be honoured as martyrs. I do not think they will, but it is possible at least that science progressed as a result of their crimes. There is certainly as much to be said in reason for allowing the dissecting-room to choose its bodies casually from the graveyards as for giving it the right to use its lancets on the un-claimed bodies of paupers. But, as most of us hope that neither we nor our friends will end even in these costly days in the workhouse, we are content with the present compromise, and we scarcely ask ourselves how the dissecting-rooms are to be supplied when poverty has been abolished. No doubt there will always be enough men and women with such a religious devotion to science that they will volunteer for the dissecting-room in their wills. But our first instinct, if volunteers were called for, would be to shrink as if from a painful sacrifice.

I, for one, should find it difficult to bequeath my body into the reckless hands of medical students. I do not know why, except that I cannot help somehow or other identifying my body with myself. Socrates was philosopher enough, on the eve of his death, to see his body as a shell and to say to himself: 'That is not I.' Most of us, however, though we might admit in our intelligences that our bodies were not we, would continue to think of them as ourselves in our imaginations. Whatever our essence, it is through the body that we have visited the earth, and we cannot dissociate from it any of the experiences that have made life so well worth living that we wish to go on with it. Our body was at least our inseparable consort, whether we went to church or to the tavern, whether we found our happiness in the sunny waist of the earth or by a coal fire at home, whether we played in the nursery or were kings of the foot-ball field, or fell in love or were rewarded with

the great public prizes of the world. There has
not been a single experience of our lives that
would have been possible without hands, feet,
heart, lungs, brain, mouth, eyes and ears. It is
no wonder that St. Francis, on his death-bed,
apologised to his body for having used it so ill,
for without it there would have been no St.
Francis, and the birds would have gone without
their only sermon. How, then, can we be indifferent to such an associate? If a church made
from the stones of the hills becomes sacred
through associations, so that men, on entering it,
take off their hats out of reverence for the temple
of God, how much less surprising is it that a man
should take thought for the fate of his body that
is made of flesh and bones? Many men even
leave instructions that honours shall be paid
to their dead bodies such as they never demanded
during life, like the Ulster Unionist who asked
that his body should be wrapped in a Union
Jack and taken out and buried in Britannia's sea.
Others have died the more easily because they
knew that their remains (as the phrase goes)
would be buried in some particular place—on
the top of a hill, or in a cemetery with ghostly
headstones visible from the sea at evening, or
under the trees by an old church in a half-
deserted village. I myself should feel melancholy
if I thought I was to be buried in the Sahara or
even in one of the colonies, and for a long time
I should have felt a sharp pang if it had been
foretold that I should be buried anywhere
except in my own country, and I was particular
even as to the exact spot in that. I do not know

if I care so much as I once did. I fancy I have a growing objection to being buried anywhere at all. Nor do I take to the prospect of being burned. So long as one thinks of one's body as a living thing, one can hardly imagine an end to it that does not seem almost as horrible as the dissecting-table. To be perpetuated as a mummy —who would care for that? Better to be cleansed swiftly by the earth into a skeleton in a Christian grave. When I had just left school and thought I was a pantheist, I used to take a sentimental pleasure, as other boys have done, in the prospect that flowers would spring from my tomb. I even liked the thought that I should help to fertilise the earth for those flowers. I cannot comfort myself so easily now, though I should be the happier if I thought the gardener would occasionally pay some small attention to my coverture. But I have really no taste for the underworld, and, if it were possible, I do not think I should ever visit it, but should continue on the floor of this excellent earth as long as the Wandering Jew. It is said that in the end men grow tired of the body, and are glad enough to leave it. Those who do, I fancy, are bolder spirits than I. I am naturally a stay-at-home, and the only home in which I have lived all my life is my body. Born under Saturn, I have nevertheless been happy enough never to wish to change it for a better. If I have wished to be a better man, I have still wished for the new spirit to inhabit the same body, for, though it is a body that no man could be proud of, not being built in any of the noble styles of architecture,

I am used to it and am bound to it by all manner of sympathies. Not that I have looked after it as well as I might have done. I have allowed it to sink into dilapidation and disrepair, so that it already resembles more than it should a piece of antiquity. But even the crooked man with the crooked cat probably lived happily enough in his crooked little house, and would not have left it without compulsion. Hence, though I cannot share their faith, I should not be sorry to think that those Christians were right who believe that on the last day the body will be whisked through the air to become the house of the soul again in a better world. I do not defend myself or pretend that this is a laudable attitude. I admire Socrates, indeed, and all those who have despised the body as a fragile pot or as grass that withers, but I cannot help recognising the fact that I am not of their company.

On the other hand, I cannot go so far as those people who shrink from the grave all the more because they cannot endure the thought of the rain beating down upon them by night and chilling their senseless bones. I read somewhere lately that, when the woman he loved died, Abraham Lincoln was almost driven mad during a storm by the feeling that the wind was howling and the rain falling on her grave. Others have told me that they share this feeling, and I know a man who said that he would hate to be buried in a certain graveyard because it was 'very damp.' But then he was subject to rheumatism. His objection was as valid, however, as is the objection of most of us to lie, misshapen and skinny, under the eyes of a professor on the dissecting-table. We impute to our dead bodies many of the senses and shames of the living, and we shudder without reason at the thought of things occurring to them that could injure us only while we are alive. Thus do we give ourselves an extension of life in our fancies. It seems as though we must be surer that life is worth living than that death is worth dying. But, even on this matter, there is room for hope.

Gilbert Norwood

1880–1954

TOO MANY BOOKS

WHEN Julius Cæsar allowed the Library of
Alexandria to burn, excellent people no doubt
exclaimed: 'Lo, another cord added to the
scourge of war!' Certainly countless students
since the Revival of Learning have looked upon
that conflagration as one of the world's disasters.
It was no such thing, but a vast benefit. And
one of the worst modern afflictions is the print-
ing-press; for its diabolical power of multiplica-
tion has enabled literature to laugh at sudden
mischance and deliberate enmity. We are
oppressed, choked, buried by books.

Let not the last sentence mislead. I do not
mean that we, or some few of us, are asphyxiated
by barren learning; that is another story. Nor am
I adding yet another voice to the chorus which
reviles bad literature—the ceaseless nagging at
Miss Ethel M. Dell. I have read none of her
books; and in any case that, too, is another
story. No; I mean good literature—the books
(to take contemporary instances) of Mr. Arnold
Bennett and Pierre Loti, of Schnitzler and Mr.
Max Beerbohm, and countless others ancient
and modern, European, American, Asiatic, and
Polynesian (an epoch-making novel from Ota-
heite is much overdue). And when I say 'good,'

I mean 'good.' I have no intention of imitating those critics whose method of creating a *frisson* is to select the most distinguished author or artist and then, not call him bad, but imply that he is already recognised as bad by some unnamed and therefore awe-inspiring coterie. They do not write: 'Mr. Hardy is a bungler,' but: 'Unless Mr. Jugg takes more pains, his work will soon be indistinguishable from Mr. Hardy's.'

It was a famous, almost a proverbial, remark that Sappho's poems were 'few, but roses.' What should we say if we found roses on every table, rose-trees along the streets, if our tramcars and lamp-posts were festooned with roses, if roses littered every staircase and dropped from the folds of every newspaper? In a week we should be organising a 'campaign' against them as if they were rats or house-flies. So with books. Week in, week out, a roaring torrent of novels, essays, plays, poems, books of travel, devotion, and philosophy, flows through the land—all good, all 'provocative of thought' or else 'in the best tradition of British humour'; that is the mischief of it. And they are so huge. Look at 'The Forsyte Saga,' confessedly in itself a small library of fiction; 'The Challenge to Sirius' is four short novels stitched together; consider the 'Golden Bough,' how it grows. One is tempted to revolt and pretend in self-defence that these works are clever, facile, and bad. But they are not; far from it. The flood leaves you no breath. Hardly have you recovered from Mr. C. E. Montague's dazzling 'Fiery Particles' when Mr. Guedalla comes at you with 'Masters and Men.'

Stop reading for an instant and you miss something really first-rate. Have you finished Anatole France? Thank Heaven therefor, because 'Batouala' awaits you. 'From the four corners of the earth they come': Tagore whispers from Bengal, Sinclair Lewis from the Middle West, Olive Schreiner delivers her Thoughts on South Africa, and from the icy North stalks a Jötun of a book by Knut Hamsun.

Only a creature possessed of Macaulay's reading-power and the leisure of St. Simeon Stylites could keep his head above the stream of contemporary literature. Yet even he would be in miserable case. There is 'our magnificent heritage' to be dealt with—the accumulation of classical English literature. And, vista behind vista, one sees the literature of other European nations, stretching back to the Greek and Roman classics and frowned over by those august nightmares, the Sacred Books of the East.

What is to be done about it? Even if we allow no time for frivolities and read only those works which 'you really *must* read,' it has now become impossible for the longest-lived, the most methodical and resolute mortal to get through the excellent literature which stares at him from the shelves with mute entreaty and reproach. Of course some people pretend that they can manage it. The professional critics imply not only that they themselves do so, but also (infuriating trick!) that every other decent person does it. If they were simple-hearted and began their essays with the statement: 'I have read all Samuel Richardson's novels,' we might admire, envy, or disbelieve, according to our taste or experience, and no harm would be done. But that would be vulgar boasting. On the other hand, we really must have some reward for reading Richardson to the end. So we advertise our exploit by an apparent accident. Hence the ritual opening: 'Everyone remembers the touching climax of "Pamela."' It is nonsense, of course. Everyone does *not* remember the passage in 'Pamela.' In fact, only one in a hundred English people knows that there is such a book; only one in a hundred thousand has read it; and of those few, quite ninety per cent. have done so because circumstances (to be described below) have compelled them. I do not believe that, of persons now living, more than ten really know and love 'Pamela' for its own sake. So far, again, no harm is done; there are plenty of other excellent books, as I have remarked already. But observe. The 'everyone remembers' sentence is read by thousands. Each of them (save the Ten) suddenly sees a spectral finger pointing out from the page; a Voice sounds in his spirit's ear: 'Everyone—except you!' He beholds himself as the one miscreant in a world of Pamelarians—undetected for the moment, but how long will his precarious safety continue? The first man whom he meets in club or train may ask: 'Don't you think Pamela is splendid when she . . .?' Who but a slave would go through life saying, 'Oh—er—yes'?

So the horror begins. That one sentence drives hundreds of people bounding like hunted

fawns to the Free Library. After a three-months'
seclusion they emerge into the light of day, safe.
Then with a masterful smile they once more
pick up their weekly paper, only to drop it with
a strangled moan. They have caught sight of
the jaunty statement: 'Few will accept the
author's suggestion that Gogol is the Russian
Hergesheimer.' Here is a Russian, Gogol—
poet, painter, novelist?—and one Hergesheimer,
apparently not a Russian. Heavens! 'Will the
line stretch out to the crack of doom?' What,
I repeat, is to be done? Various remedies are
in vogue, none efficacious, indeed—that is my
point—all deleterious. There is nothing for it
but burning nine-tenths of the stuff. For consider these remedies.

First, of course, comes the man who simply
gives up, who says: 'I haven't the time,' and
goes under. Virtue, they say, is its own reward.
Not for him. He tries to pass it off blusteringly,
but he is ashamed of himself till death.

Second is the man who, swindler though he be,
yet merits applause as paying back the 'everyone' journalist in his own base coin. He defines
in his mind the little patch of literature that he
can read, then condemns all the rest on general
grounds, evolving a formula which shall be
vaguely tenable and shall vaguely absolve him.
An eager youth asks: 'Pray, Sir, what is your
opinion of Mrs. Virginia Woolf?' He replies:
'No opinion of mine, my dear Guildenstern,
would be of much use to you, as regards Mrs.
Woolf. I fear I am an old fogey. These modern
people seem to me to have lost their way.

Fielding and Jane Austen are good enough for me.' Guildenstern retires, suitably abashed, and vaguely classing Mrs. Woolf with Mr. Bertram Atkey, Alice Meynell with Ella Wheeler Wilcox.

The third man gallantly faces the insoluble problem by following the fashion. Setting his jaw, he specialises in the moderns of whom one reads most in the *Times Literary Supplement*. Feverishly he cons the work of all the authors enshrined in that austere mausoleum; feverishly, because he may at any moment be caught napping by some more alert practitioner. This third section forms the bulk of the educated class. Members are everywhere, and spoil everything. Literature has two great uses: the fundamental use is that it creates and satisfies a keener taste for life; the superficial use is that it provides a precious social amenity. Our third man not only knows nothing of the first; he ruins the second. Decent people converse about books with a view to finding common ground and exchanging delight (deep or frivolous) thereon. But the Third Man is mostly antisocial. He selects some voluminous author and catechises his victim till he has found a work which the victim has not read. With a hoot of joyous disgust he leaps upon the confession and extols the unread book as the finest of the list. Such a man will always be found smacking his lips in public over Stevenson's 'Wrong Box' or Lewis Carroll's 'Sylvie and Bruno.' Chief of this tribe, apparently, was no less a person than Coleridge, of whom Hazlitt reports: 'He did not speak of his [Butler's] "Analogy," but of his "Sermons at the Rolls Chapel," of which I had never heard. Coleridge somehow always contrived to prefer the *unknown* to the *known*.' Exactly; for the great aims of such people are (1) to avoid being scored off; (2) to score off others. It is this ignoble competition which has ruined taste, for to carry it on we must needs follow the crowd. It would never do to enter a room full of persons discussing Masefield or Walter de la Mare and explain wistfully: 'I've been reading Whittier all day.' Masefield and de la Mare are good—yes, maybe; but we keep up with them not for that reason, but because they are the gods of the literary weeklies. Our notion that commerce is the first of human activities has ruined the noble art of reading; for, though competition is the life of trade, it is the death of social intercourse and of social arts. The greatest things in life flourish by being shared, not by being monopolised.

Our Fourth Class is far the most respectable. It advocates what may be termed the Cream Theory. 'Since we cannot read all the good books, let us attempt to know the best that has been written in all times and places.' So after a solid banquet of English, they move off to Dante (a great man for this class, and read by scarcely anyone else), Goethe, Tolstoi, Racine, Ibsen, Cervantes, Virgil, Homer. A respectable kind of person, we said; but not necessarily sagacious. In fact, they are utterly, almost horribly, mistaken.

For it is an error to suppose that because an

author has by the world in general been placed upon a pinnacle, every reader can derive much good from him. Do we not see that a bright boy of twelve finds nothing particular in Milton or Thackeray? (Someone objects: 'Oh, but he does!' One in a million, my friend; anything beyond that is propagandist falsehood.) Why? Because he is not yet ready for them. They are magnificent, but they wrote for adults—as, unfortunately, most great authors have written. Let him gain by experience the needful equipment, and he will appreciate them well enough. And the analogous proposition is true of the Cream Theory. Take a person who has completed the first stage, namely a reading of English, and place him suddenly before those foreign Great Ones. They will bore him to tears. Any dramatic canons drawn exclusively from Shakespeare prove that Racine is a simpleton; any poetical canons, that Virgil is affected, Homer childish, and Dante no poet at all; any psychological canons, that Ibsen is 'a dirty old blackguard' (a quotation, this, from a man deeply read in English). Yes, they are bored to tears; but since our national temperament understands not æsthetic right, only moral right, they feel that they must be wicked if they are bored by great authors. The familiar result follows. Thousands of otherwise honest folk who are hungering for Edgar Wallace sit flogging themselves through 'Andromaque' or 'Don Quixote' with a dazed sense that they are making the Almighty somehow their debtor. Works like these depend for their true effect upon a whole literary tradition, a whole national culture, unrevealed to the worshipper. Every writer needs a considerable equipment in his reader, and it is precisely the greatest writers ('simple' though they are called by the critics) who demand most. They sum up gigantic experiences of the race in politics, religion, philosophy, literature.

Nevertheless our friend plods on, head bowed and muscles tense. It is heartbreaking to see an intelligent artisan seeking to 'widen his outlook' by patient study of Æschylus in a prose translation; the spectacle reminds one of the hunting-attic in Ibsen's 'Wild Duck.' The Cream Theory, even for its most genuine and respectable adherents, is a delusion. That is not the way in which literature 'works,' or life. As well saw off the topmost six feet of the Jungfrau, set the mass up in your back-garden, and take your guests out to admire the terrific grandeur of the scenery. As well select the profoundest philosopher in China and rush at him with a request for his views on Marcus Stone's pictures or the dramas of Pinero. It is hopeless to expect any particular benefit from Virgil or Cervantes without a sound European education. The method is recognised as futile when applied to travel. A man who 'knows' London, Paris, Rome, New York, and nothing else about the countries which contain them, knows only what he brings with him. And, further, in literature, as in life, it is the details which really interest. To grasp the topography of Hell is one thing, to make Dante part of your spiritual experience is quite another, to be compassed by noting, understanding, and digesting, just those oddities for which 'one has no time.' Far better than the Cream Theory is the Patch Theory—to know one area of literature really well, diaries, minor verse, table-talk; but then we only betray our 'heritage' in another, equally effectual, manner.

At the very moment of writing I note, in the current issue of the *Observer*, a remark by Mr. St. John Ervine which gives excellent support (if support be needed) to what I have just been saying:

> 'Benavente's plays are sometimes too national in quality. The foreigner has to project himself into the mind of the Spaniards more than most people are willing to do. Benavente, perhaps, recognises this, for he is reported by his translator, Mr. Underhill, to have said, "When we read 'Don Quixote' or 'The Divine Comedy' or Shakespeare's plays for the first time, were we not upon the point of finding them a little tiresome?"'

I confess that Señor Benavente goes on:

> 'If we had permitted ourselves to be overcome by the first impression, and had ceased to read, should we not have sacrificed the most profound artistic emotions of our lives?'

But my honesty in completing the quotation ought not to count against me. For all I know, Señor Benavente may be deluding himself, or (more probably) he may have acquired by the time of his second reading the equipment which a Spaniard needs if he is to appreciate Shakespeare and Dante.

The Cream Theory finds its best expression in those dreadful lists of the World's Best Books. Everyone who has glanced through those catalogues knows how repellent they are; but does he realise why? It is because they are inhuman. The list is nobody's list, though it contains something which would be in everybody's list; it is the greatest common measure of Books That Have Helped. Just so one might compose a statue of the best head, the finest arm, etc., to be found among the world's sculptures. The catalogue will contain, let us say, the 'Sakuntala' and 'The Path to Rome.' Now both may be capital books, but the point is that nobody—no real individual person—reads both. It can't be done (I mean, not normally and humanly; after the publication of such a list people will insist on doing it—see below); it can't be done any more than you can be both a jockey and a botanist. And any list, to be real, must, at whatever cost, correspond to some conceivable personality.

But in our time there the catalogues are, and what is their effect? Thousands of people pursuing synthetic culture just as some buy synthetic pearls, and loading their commonplace Occidental brains with bits from the Rig-Veda, like a Hottentot parading in a silk hat. In this way certain august but essentially unreadable books are kept 'in the hands of the public'—books which nobody now on earth likes or would read for ten minutes ungoaded by snobbery. The phases of that snobbery are indicated by the three sentences: (1) 'Everyone knows . . .'; (2) 'I've begun the thing and by George I'll finish it'; (3) 'Now that I've got through it, I'm going to have the credit.' When British culture regains its health some truthful critic may draw up the list for the astonishment and warning of book-lovers. Some entries are obvious. Far beyond the rest, like Achilles in battle, leap forth the 'Meditations' of Marcus Aurelius, that prince of bores. Next come the writings of Epictetus and Samuel Richardson, most works on religion, the 'Faery Queene,' 'Sartor Resartus,' 'The Shaving of Shagpat'—and here I cease, since the reader (in a happy dream) is continuing the list for himself.

About once a year some bright journal asks each of our leading men and women for a few lines on the topic, 'If I were forced to live on a desert island with permission to take only one book, what would that book be?' They all answer on Cream Theory lines, except that Mr. Bernard Shaw probably elects for a large note-book. A disillusioned statesman chooses the 'Pilgrim's Progress' (because he means to write, when he 'comes out,' a work entitled 'Morality in Theory and in Practice'); a fashionable actor chooses Plato's 'Republic' ('Thirty Years of Mimesis,' by an Old Mummer); a woman novelist chooses the works of Shakespeare ('Caliban at Home,' by Miranda). Very impressive; but if they were truthful they would all select some manual in varnished picture-boards called *Practical Boat-Building for Amateurs.* If the aim is to discover what people like, the test is wrong, for the patients are all given a chance to show off when they return to civilisation. The real test is to promise anonymity for the replies, and ask: 'If you were the last survivor of the human race, what kind of book would you read?' Practically all of us would answer, 'Detective stories, till I had read every one three times; then humorous novels; then I should go to the bad, give up books, and read the private correspondence of my deceased neighbours and friends.' How many classical authors should we read if we knew with certainty that we should never be questioned about them? Educationists condemn, and outsiders ridicule, students who 'cram' for examinations. How many 'book-lovers' do anything else? Charles Lamb indeed, a great reader, nevertheless read to please himself, with no shame, no stint, no plan, and no faintest desire to get marks. But he chatted so charmingly about his books that the literature which was a light-hearted hobby for him became a light-headed cult for others. He cherished a whimsical affection for Elizabethan playwrights, some of them rubbish; and (as one result) arid nincompoops are obtaining doctorates for research into the 'outlook,' 'Italian sources,' and the like, of such wretches as Glapthorne and Shakerley Marmion, whose cleverly constructed name is his only asset. St. Jerome, writing from his hermitage near Bethlehem, laments that his reputation has brought so many fashionable recluses to the place that there is no privacy in the desert. Poor Lamb's at first unfashionable hobby has become a stamping-ground for people who, were he alive now, would despise him for reading Longfellow and Hannah More.

So much for the various types of reader. None of them solves the difficulty. What, then, is to be done? It is no answer to say: 'Read what you can, and leave the rest,' because the size of the unread mass has positive and evil effects. In the honest it causes worry, a sense of waste; in the dishonest it causes snobbery and the desire to outshine. There is but one remedy: a wholesale destruction. Quite nine-tenths of the good books should be burnt; of the bad we need say, here as elsewhere, nothing—they are drawn towards the pulping-machine by a force persistent as gravitation. 'But,' say some, quoting perchance their own reviews, 'your suggestion raises more difficulties than it solves.' Scarcely; but I see two problems, which are by no means so hard to solve as might appear: What are we to destroy? How are we to destroy it?

Let me answer the second question first. When a book is condemned, all public libraries burn their copies with whatever rites may seem fitting to its subject-matter and the occasion. It becomes illegal to possess, buy, sell the book or to expose it for sale. All copies secretly preserved are stripped of their value by an enactment that any person quoting them, referring to them, or in any manner whatsoever seeking personal credit from them, shall be prosecuted under a Disturbance of the Realm Act. A fixed sum should be paid for each copy handed over to the police; that is the way, more or less, in which wolves were extirpated, and it should serve the State well again. That great army of persons who thrive on the various forms of bibliography, the booksellers, the librarians, the makers and printers of catalogues, the ghouls who (like vultures on the battle-field) hover over the two-penny box fingering and tumbling gritty copies of 'La Canne de Jonc,' Blair's 'Sermons,' and cookery-books with long esses, should be told that the State is not robbing them either of livelihood or of excitement. 'Of whatever thing a man is a smart guardian,' says Plato, 'of that he is also a smart thief.' Let these experts continue their function of tracking books, but for destruction, not preservation. They will not care. What they love is their hard-won knowledge of the quarry, its appearance, methods of concealment, and habitat; not its ultimate destiny. Does the enthusiast who follows the scent of a First Folio across England and at last runs it to earth in an apple-loft, sit down forthwith and read *The Merchant of Venice*? Not he. If he ever reads the play at all (which is highly doubtful) he prefers a popular edition with pink pictures of the Rialto. For him the chase is all. The new régime will alter his life and enjoyment surprisingly little. He will give interviews with the title: 'How I Stamped Out Fielding.' Nor is this the only way in which our newspapers will be brightened. During the first years of the new Golden Age we shall read of a fanatic who, hearing a Cabinet Minister quote the words 'as well almost kill a man as kill a good book,' instantly shot him through the head, and of detectives at peril of their lives raiding a den of Wordsworth-printers.

Before we consider the second problem in its main aspect, the selection of the extant works which are to be banned (for Milton and Wordsworth were mentioned just now only as examples), let us complete the minor task of diminishing heavily the future output. I should favour the absolute prohibition of all novels for the next ten years. Then, during five years, only those novels, hitherto held up, should be issued which both publisher and author still thought worth while. After that, if people persisted in writing novels, the Government might refuse permits to those treating the following topics: (*a*) the Great War, (*b*) girls dressed in salad and living beside lagoons, (*c*) imaginary kingdoms with regents called Black Boris, (*d*) any type of 'lure.' Next, no work of any sort should be translated into English unless it were approved by the Problems Editor of the *Westminster Gazette* (the man who 'throws away' all the entries). As for indigenous works other than novels, they might be allowed freedom of publication so long as the price were not less than one penny a page. This would keep down the output effectually and would also give the Cambridge University Press an equal chance with other publishing concerns.

There remains the chief and most arduous task, to decide which books already extant should perish. The work is enormous, and must be spread over many years. Ten thousand *per annum* seems a likely figure, which could be

rapidly increased as the public grew accustomed
to the system and observed that the sky did not
fall. A committee of fifty (ten of whom must,
and all of whom might, be women) should each
year promulgate its list, to appear simultaneously
with the New Year Honours List. But of the
committee more anon. In order to popularise
the scheme and provide incentive to individual
effort, any person who greatly distinguished
himself should be rewarded by permission to
select a book or books for slaughter. How much
more eagerly would a woman strive to swim the
Channel did she know that as she waded ashore
at Cap Grisnez she could delete (from English
at any rate) three plays of Strindberg! Imagine
an undergraduate, longing for a First in Greats
but weak in Kant, who should by titanic efforts
win the Amateur Golf Championship and
abolish the 'Critique of Pure Reason' even as he
faced the camera! Word would go round that
Captain A., who was preparing to reach the
North Pole by aeroplane, intended to select
Browning as a reward. Instantly the Browning
Society would organise a rival expedition and
would be accused of doping his petrol. Life
would become even more fascinating, and some
people would deliberately read Browning from
cover to cover. Some exploits would be so
sublime that five, ten, nay, a hundred books
should be awarded. Miss Mary Pickford might
by a stroke of the pen free us from dialect poetry;
and the genius who settled the Reparations
Question to the satisfaction of all parties might
be allowed to exclaim in Tennysonian phrase:

'I care for nothing: all shall go!' Neither Mr. Gosse nor Mr. Birrell would be ungracious enough to annul his decision by writing 'Memories of a Dismantled Study.'

But, as a fact, these sensational privileges would have small effect upon that overwhelming mass. Nearly all the work would be executed by the humdrum public service of the Committee. When the 'republic of letters' realised that the law was to be enforced, there would begin a furious attempt to pack the committee with critics, writers, book-fanciers of all kinds who would seek to ruin the scheme by concentrating upon obsolete Bradshaws, atlases, old school-books, 'Who's Who,' and Walt Whitman. This would not be permitted. The Committee should contain representatives of every class and —an unusual thing in committees—every age. First, that the more nervous might be in some degree reassured, they would make a list of books which in any case should be preserved— books which almost everyone really likes and really reads. It would be a surprisingly small list, but there is no danger of our losing Shakespeare, most of Dickens, the Sherlock Holmes stories. This done, they would on each New Year's Day promulgate their list of ten thousand books.

Nothing, however, is further from my intention than tyranny. All I aim at is effecting what the public in its heart desires. Therefore any of these ten thousand may be saved if it can be shown that the public really wishes to save it. The proof must, however, be given in deeds, not words as heretofore and should be conducted on the following lines. The list is promulgated on January 1st, but the destruction does not begin until August 1st. During July all publishers and librarians are to make a return of the number of persons who during the preceding six months have purchased or read each of the books proscribed. Anyone claiming to have read a book owned by himself would be subjected to a brief oral examination. The works would then be arranged in three categories. Any which had been read by ten thousand people should be struck from the list and given immunity for fifteen years. Those which had been read by less than ten but more than five thousand should be immune for five years. Each work which had found less than five thousand supporters should be retained for one year if any single person could be found to prove his love for it by making a sacrifice to ensure its preservation. This would form the sound test of that 'revelling in' authors of which we hear so much. The sacrifices demanded would, of course, vary according to the original support. A book with four thousand adherents would escape if £100 were paid into the Treasury; the rescue of one with only a thousand would mean fifty years' penal servitude —often a mere bagatelle if all the essayists and editors contributed. At the end of the scale books with less than ten readers could survive only if one person consented to go to the scaffold. The executions would take place on August 15th in public, and it would be an uplifting sight when some grey-haired fanatic passed into the Beyond crying, 'Long live "Butterflies of North-East Bucks"!' Nor would this heroism be needed in the following year for the same work. Such a public confession would kindle popular curiosity, and the book might easily leap up into the fifteen-year class. We should have great families in which it was the tradition for the eldest son to give up his young life for some Portuguese grammar or volume of *vers libre* which his forbears had protected from the committee for centuries.

R. W. Chapman
1881–

THE PORTRAIT OF A SCHOLAR

His studies had been so various, that I am not able to name a man of equal knowledge. His acquaintance with books was great, and what he did not immediately know, he could, at least, tell where to find. Such was his amplitude of learning, and such his copiousness of communication, that it may be doubted whether a day now passes, in which I have not some advantage from his friendship.—JOHNSON'S *Character of Mr. Gilbert Walmsley.*

My old friend was no walker. Yet the picture which recollection chiefly invokes is of a spare figure, much swamped and muffled in great-coats and a soft hat, stepping delicately down the High Street of Oxford, and pausing to regard the windows of booksellers and antiquarians with a chill glance of recognition and dispraise. There was an unconscious *fastidium* in that walk, and in the aquiline cast of his old face in repose, which expressed the innocent arrogance of his mind. A natural aristocracy spoke in his bearing, to the exclusion of any mark of occupation. He was no more like a great scholar than anybody else; but he might have been an ambassador, or the head of a great banking house. He might have been a duke of the premier line.

He was in fact a very great scholar. Many who knew him by his recensions of the text of

Aristotle and by his casual conversation—his copious memory was stored with the lapses of lesser scholars—thought of him as profoundly versed in the diction of Greek philosophers and the principles of textual criticism, and by the same token preoccupied to excess with minutiæ of idiom, inordinately solaced by professional scandal. The travesty is risible, but it is fostered by a vulgar error. There is no humaner science than grammar and few more exciting pursuits than textual criticism; but the dry bones of both studies attract the spade of unenlightened industry, and the fair name of classical scholarship suffers from the multitude of its drudges.

The subject of my portrait was a great scholar, as only those few can be who laboriously cultivate a rare natural gift. The penetralia of the ancient world are not to be reached save through the long and dusty corridors of modern learning; and only by a saving grace of genius will the student reach the farther end with senses unimpaired. Our scholar knew the history of classical learning as it is unlikely it will ever be known again, and read ancient literature with a taste and feeling undimmed by a cobweb. He told me once, he had read the 'Choephoroe' in the train that morning: 'You know, it's monstrously good.' The quotation does feeble justice to my vivid sense of his being as intimate with Æschylus as he was with Browning, and as intimate with Politian as with either. He was so profoundly versed in the literature and the manners of many ages, that he would speak of Sir Thomas More, or of Burke, very much as he spoke of Swinburne; as if he had known them.

Few even of his friends, I imagine, suspected the prodigious range of his attainments. He did not suspect it himself. He had no vulgar avidity of information or conceit of versatility, and of many branches of modern scientific and mechanical knowledge was content to remain as ignorant as a gentleman need be. He acquired his knowledge with an easy deliberation, and kept it by mere tenacity and a sure instinct for selection. In conversation his native courtesy chose subjects with which he knew his interlocutor to be familiar; and the Renaissance scholar who knew that he lived on terms of close intimacy with Erasmus and the Scaligers might well remain in ignorance of his equal familiarity with Diogenes Laertius, or the Elizabethan dramatists, or the historians of the Peninsular War. Till he warmed to a subject his knowledge was always shy; he was not to be drawn; and it was felt that the attempt would be indecent. The loftiness of his own standard was more surely betrayed by the alarm he evinced at the rare discovery of a gap in his knowledge. At a meeting of a learned society over which he presided, a member, while reading a commentator's note, boggled at a word and applied to the president for its meaning. '*Sicilicus—sicilicus!*' There was a silence as he made his way to the dictionary. '*Sicilicus.* It means the forty-eighth part of an *as*, and, by metonymy, it means a comma.' Then, replacing the book and turning to his audience, in accents of unfeigned dismay— 'I didn't *know that!*'

Circumstances allowed me to spread my net wide. My relations with him were in part professional, and it was often my business to seek from him information or counsel on various projects of learning. This required a degree of tact, and even the most careful application was not always successful. He would sometimes profess nescience, or preoccupation, or even indifference. But when his interest was stimulated the results were surprising. He liked to have notice of awkward questions. If his mind was a well-stored encyclopædia, it was an incomparable bibliography. His cash resources were as nothing to his credit. He had a rare nose for books, and anything that lurked in a book he could track to its lair. He was seldom visible before lunch time; and I think of him as spending long mornings in his library, pacing the floor with his delicate step, lighting and relighting his big pipe, and ever and again pouncing hawklike on his quarry. Scholarship and lexicography owe much to those unrecorded searches.

. . . .

His published works, though their volume is respectable, afford but rare glimpses of the range of his learning or the play of his discursive judgment. They are confined strictly to his professional avocation, and are the best illustration of his favourite censure, 'It isn't a businesslike book.' But their quality, if severely, if even regrettably restrained, is the mirror of his exact, profound, and laborious scholarship. Of its exactness I once made a searching experiment. He had commissioned me to read the proofs of

his last and most important book. So honorific
an invitation could be received only as a command; but it was embarrassing, the more so as
a handsome and equally obligatory honorarium
was attached. The substance of the commentary
I could not presume to criticise; and how should
I earn my guineas by the barren labour of verify-
ing references which I was sure had been tested
again and again, any time those twenty years?
I cast here and there; but the most assiduous
angler will flag under the conviction that there
are no fish in his waters. I fell in despair upon
the *index verborum*; and by erasing a word in the
text, as I checked each entry, hoped at last to
reap a harvest of *paralipomena*. A grotesque, but
perhaps a unique labour; I pursued it with zeal.
My mind misgave me when I got to ϕ, and found
the pages of the text all but obliterated; and
when I reached the last word in the index, and
turned to the text for my reward, all I had to
show for my toil was one lonely word overlooked,
a single islet in a sea of erasure.

If the old man had a vanity, it was that, being
a great scholar, who lived to celebrate as a
Regius Professor the jubilee of his matriculation,
he preferred to envisage himself in a metro-
politan setting. Affectionate loyalty forbade a
hint that Oxford was parochial; but there was
a modest gratitude in the explanation, 'I have a
house in London.' Certainly those who knew
him only in the streets of Oxford, in the high
gloomy room in Wolsey's Quad, or the very
ordinary villa in the Parks, missed the cream of
his urbanity. But I think fondly of the Oxford

house. It was there I first enjoyed his familiar conversation, and heard him quote the saying of Chandler—'a better Aristotelian than I shall ever be'—that 'the first half-dozen chapters of any book of Aristotle are really very well done.' It was there that on the eve of his leaving Oxford he invited me to call on him at five o'clock, 'when I shall be still able to give you some tea.' I have often smiled, as I smile now in fond amusement, at something engaging in that phrase. The amenities of tea were unruffled by any squalor of packing; and the object of the invitation was to load me with books. They were duplicates, he explained, and it was therefore in my power to do him a kindness.

But the house in Kensington was more amply expressive. A house is infinitely communicative, and tells many things besides the figure of its master's income. There are houses that confess intellectual penury, and houses that reek of enlightenment. The habitations of professors are in general, perhaps, too apt to emphasise the dignity of labour. This, on first showing, was merely the house of a cultivated gentleman of easy fortune, liberal tastes, and ample leisure. Here were no telephones or lists of engagements, no display of the apparatus of research. The study at the top of the house confessed itself a workroom; but even there his guests breathed a serene atmosphere. If there was any litter it was a litter of pipes and tobacco jars, and if any books lay on chairs or tables they were probably recent acquisitions which had not yet been assigned their places. If the house was unlike a laboratory it was equally unlike a museum; the responsive visitor felt that his senses were agreeably amused, but became only by degrees aware that the furniture was more than good, the silver better than old, the books not only handsome but rare and precious. Of books, and especially of early Greek books, he was a systematic collector; his other possessions he had acquired by the same gift which gave him his miscellaneous information; he never seemed to know anything that was not worth knowing, and his house, by the same *flair*, held nothing one might not have been tempted to covet.

Of his tastes and opinions I can qualify none as prejudice, unless it be his dislike of chrysanthemums; but there were proclivities and avoidances as characteristic and as amiable as the best of prejudices. I do not think he had any love of the sublime in nature; I have heard him avow a distaste for mountains, and he never spoke of Switzerland except as a natural obstacle. He loved the ordered landscapes of South England; he loved Paris, and he loved the Mediterranean. He never visited Greece, and did not regret the omission. I think he had his own vision of the Academy and the Lyceum, and shrank from the desecrated temples and the spurious pretensions of modern Athens. But he travelled much in Italy, and more in Spain; and his mind was stored with rich impressions of old cities, of noble libraries, gorgeous palaces, solemn rituals. Perhaps the disapprobation of mountains extended itself to the lesser pinnacles of human architecture; I think of him, at all events, as less moved by domes and buttresses than by the dim magnificence of interiors, by porphyry and bronze and incense and the pomp of the Mass. He told me once that were he a pious millionaire desirous of raising a monument to the glory of God and for his soul's good, he should not spend his money on spires and arches, but should buy a building in a street, with no exterior but its modest frontage, and lavish his resources on gorgeous incrustations.

To see him among his books was to learn a lesson in piety. When he described the printed catalogue of his choicest volumes as *Elenchus librorum vetustiorum apud . . . hospitantium*, he was guilty of no affectation of modesty. He did not conceal a collector's just pride of possession; but you need only see him take a book from its shelf to know that he felt himself the ephemeral custodian of a perennial treasure. There is a right way and a wrong way of taking a book from the shelf. To put a finger on the top, and so extract the volume by brutal leverage, is a vulgar error which has broken many backs. This was never his way: he would gently push back each of the adjacent books, and so pull out the desired volume with a persuasive finger and thumb. Then, before opening the pages, he applied his silk handkerchief to the gilded top, lest dust should find its way between the leaves. These were the visible signs of a spiritual homage. His gift of veneration was as rich as his critical faculty was keen; if a book was of the elect it was handled with a certain awe.

He was easily persuaded to do the honours of

his collection. One book would suggest another, which would be taken down in its turn to prompt further comment and reminiscences. He did not disdain the collector's foibles; he liked to point out that this was a clean copy and that a tall copy; or even, with a smile that confessed a weakness—'It has the blank leaf at the end!' The importance of these qualities may seem to be exaggerated by booksellers' catalogues, when they deplore a missing dedication or measure values with a millimetre scale; but an accurate regard for them is common to connoisseurs, and should not be held to argue an undue concern for externals. Here, at all events, was no room for such a suspicion; for it could not be supposed that he had not read his books.

His standard was as high in this as in less important matters. He condemned as ignorant the modern passion for old Sheffield plate. Old Sheffield might be very well; but no one of the period bought Sheffield for any better reason than that he could not afford to buy silver. He was equally contemptuous of the exaggerated value now set upon old English cottage furniture, which he regarded as barbarous. He named a lady who had filled her rooms with it: 'You know, the house of a baronet's widow oughtn't to be like the bar parlour of the *Pig and Whistle*.' His taste in books was as severe. He often mentioned an excellence—'It's a good copy; it's a better copy than the one in the British Museum' —but I do not remember his owning a defect. I must suppose that he had no poor copies. The same standard was applied to the discrimination of the products of presses and centuries. He loved the best, and had no reason for putting up with what was inferior. I do not think anything later than the sixteenth century had much power to stir him.

I was very sensible of the beauty of his books— the fine old Italian print, the fair margins, the armorial bindings eloquent of worthy ownership. I felt myself incompetent to appraise the rare industry and rarer learning by which the collection had been formed. But no profound acquaintance with a subject or a period was required to appreciate his knowledge of books in general, their every circumstance and attribute. He answered to any and every test, 'Yes. I know the book. I have a copy. It isn't a rare book.' It has been said of him that if he had not been a great scholar he might have been one of the greatest of all booksellers. His instinct for prices was uncanny. Of imprints he could talk by the hour; whether *Londini* or *Londinii* were the preferable form; of the Paris imprint, which at a certain date appears as *Parisius* (a fact not generally known); of a well-known scholar who imagined that *Hafnia* was Hanover, but might have remembered Campbell—'Hafnia and Trafalgar.' His regard for myself, I cannot doubt, had at least its origin in my unfeigned appreciation of such particulars of controversy, obscurity or scandal. My memory, by the same predilection, retains these anecdotes, while preserving only a vaguer sense of the range and charm of his talk, the mordant perspicacity of his judgments. We are accustomed to associate candour and charity with an amiable character; but greatness of mind is allowed to justify a measure of cynicism; and his censorious worldliness was so rooted in wisdom, and so divorced from all vanity and pettiness of spirit, that I found it not only more entertaining, but even more lovable, than the most good-natured disposition to see the best in everything. He had no regard for established reputations, or none that he allowed to obscure his judgment; and the surprise with which he recognised the ignorance and mendacity of mankind was the measure of his intellectual probity.

> Scorn looked beautiful
> In the contempt and anger of his lip

as he pronounced the final verdict, 'It's a shoddy book.' Most books, if not shoddy, are yet, in his other phrase, 'not important'; and if his admiration was less often exercised than his censure, it was less often deserved. It was the more impressive. He seldom quoted a saying of his own; but he was fond of relating how, in an academic committee, some one who should have known better had suggested, on a proposal to further the study of inscriptions, that people who dabbled in inscriptions were always charlatans. 'Do you call MOMMSEN a charlatan?' It is probably a legend that he used to take his hat off when, in lecture, he had occasion to name Bernays; but I can hear the tones of his voice when he invoked the authority, or appealed to the example, of Erasmus, or Bentley, or Gibbon.

Johnson has been reported as saying that 'the

happiest conversation is that of which nothing is distinctly remembered, but a general effect of pleasing impression.' I comfort myself, in the face of my poverty of recollection, with an impression, as rich as it is doubtless incommunicable, of my old friend's wit and wisdom, his courtesy and kindness. He was an admirable host; exacting only in the attention invited to his cellar and his cigars, and in the inordinate hours at which one was expected still to converse, or at least to listen. It was difficult to resist that glass of claret which wasn't a dinner claret but an after-dinner claret; and I have a shameful memory of being once caught in a yawn, and politely escorted to my candle, at about half-past one. When I dined with him last he had been very ill; his servant met me with an anxious face, and a request that I would not keep him up. He looked old and frail, and was unusually silent; but over the second glass of port—the doctors were building him up—he began to mend; and when the second cigar had been smoked the flame of discourse was burning with its old mild radiance. He would not speak of the war; I think he already knew he should not see its end. But the recent publication of a volume of Professor Oman's 'History' evoked his interest in the great days of the Peninsula; and I heard for the last time the old stories of San Sebastian and Salamanca.

The graces of civilisation and the delights of learning are far from me now.[1] But my nomadic and semi-barbarous existence is still solaced by a

[1] [Written in Macedonia, 1917.]

few good books; and the best odes of Horace, the best things in Boswell or Elia, often awake memories of Attic nights. Memories and visions, in which gleaming mahogany and old morocco are seen darkling in a haze of smoke, and an old man in his big chair by the fire draws forth, for my pleasure and his, the hoarded treasures of his rich old mind.

J. C. Squire

1884–

RAILROADIANA

I WAS looking over a list of sales to be held this spring in New York by the American Art Association, the Sotheby's of America. All the usual things are to come up: incunabula, illuminated manuscripts, first editions, four Shakespeare folios, etchings by Whistler, eighteenth-century illustrated books. My eye lingered lovingly on some of these categories. I mused on these treasures three thousand miles over the horizon, most of them emigrants from their English homes. But one entry aroused in me not a sentimental hankering, but wonder. A gentleman, or the executor of a gentleman, is disposing of a collection of what, with fine courage, the cataloguer calls 'Railroadiana.' Why should he not? We have Shakespeariana, Baconiana, and Johnsoniana; nevertheless it looks odd—almost as odd as 'aeroplaniana' and 'oilenginiana' will look fifty years hence.

I suppose that this hoard of 'railroadiana' (we should still call them 'Railway Items' or 'Books, etc., Bearing on the History of Locomotive Traction' in this country) will probably consist mainly of works illustrating the development of railways from George Stephenson onwards. It is early as yet, and the chances are

that the man who made the collection was himself a railwayman or what is called a railway
magnate. I don't think that railways have yet
got into the field of vision of the collector proper.
But they undoubtedly will when they are slightly
more venerable and when information about
their origins is more patently useless and recon-
dite. To-day it is the railwayman who forms
libraries about his industry. When railways
have been transformed or, better, abolished,
it will not be the traffic experts who will know
about nineteenth-century railways. It will be
the bookworms—men who could scarcely drive
a perambulator, much less an engine; just as
if anybody is collecting information about
Alexander's campaigns we may be sure it is
not a soldier. Everything, when it gets hoary,
falls into the net of this one class of enthusiasts,
the dustmen, the rag, bone, and bottle men
of human history. In our great-grandsons' day
there will be bald and spectacled collectors who
will know by heart the names of the railway
systems of our day, and will spend fortunes upon
precious scraps of information about those half-
forgotten institutions. And the queer thing will
be that they will search with most zeal not for
large and authoritative books but for odds and
ends that we regard as negligible. Posterity's
tastes are always surprising.

To-day men collect, and will give large sums of
money for, horn-books: little contraptions from
which Queen Anne's children, numerous but
early dead, learned their alphabets. Children's
books of a later date form the substance of

specialised collections; where (as with some of
the early compositions of Charles and Mary
Lamb) they bear famous names they will fetch
their hundreds of pounds, enough money to
keep a labourer's family for a year. There are
always collectors who go off the beaten tracks
of early printing and first editions of the dramatists and prefer to devote themselves to out-of-
the-way literature which will illustrate some
aspect of social life. The more ordinary and
common the literature was in its own time the
more likely, as a rule, it is to be scarce; yet it is
from this sort of thing that we are likeliest to
get a peep into the minds of the generality of
our ancestors or a notion of their day-to-day
lives. The antiquary of the future who wishes
to know what our own time was like will get a
very distorted picture if he possesses the works
of Mr. Swinburne and Mr. Conrad and has
never heard of *Home Notes* or Mr. Garvice; if
Sir Edward Elgar's symphonies survive, but not
'Get Out and Get Under' or 'Pack up Your
Troubles.' Yet copies of these will be few and
hard to get at. The hawkers a hundred years
ago sold chapbooks in the streets; elderly dons
now accumulate collections of chapbooks with
the utmost pains. The old ballads were hawked
to the poor at a penny or twopence; to-day 'a
really fine collection of Broadsides' will make
the dealers of two continents prick up their ears.
Almanacks were common enough, being things
useful to everybody in the days of the Tudors.
But people bought them to use them, not to
stack them on shelves or stow them away in

lavender, and the Bibliographical Society was performing an important service to research last year when it published a catalogue of Early English almanacks, many of them of the first rarity. So it will be with the commonest printed wares of our own generation.

Railroadiana! Yet in a century or two some of these very railroadiana may be in wide demand by classes of people who at present think railways beneath a scholar's or an artist's notice. Books about mechanical locomotion will be valued in their degree according to age, scarceness, and intrinsic interest. But it may well be that the real gems will not be books, properly so called, but literature which we see but scarcely notice on every table and on every wall. Men hang up to-day as curiosities, in the dining-rooms of old coaching inns, time-tables, yellow and quaint, giving the arrivals and departures of the York or the Exeter Mail. The proprietors of our most venerable theatres point with the greatest pride to play-bills of the eighteenth century, common printed sheets once thrust (for I suppose they did such things) under every door, and now almost as rare as primroses in December. If our odd civilisation continues, as much will happen to the announcements and the time-tables of 1920. I can visualise entries in Sotheby's or Hodgson's catalogue of 2120:

Lot 2140: Board of Trade Regulations for the Carriage of Live-Stock by Rail Dated 1920 and signed by H. Jones, Permanent Secretary. Brilliant Impression in perfect

order. This document throws a great deal of
light on much-vexed questions relating to
social life under George V, and some of the
detail is very entertaining. Much of it relates
to dogs, cats, pigs, etc., the transport of which
seems to have engaged much of our ancestors'
attention. To the precise determination of
charges they seem to have devoted a dialectical
subtlety which would do credit to Socrates.
Only one other perfect copy of this most
curious record is known to exist, and there
is none in the British Museum.

Lot 2642: A series of six 'Posters' bearing
on various aspects of the war against the old
Empire of Germany. No. 1—A Soldier's Cap,
with inscription 'If the Cap Fits Wear It';
No. 2—Picture of Britannia fighting the
Dragon of Prussianism; No. 3—Rescue of
British child carrying basket of food, from
German by Englishman; No. 4—Picture of
typical twentieth-century cottage, 'Is not this
worth fighting for?' etc., etc. The two first
are not known to exist elsewhere.

Lot 5621: Election 'Poster' dated 1918.

The picture is torn across and its exact
nature cannot be deduced, but the text—an
appeal to the voter to return the Duke of
Walton (then Mr. Lloyd George)—is intact.

These things will come up on some afternoon
of 2120; but the pearl of the sale will very likely
be a set of 'Bradshaws' and 'A.B.C.s' covering a
period of years. What a mine of information
our posterity will find those despised guides,

which we regard as purely utilitarian, and throw away as soon as we think them out of date! What numbers of stations, and trains, and routes, and fares they specify! Where else will the scholar, where else the investigator of Social Development, be able to look for information at once so accurate and so comprehensive concerning an important department of our lives? And where else will the antiquary, the bibliophile, the collector be able to recover so much fragrant detail, such countless suggestions of the lives that we, a quiet, jaded, picturesque, slow-going, but robust, simple and merry race of people led in an England not yet urbanised, modernised, or developed in accordance with the later conceptions of applied science? Men often lay up money or lands in order to insure the fortunes of their descendants; men have been known, trusting to their ability to scent a rising market, to stock their houses with pictures with the same object; it is reported that in America of recent months prudent men have been doing their best for their progeny by laying down cellars of wine. But I doubt if a man who is willing to take really long views and can trust his children to obey the terms of his will, could do better than lay down in dry, warm bins, not to be disturbed for two centuries, a complete file of 'Bradshaw's Railway Guide.' That is what will be rare; that is what they will really appreciate and covet; that is what will fetch the money. Failing that, any non-literary relics, provided these are sufficiently common and (at present) insignificant, will do. An air-gun, a few sets of Ludo and

Halma, an opera-hat, a football cap, a signed photograph of Sir Henry Irving, a few pairs of flannel trousers—a collection like that, kept in good condition, would some day be worth its weight in gold. These things would be regarded as—and perhaps they really are—the bones of history.

ON DESTROYING BOOKS

'It says in the paper' that over two million volumes have been presented to the troops by the public. It would be interesting to inspect them. Most of them, no doubt, are quite ordinary and suitable; but it was publicly stated the other day that some people were sending the oddest things, such as magazines twenty years old, guides to the Lake District, Bradshaws, and back numbers of *Whitaker's Almanack*. In some cases, one imagines, such indigestibles get into the parcels by accident; but it is likely that there are those who jump at the opportunity of getting rid of books they don't want. Why have they kept them if they don't want them? But most people, especially non-bookish people, are very reluctant to throw away anything that looks like a book. In the most illiterate houses that one knows every worthless or ephemeral volume that is bought finds its way to a shelf and stays there. In reality it is not merely absurd to keep rubbish merely because it is printed: it is positively a public duty to destroy it. Destruction not merely makes more room for new books and saves one's heirs the trouble of sorting out the rubbish or storing it: it may also prevent posterity from making a fool of itself. We may be sure that if we do not burn, sink, or blast all the superseded editions of Bradshaw, two hundred years hence some collector will be specialising in old railway time-tables, gathering, at immense cost, a complete series, and ultimately leaving his 'treasures' (as the Press will call them) to a Public Institution.

But it is not always easy to destroy books. They may not have as many lives as a cat, but they certainly die hard; and it is sometimes difficult to find a scaffold for them. This difficulty once brought me almost within the Shadow of the Rope. I was living in a small and (as Shakespeare would say) heaven-kissing flat in Chelsea, and books of inferior minor verse gradually accumulated there until at last I was faced with the alternative of either evicting the books or else leaving them in sole, undisturbed tenancy and taking rooms elsewhere for myself. Now, no one would have bought these books. I therefore had to throw them away or wipe them off the map altogether. But how? There were scores of them. I had no kitchen range, and I could not toast them on the gas-cooker or consume them leaf by leaf in my small study fire—for it is almost as hopeless to try to turn a book without opening it as to try to burn a piece of granite. I had no dust-bin; my debris went down a kind of flue behind the staircase, with small trap-doors opening to the landings. The difficulty with this was that the larger books might choke it; the authorities, in fact, had labelled it 'Dust and Ashes Only'; and in any case I did not want to leave the books intact, and some dustman's unfortunate family to get a false idea of English poetry from them. So in the end I determined to do to them what so many people do to the kittens: tie them up and consign them to the river. I improvised a sack, stuffed the books into it, put it over my shoulder, and went down the stairs into the darkness.

It was nearly midnight as I stepped into the street. There was a cold nip in the air; the sky was full of stars; and the greenish-yellow lamps threw long gleams across the smooth, hard road. Few people were about; under the trees at the corner a Guardsman was bidding a robust goodnight to his girl, and here and there rang out the steps of solitary travellers making their way home across the bridge to Battersea. I turned up my overcoat collar, settled my sack comfortably across my shoulders, and strode off towards the little square glow of the coffee-stall which marked the near end of the bridge, whose sweeping iron girders were just visible against the dark sky behind. A few doors down I passed a policeman who was flashing his lantern on the catches of basement windows. He turned. I fancied he looked suspicious, and I trembled slightly. The thought occurred to me: 'Perhaps he suspects I have swag in this sack.' I was not seriously disturbed, as I knew that I could bear investigation, and that nobody would be suspected of having stolen such goods (though they *were* all first editions) as I was carrying. Nevertheless I could not help the slight unease which comes to

all who are eyed suspiciously by the police, and
to all who are detected in any deliberately
furtive act, however harmless. He acquitted
me, apparently; and, with a step that, making
an effort, I prevented from growing more rapid,
I walked on until I reached the Embankment.

It was then that all the implications of my act
revealed themselves. I leaned against the para-
pet and looked down into the faintly luminous
swirls of the river. Suddenly I heard a step near
me; quite automatically I sprang back from the
wall and began walking on with, I fervently
hoped, an air of rumination and unconcern.
The pedestrian came by me without looking at
me. It was a tramp, who had other things to
think about; and, calling myself an ass, I
stopped again. 'Now's for it,' I thought; but
just as I was preparing to cast my books upon
the waters I heard another step—a slow and
measured one. The next thought came like a
blaze of terrible blue lightning across my brain:
'What about the splash?' A man leaning at
midnight over the Embankment wall: a sudden
fling of his arms: a great splash in the water.
Surely, and not without reason, whoever was
within sight and hearing (and there always
seemed to be some one near) would at once rush
at me and seize me. In all probability they
would think it was a baby. What on earth
would be the good of telling a London constable
that I had come out into the cold and stolen
down alone to the river to get rid of a pack of
poetry? I could almost hear his gruff, sneering
laugh: 'You tell that to the Marines, my son!'

So for I do not know how long I strayed up and down, increasingly fearful of being watched, summoning up my courage to take the plunge and quailing from it at the last moment. At last I did it. In the middle of Chelsea Bridge there are projecting circular bays with seats in them. In an agony of decision I left the Embankment and hastened straight for the first of these. When I reached it I knelt on the seat. Looking over, I hesitated again. But I had reached the turning-point. 'What!' I thought savagely, 'under the resolute mask that you show your friends is there really a shrinking and contemptible coward? If you fail now, you must never hold your head up again. Anyhow, what if you *are* hanged for it? Good God! you worm, better men than you have gone to the gallows!' With the courage of despair I took a heave. The sack dropped sheer. A vast splash. Then silence fell again. No one came. I turned home; and as I walked I thought a little sadly of all those books falling into that cold torrent, settling slowly down through the pitchy dark, and subsiding at last on the ooze of the bottom, there to lie forlorn and forgotten whilst the unconscious world of men went on.

Horrible bad books, poor innocent books, you are lying there still; covered, perhaps, with mud by this time, with only a stray rag of your sacking sticking out of the slime into the opaque brown tides. Odes to Diana, Sonnets to Ethel, Dramas on the Love of Lancelot, Stanzas on a First Glimpse of Venice, you lie there in a living death, and your fate is perhaps worse than you deserved. I was harsh with you. I am sorry I did it. But even if I had kept you, I will certainly say this: I should not have sent you to the soldiers.

J. Middleton Murry

1889-

SHAKESPEARE AND LOVE

IN a very interesting essay recently published
Professor Herford discusses Shakespeare's attitude to love and marriage, and insists upon what
he calls the profound 'normality' of the poet's
conception of love. He points out that love is
but seldom the substantial theme of Shakespeare's greater tragedies, and that Shakespeare
conceives it as a condition which, so far from
inevitably containing the seed of its own disruption, is so naturally strong that it needs the
invasion of an alien power to be prevented from
the bliss of perfect fulfilment. If we may translate
Shakespeare's idea of love into terms he would
certainly not himself have used, we may say,
following out Professor Herford's view, that
Shakespeare instinctively thought of love as a
principle of order in the human world, which
could be thwarted from its true purpose only by
forces foreign to itself. Professor Herford con-
cludes:—

'Shakespeare certainly did not, so far as
we can judge, regard sexual love (like some
moderns) as either the clue to human life or
as in any way related to the structure of the
universe. But if instead of these abstract
questions, we ask whether any poet has united

in a like degree veracious appreciation of love in its existing conditions with apprehension of all its ideal possibilities, we shall not dispute Shakespeare's place among the foremost of the poets of love.'

That is, in substance, a singularly just conclusion, and yet, we think it will strike a reader of Shakespeare as a little cold. It would, perhaps, scarcely have occurred to him that Shakespeare's place among the foremost of the poets of love should be disputed; and it is not unlikely that his natural impulse would be to call Shakespeare the greatest love-poet of them all. For the love of many other great poets, 'the love which moves the sun and the other stars,' is a wonderful and mighty power, but it is hardly love. It bears the name only by a sublime analogy; it is no native of the earth. Shelley's distracted life was proof of that, if proof were needed.

But in Shakespeare love is not cold and celestial; no icy flame of the *amor intellectualis dei* burns frozen at its heart. It is warm and human, and generation after generation of men and women to whom the intellectual love of a Dante, a Spinoza, or a Shelley would be an unintelligible fantasy have recognised it as a reflection of something they had felt or might hope to feel. If we take that which ninety-nine out of a hundred of all sorts and conditions of men feel or dream or understand at the word love, as the rough ore of the mysterious element, and if we refine this to the utmost of our power, casting nothing away that truly belongs to it, then of the recognisable universal love which remains Shakespeare is the pre-eminent poet. Nor is this love less ideal because it has nothing of the abstract-metaphysical in its composition, unless we are to hand over the word 'ideal' to the tender mercies of the philosophers. Shakespeare's conception of love is ideal in the most humane sense of the word, an enchanting and attainable perfection of the real.

Tradition, the popular voice, the judgment of the critics are at one in regarding Shakespeare as the poet of the earthly felicity of love. For this he was 'sweet' and 'gentle' in his own day, as he is in ours. The evidence of the plays is beyond all doubt. It is not a question of scattered lines or single characters, but of the general sentiment pervading all his plays: it cannot be escaped; it is the very air we breathe in them. Yet in this there is something strange, something miraculous almost; for whatever may be our estimate of the precise value of the Sonnets as autobiography, it is impossible for any one but a briefed advocate to assert that they do not substantially contain the record of the poet's own disaster in love. That earthly felicity of love between man and woman which runs, with but a single moment of interruption, like a thread of gold through the work of Shakespeare the dramatist, would seem to be the one aspect of love of which knowledge was denied to Shakespeare the sonnetteer. He seems to have tasted only the despairs, the degradations and the bitternesses, even though it was he also who declared his faith in the loyalty of a true lover's heart.

> 'Love is not love
> Which alters when it alteration finds
> Nor bends with the remover to remove.'

If we seek a simple explanation of the fact, we shall say, well knowing that we trespass against Signor Croce's canons of criticism, that the sonnets of tormented love belong to the moment when the golden thread in the plays is suddenly and unexpectedly snapped. We shall hold that the Sonnets represent an episode in Shakespeare's experience which caused a momentary but a complete overclouding of the reflection in the mirror of the plays. The episode passes and the reflection becomes calm and serene once more. The Sonnets give us, as it were, a year of Shakespeare's attitude to love; the plays give us a lifetime. In other words, even in this single matter of love, it is a mistaken effort to measure the plays by the Sonnets; what we have to do is to measure the Sonnets by the plays. If we do this the sonnets of disastrous love seem to fall naturally into place in that period of profound disturbance which is expressed in *Hamlet*, in *Measure for Measure*, in *Troilus and Cressida*, and in *All's Well that Ends Well*. No doubt this disturbance had its manifest reactions in realms of Shakespeare's faith other than his faith in love; it may have been the proximate cause of his greatest tragedies. But for these we need not assume an origin in personal catastrophe. Moreover, in the great tragic period Shakespeare's faith in love has manifestly begun to reassert itself. We have only to imagine *Antony and Cleopatra* written in the mood of *Troilus and Cressida* to understand what Shakespeare actually chose to do with a theme that would have lent itself magnificently to all the bitterness of an outraged heart.

If we put aside the plays of this period of disturbance, which ordinary readers and literary critics alike have felt to be discordant with Shakespeare's work as a whole, we discover pervading the rest an attitude to love which all cynics and most critics have conspired to describe as romantic. It is true that it appears to flower most divinely in what we call the romantic comedies; but that does not mean that the love portrayed in them is romantic in essence. Classification of this kind is superficial and confusing. A poet uses the most convenient plot as the foundation on which to build up the expression of his emotional attitude. The mere accident that the plot contains improbable coincidences and enchanted islands cannot affect the substance of the attitude expressed by its means. The romantic comedy of one poet may be a trivial indulgence of the fancy, while that of another is the flashing of a warm light into the verity of the human soul. We have only to compare Shakespeare's comedy, on the one hand with Beaumont and Fletcher's, and on the other with Ben Jonson's, to discover how far asunder they are in their poetic truth. The segregation of Shakespeare's comedies is misleading unless it is considered merely as the distinction of an aspect within the whole work of Shakespeare. The most immature of his comedies is nearer in spirit to the most perfect of his tragedies than it is to the comedies of Jonson or Fletcher, whatever merits of their own these may possess.

To call the love of Shakespeare's romantic comedies itself romantic is meaningless, or it is the expression of a private and personal conviction concerning the nature of love. It may mean that in the opinion of the judge love is not in fact so happy, nor so secure, nor so deeply irradiated with the heart's delight as Shakespeare represented it; but it can mean nothing more. And we cannot tell whether Shakespeare himself believed that love actually was as he chose to represent it. But we can say that he did believe either that it was so, or that it ought to be so; and that he found it natural to create men and women who are alive with a reality no other created characters possess, who love in the way he chose to make them love, with a tenderness and a gaiety, an open-eyed confidence in themselves and the future, a shyness and a humour, a marvellous equality in affection, which have made them for a whole world of mankind the embodiment of their experience if they were happy in love, or of their dreams if they were disappointed. And this love, which is as solid and as ethereal, as earthly and as magical as a rose in full bloom, is in all his early comedies; it is essentially the same in *A Midsummer Night's Dream* as in *Much Ado about Nothing*. We can hardly say more than that the light changes from moonlight to full sunshine as we pass from

Lysander and Hermia, through Orsino and Viola, to Benedick and Beatrice, and that when we reach *As You Like It* the midday brightness is faintly mellowed with afternoon. Nor is it possible to say that the love of the *Merchant of Venice* or of *Romeo and Juliet* is of another kind, though the one is calm and the other tempestuous. It is only the tempest of circumstance which wrecks the love of Romeo and Juliet. There is a peculiar ecstasy in their surrender to the enchantment, which bursts out like a flame at the clash of contact between the enemy houses; but in their love no seed of disruption or decay is visible, much less of disaster. Theirs is a love of which all human foresight could prophesy its

'Outliving beauty's outward with a mind
  That doth renew swifter than blood decays.'

They are the victims not of their passion but of crass casualty; they are fortune's fools, not their own. '*Romeo and Juliet*,' as Professor Herford truly says, 'appears not to be the tragedy of love, but love's triumphal hymn.'

The love which shines so gloriously through this period of Shakespeare's work is as mysterious and natural as birth. It is a thing that happens; to ask why it happens is to wait till doomsday for an answer; and if these lovers ask each other, they can only make up jesting replies. When Phebe applies Marlowe's line to her own love of Rosalind-Ganymede, she speaks for them all, men and women alike.

'Dead Shepherd, now I prove thy saw aright:
  Whoever loved, that loved not at first sight?'

For the most part they know themselves what has happened; and even where, as with Benedick and Beatrice, we seem to know it before they do, it is only because of their shyness of themselves and each other, which will not suffer their heads to confess the truth of their hearts. The moment that Benedick and Beatrice open fire on one another we know that they are caught. It is only love that makes a man and a woman single out each other for such teasing.

> *Beatrice.* I wonder that you will still be talking, Signior Benedick; nobody marks you.
> *Benedick.* What! My dear Lady Disdain, are you yet living?

Benedick might have called her the dear lady of his heart and had done with it, for he gave himself as completely away in that address as he could ever have done in the sonnet they found in his pocket at church, in which no doubt he rhymed, as he feared to rhyme, 'ladies' and 'babies.' Yet, though *Much Ado about Nothing* has precisely the same radiant substance as the rest of the love-comedies—love at first sight—it stands apart from them because the drama itself consists in the delicate working out of the psychology of this heavenly condition. It is not entangled with alien accidents, and owes nothing to the enchantment of disguise; it deals with an absolute perfection of art, with the process by which the message of unhesitating love steals from the heart to the mind. For this cause it is at once the simplest and the subtlest of all Shakespeare's comedies of love. For once Shake-

speare chose to communicate the reality of love
to us realistically: we can imagine the essence
of the play—for what does Don John matter?—
being played in real life at this very moment in
the garden of any kindly country house; the
process is as old as the hills and as new as the
morning.

But generally Shakespeare preferred to let one
of his lovers or both know at once what had
happened to them. The recognition is as quick
as the love of Celia and Oliver.

'Your brother and sister no sooner met but
they looked; no sooner looked but they loved;
no sooner loved but they sighed; no sooner
sighed but they asked one another the reason;
no sooner knew the reason but they sought the
remedy.'

The condition is presented to us a thing elemental, inscrutable, which either is or is not.
But if it is, Shakespeare can prove to us immediately that it is the true metal. He does not
profess to show how it happens; he does something far more difficult; he convinces us that it
has happened. He makes his lovers say the
simplest and divinest things; they seem to drop
sunbeams from their lips. In reality love is too
often tongue-tied: Shakespeare gives it speech
that seems as natural and magical as love itself.
When Orlando says of Rosalind that she is 'just
as high as his heart,' when Rosalind says that
'men have died from time to time, and worms
have eaten them, but not for love,' when Beatrice

answers the Prince's 'Out of question you were born in a merry hour,'

> 'No, sure, my Lord, my mother cried, but then there was a star danced, and under that I was born,'

we recognise the speech of love as surely as the old prophets recognised the voice of the Lord. This is how lovers would speak if they could. What wonder that they should have recognised their spokesman, and with a single voice elected him the poet laureate of love?

So natural is this flowering that we cannot imagine any end to it but the perfect happiness of marriage. These lovers are too open-eyed to be victims of the sad illusion; their felicity is destined to outlive beauty's outward. They seemed to be poised in a balance of perfect equality; yet if we have to pronounce which way the scale imperceptibly inclines we must say it is to the woman's side. The Duke says to Cesario:—

> 'For, boy, however we do praise ourselves,
> Our fancies are more giddy and unfirm,
> More longing, wavering, sooner lost and worn
> Than women's are.'

Certainly the Duke himself changed his affection quickly from Olivia to Viola; but then we may truly urge that he was in love with Cesario all the while. Claudio suspected Hero suddenly and condemned her violently. But these, after all, are only the subordinate necessities of the romantic fable; they do not determine the quality of the belief with which Shakespeare charged it.

The happiness of the love of the mature comedies passes undisturbed into the married security of *Henry IV.* and *Julius Cæsar*. Kate and Hotspur are the proof that marriage, which is the inevitable end of Shakespeare's lovers, born not merely under a lucky but a dancing star, does not mean the end of love-making.

'I' faith I'll break thy little finger, Harry,
   An if thou wilt not tell me all things true.'

They are married, and as much in love as when first they met. There is no room for such gaiety between Brutus and Portia. Brutus is caught in a conspiracy, and is venturing his life in an enterprise which Portia feels must bring disaster. Only the anxiety and devotion can appear, but it is equal. Portia knows that her husband cannot resist her appeal to 'the great vow which did incorporate and make them one.'

'Dwell I but in the suburbs
Of your good pleasure? If it be no more,
Portia is Brutus' harlot, not his wife.'

And even in the relation of Mistress Quickly and Doll Tearsheet to Falstaff we catch the undertone of a fidelity not really unworthy to be compared to this. Both these women loved the genial old ruffian, who in his way loved them; and there are moments when nothing in Shakespeare seems to reveal more clearly his faith in the loyalty of love than the words he makes the cockney landlady say of Falstaff's death:—

> *Nym.* They say he cried out of sack.
> *Host.* Ay, that a' did.
> *Bard.* And of women.
> *Host.* Nay, that a' did not.
> *Boy.* Yes, that a' did; and said they were devils incarnate.
> *Host.* A' never could abide carnation; 'twas a colour he never liked.
> *Boy.* A' said once, the devil would have him about women.
> *Host.* A' did in some sort, indeed, handle women; but then he was rheumatic, and talked of the whore of Babylon.

Then comes an abrupt and startling change. Suddenly the steady, shining stream of Shakespeare's presentation of love as happiness and loyalty is disturbed and muddied. The moment coincides with a sudden check in the confident advance of Shakespeare as a poet and a dramatist. We are confronted with what we may roughly call 'the Hamlet period,' which includes that strange *sosie* of *Hamlet, Measure for Measure,* and *Troilus and Cressida,* and *All's Well that Ends Well.* In all these plays there are sustained passages of poetry, of poetry of form and content incomparable, in which Shakespeare definitely passes beyond the highest point that poetry had reached before him, or has reached after him. It was no even temporary weakening of his purely poetic powers that assailed him; but we have a sudden sense of loss of all direction, an invasion of bitterness, of cynicism, and of a conscious helplessness. We feel we are in contact with a wounded and bewildered spirit that can see life steadily and whole no more. Shakespeare managed to project this bewilderment out of himself most completely and almost to master it in the realm of art in *Hamlet*. He concentrated it all in a character, divided in his deepest being against himself, but yet one; nevertheless the play is bewildering: not, we believe, because there may be remnants of an old play in it—Shakespeare had rewritten old plays before without leaving us in any doubt of his dramatic intention—but simply because the attitude to life which every great poet must convey had suffered a chaotic disturbance. We feel the same indecision in *All's Well*. Here also we are told that the unsatisfactory nature of the whole composed of such brilliant parts is due to its being a revision of an earlier *Love's Labour Won*. Again we must reply that Shakespeare knew how to rewrite plays; he had spent his life at the business. What we seek to know is the reason why he suddenly began to fail in a task he had performed for years with brilliant success, and was to perform again more marvellously still.

When we find precisely the same fundamental indecision, the same deep hesitation of a mind that can by nature never be more than half-cynical, in the two other plays of this period, against which the defect of rehashing has not yet been urged; when we find that those four plays are as closely united to each other as they

are separate from the whole of the rest of
Shakespeare's work, we may fairly neglect the
hypothetical 'Ur-Hamlets' and earlier versions
and stick to what we have. Of these four plays
we may say that we do not clearly understand
Shakespeare's dramatic purpose or the direction
of his sentiment in any of them. Whether the
cause of this clouding actually lay, as we ourselves incline to believe, in the love-catastrophe
recorded in the Sonnets, is a minor matter; but
the fact is that the disturbance is most clearly
to be distinguished in his treatment of love. The
main intention of *Hamlet* is on the whole fairly
clear. But who has ever spoken convincingly on
the significance of Hamlet's love for Ophelia?
It remains mysterious to us. The final effect of
Troilus and Cressida is a feeling that again Shakespeare could not really face his own subject.
For a moment he handles the love of Troilus and
Cressida firmly, then he appears to let it drop
as though it were unbearable and to turn away
to deride the Homeric heroes and the idea of
chivalry. In a play which contains, in Ulysses'
speeches and Troilus' love addresses, some of
Shakespeare's finest poetry, we are struck at the
last chiefly by its strange inferiority to Chaucer's
wonderful poem. Shakespeare could have
handled the love theme with the mastery of his
great predecessor; but something prevented
him, and the consequence of his hesitation is
that essays are now written to prove that he
meant only a satire on hero-worship. Seeing
that Shakespeare put his finest declaration of
the ideal of love into the play, we may assume

that this master of love would have worked out the tragedy of love if he could have borne to do so.

Measure for Measure is that one of Shakespeare's plays which Coleridge could never bring himself to like. The treatment of love in it is as near to pure cynicism as Shakespeare could get. Claudio, who really loves, and is loved by Julietta, is sentenced to death for anticipating the marriage he intends. Isabel, who will not sacrifice her icy chastity to save her brother, ends by acting like a woman of the town, but one utterly devoid of the humanity which glows in Doll Tearsheet or Bianca. Believing her brother dead, she pleads for Angelo, the reverend justice who has killed him and would have ravished her, in these terms:—

'Look, if it please you, on this man condemn'd,
  As if my brother lived: I partly think
  A due sincerity govern'd his deeds,
  Till he did look on me; since it is so,
  Let him not die. My brother had but justice,
  In that he did the thing for which he died:
  For Angelo,
  His act did not o'ertake his bad intent,
  And must be buried but as an intent
  That perish'd by the way: thoughts are no
    subjects;
  Intents but merely thoughts.'

It would be difficult to conceive anything more revolting. Dr. Johnson's note on it is properly cynical, but it is too good-humoured. The lines contain a fierce and bitter caricature of love, and

we must believe that Shakespeare meant it.
Then there is the trick, significantly repeated in
All's Well, by which Angelo possessed the faithful
Mariana in the belief that she was Isabel. And
over the whole play hangs the sinister cloud of
preoccupation with death, suddenly crystallised
into the sardonic figure of Barnardine. Whatever may be the dramatic purpose of this
singular 'comedy,' the condition of mind from
which it sprang is manifest. Life is hateful and
contemptible; and as for love, your bawd is your
only honest man.

In *All's Well that Ends Well*—supremely cynical
title—Shakespeare seems deliberately to take
revenge on his own idealism of love. He deliberately makes Bertram detestable and shows that
the bragging coward, Parolles, is the better man.
Then he makes Helena fall in love, passionately,
tenderly, delicately, with the unpleasant young
nobleman, builds her up as surely as Beatrice or
Rosalind, puts into her mouth the divinely
hesitating reply to Bertram's purely brutal
'What would you have?'

> 'Something; and scarce so much: nothing,
>   indeed.
> I would not tell you what I would, my lord:
> Faith, yes;
> Strangers and foes do sunder and not kiss.'

Yet after all this she plays the Mariana trick.
One wonders what can be the conception of the
poet in the minds of those who imagine that he
had written a romantic comedy with a happy
ending. The self-torturing mood of the play, the

bitter mood of 'I'll show you a happy ending,' is only too apparent. But Shakespeare, it seems, could never succeed in projecting an attitude of embitterment completely: his hand weakened, his idealisation of love and humanity interfered. That is why the fascination of the plays of this strange tormented period is out of all proportion to the sureness of their achievement as works of dramatic art.

We may speculate that the true poetic realisation of this period, whose stress we imagine we can measure by Othello's words—'when I love thee not Chaos is come again'—is to be found in the great tragedies. The shattering personal experience there found its place in a vision of life as a whole. There is no bitterness any more; and in the microcosm of his vision of life which is his attitude to love it is apparent that Shakespeare has regained his belief. The love of Othello and Desdemona is in itself unclouded. No human mind could resist the villainy of Iago. Their perfect happiness is overwhelmed by no defect of their love, and Othello's very act of murder is, as Coleridge said, an act of sacrifice to love; it is the tragedy of an ideal shattered by an alien power. Had there been no Iago their love would have endured to death. So, too, with the miniature of this great picture of married happiness, which we have in *Coriolanus*. Virgilia's reticent devotion to her proud and passionate husband is matched by his gentleness in her presence. His 'gracious silence' wields a charm over him which Shakespeare makes us feel completely in the few dozen lines he gives to her. In *Macbeth* also, though the bond holds between natures far darker than these, it holds unbreakable. Lady Macbeth may be her husband's evil genius, but she is united to him more deeply by their love than their crime. And of *Antony and Cleopatra*, with even more force than of *Romeo and Juliet*, it may be said that it is a triumph rather than a tragedy of love. At the last the mutual devotion is complete. Cleopatra in her death-scene remains what she has been, capricious as she is passionate; but her surrender is entire. 'Husband, I come. Now to that name my courage prove my title.' It is a love which may not promise the golden happiness on which Shakespeare so fondly dwelt, but it is one which transfigures the lovers and lifts them to heights of feeling and sacrifice of which neither they nor we had dreamed.

Shakespeare's final period is one of return to the love of his youth. During the great tragedies love had been on the whole—save in *Antony and Cleopatra*—a subordinate issue. He had other things to convey—the conclusion of his brooding on his experience of that life of which love is a mighty part, but only a part. Yet we may discover how great a part it was to him by his return to the theme in all his last three plays, *The Winter's Tale*, *Cymbeline*, and *The Tempest*. We feel that it was only the love scenes of the first two of these that deeply interested him. In those scenes his touch is perfectly firm, his mastery evident, while in the rest it is hesitating and perfunctory. But something ethereal is added to the love of the earlier comedies and something earthly taken away. The light is no longer golden but silver. Lovers are no more witty together; they are almost enfolded in a dream of tenderness. After the wild storm of the trage-dies, culminating in *King Lear*, we hear the poet proclaiming through Florizel and Perdita, Imo-gen and Posthumus, Ferdinand and Miranda, that love is the only light to follow. The message sounds with a magical clearness in the silver note of *The Tempest*. The wise magician throws away his book; he has seen his vision of human life.

'The cloud-capp'd towers, the gorgeous palaces,
The solemn temples, the great globe itself,
Yea, all which it inherit, shall dissolve
And, like this insubstantial pageant faded,
Leave not a wrack behind. We are such stuff
As dreams are made on, and our little life
Is rounded with a sleep.'

Yet with his wisdom and his pain of heart, Prospero gives way to the faith and the freedom of love; and his creator looks at the world not through his eyes only, but through Miranda's also.

'O wonder!
How many goodly creatures are there here!
How beauteous mankind is! O brave new world,
That has such people in't!'

So 'the world's great age begins anew.' The magic of Shakespeare's last enchantment is that he makes us believe that the eyes of love alone can see the miracle; and perhaps it is the ultimate truth of life that indeed they do.

DICKENS

I WAS struck by Mr. H. M. Tomlinson's remark, made in *The Times* a few days ago, that he was not surprised to find that a young writer and critic of his acquaintance thought that Dickens had gone the way of the wax-fruit. (Mr. Roger Fry, by the way, has told us that the wax-fruit are coming, have already come, back again.) I was surprised at Mr. Tomlinson's lack of surprise. My own impression is that in the last few years, let us say since 1914, there has been a marked revival of interest and admiration for Dickens among the younger generation. While Thackeray has been decidedly tarnished since he was put on the shelf, the splendour of Dickens, I fancy, now that he has been taken down again, shines as bright as ever.

I have a good memory for the evidences of a Dickens revival. I remember an intellectual dinner-party at which it was announced, without any manifest ill-effects upon the company, that the real test of literary taste was an admiration, not for Jane Austen (as some one had suggested), but for Dickens. And the reason given for making him the touchstone was that the lover of 'Emma' might be an intellectual snob, while the lover of 'David Copperfield' could not be. Then there was the letter of one who had been brought up in the strict Flaubert persuasion. He declared with the emphasis natural to a man who feels he has been deceived since childhood, that there was more substance in Bella Wilfer alone than in all the created characters of the great Frenchman. He was extravagant, but I know what he meant.

Again, there is the striking fact that the finest essay on Dickens which has yet been written appeared only a few months ago in an organ of ultra-modern literature, the American *Dial*. Had it not been written by Mr. Santayana, it is possible it would not have squeezed its way through the narrow door. But there it undeniably was; and it was a masterpiece of profound and appreciative criticism. Those poor slaves of fashion who have hitherto had to read their Dickens in secret, if they read him at all, may now indulge themselves in the open. And for a final overwhelming proof, a proof by miracle, as it were, a proof of the *credo quia impossibile* kind, there is the acknowledgment by Mr. T. S. Eliot in the last number of *The Tyro* that Dickens is not altogether *vieux jeu*. 'The critic', says Mr. Eliot, 'is the person who has the power to discern what, in any work of literary art, takes its place, through its expression of the genius of its language, in European literature, and what is of purely local importance. (In the case of such a writer as Dickens, for example, the dissociation remains to be performed.)'

It is rather grim. Dickens is slipped into a parenthesis, squeezed between a pair of brackets as between a pair of forceps, tied down on the surgeon's table, and warned that a serious operation is necessary. But at the cost of a certain expurgation his life can be saved. We need not despair of him. We do not yet know, of course, how much will be cut away, or whether Dickens will be recognisable when he has been pruned into a European. We hope that Mr. Eliot means nothing worse than a careful excision of sentimentality. Even that pound of flesh might have to be taken, like Shylock's, from very near the heart. Still, there is hope. I seem to remember that Mr. Eliot made a much less hopeful diagnosis a year or two ago. Now that he has granted his provisional *imprimatur*, the most advanced young man may carry a copy of Pickwick in his pocket. If he is cross-questioned about the suspicious volume, he has only to reply that he is engaged in blue-pencilling the non-European parts.

Dickens is safe, so safe indeed that within the next twelve months he may become a snobism in his turn. The permissible portions may be printed in a limited edition with a cover design by ——, but that would be implied art criticism. Let us be content with the knowledge that the offence against art and intellect is no longer to know Dickens, but to be ignorant of him. I have read the signs with care, for the simple reason that, although I have floundered into most of the artistic snobisms of my time (and, I hope, floundered out again), I have never deserted Mr. Micawber. I may have been silent, but I have not deserted him. Not through any fundamental rectitude in my nature, but simply because of the accident that 'Pickwick' was the first book I ever possessed. My copy began at page 19. I have never read those nineteen pages. They would not be real if I did. The foundation of the Pickwick Club will always be a mystery to me.

Until the day when I read Mr. Gosse's 'Father and Son,' I was persuaded that the behaviour Mr. Pickwick induced in me at the age of eight and nine was a clear proof of a peculiar madness. Even at that age I was half-ashamed of it. I used to begin to laugh before I had opened the book. (Perhaps that was as well, because the pages were so sticky that I should have lost precious time in opening them.) And I have never been able to read more than a few pages since then, because the helpless feeling of unquenchable Achæan laughter takes hold of me. I dare not let go my sanity; I am afraid of a second childhood. But Mr. Gosse reassured me, for he precisely described all my own alarming symptoms. 'I felt myself to be in the company of a gentleman so extremely funny that I began to laugh before he began to speak; no sooner did he remark "the sky was dark and gloomy, the air was damp and raw," than I was in fits of hilarity. . . . Possibly,' concluded Mr. Gosse, 'I was the latest of the generation which accepted Mr. Pickwick with an unquestioning and hysterical abandonment.' Some forty years later I was being plunged, at about the same age, into the same hysterical ecstasy. I cannot help believing that forty years hence it will happen again, and that the generations of childish Pickwick enthusiasts are perennial.

Afterwards come the phases of Dickens adulation. There is the year when Dora is woman, and the year when Squeers is the devil incarnate;

the year when Jonas Chuzzlewit makes our nights miserable, and Mrs. Gamp our days a delight; the year of confident maturity when we declare that 'Our Mutual Friend' is Dickens's only work of art; the year after when we discover that even the death of Paul Dombey has an undiminished power to harrow our souls, though our teeth are set against its illicit compulsions; there is the year of Mrs. Jellyby, the year of Little Dorrit, the year of Sally Brass and the Marchioness. And then at last come the years when we give up the insoluble problem, when we are incapable of rejecting anything to which Dickens put his hand (unless it is 'Hard Times'), when we simply know that we enter an amazing and extraordinary world, and that once we have abandoned ourselves to it the only wonder is that we could ever have been such fools as to remain deliberately outside, even for a single year.

Dickens is a baffling figure. There are moments when it seems that his chief purpose in writing was to put a spoke in the wheel of our literary æsthetics. We manage to include everybody but him; and we are inclined in our salad days to resent the existence of anybody who refuses to enter the scheme. That is why people tried to get rid of him by declaring that he was not an artist. It was an odd way of predicating non-existence. Now it is going out of fashion, I suppose because it did not have the desired effect of annihilating Dickens; and also perhaps because simple people asked why the books of a man who was not an artist should have this curious trick of immortality. There was, alas, no answer. So we are beginning to discover that Dickens *was* an artist, but, of course, only in parts. When we have discovered which are the parts we shall breathe again.

PRINTED IN GREAT BRITAIN
AT THE UNIVERSITY PRESS, OXFORD
BY VIVIAN RIDLER
PRINTER TO THE UNIVERSITY